# Critical Perspectives in
# Canadian Music Education

# Critical Perspectives in Canadian Music Education

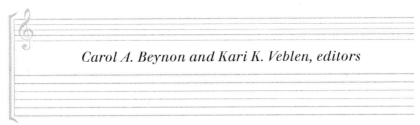

*Carol A. Beynon and Kari K. Veblen, editors*

**WILFRID LAURIER
UNIVERSITY PRESS**

This book has been published with the help of a grant from the Canadian Federation for the Humanities and Social Sciences, through the Aid to Scholarly Publications Programme, using funds provided by the Social Sciences and Humanities Research Council of Canada. We acknowledge the financial support of the Government of Canada through the Canada Book Fund for our publishing activities.

**Library and Archives Canada Cataloguing in Publication**

Critical perspectives in Canadian music education / Carol A. Beynon and Kari K. Veblen, editors.

Includes bibliographical references and index.
Issued also in electronic format.
ISBN 978-1-55458-366-9

1. Music—Instruction and study—Canada.  I. Beynon, Carol, [date]  II. Veblen, Kari K.

MT3.C35C93 2012        780'.71071        C2011-907477-X

———————

Electronic monograph in PDF format.
Issued also in print format.
ISBN 978-1-55458-386-7

1. Music—Instruction and study—Canada.  I. Beynon, Carol, [date]  II. Veblen, Kari K.

MT3.C35C93 2012        780'.71071        C2011-907478-8

Cover design by Martyn Schmoll. Cover images: iStockphoto. Text design by Daiva Villa, Chris Rowat Design.

This book is printed on FSC recycled paper and is certified Ecologo. It is made from 100% post-consumer fibre, processed chlorine free, and manufactured using biogas energy.

Printed in Canada

# Contents

**Foreword:**
Questioning Traditional Teaching and Learning in Canadian
Music Education  vii
*R. Murray Schafer*

**Preface and Acknowledgements**  xi
*Carol Beynon and Kari Veblen*

ONE **The "Roots" of Canadian Music Education:**
Expanding Our Understanding  1
*Betty Hanley*

TWO **Cross-Country Checkup:**
A Survey of Music Education in Canada's Schools  21
*Benjamin Bolden*

THREE **Canadian Music in Education:**
"Sounds Like Canada"  39
*Patricia Martin Shand*

FOUR **Manitoba's Success Story:**
What Constitutes Successful Music Education in
the Twenty-First Century?  49
*Wayne D. Bowman*

FIVE  **Traditional Indigenous Knowledge:**
An Ethnographic Study of Its Application in the
Teaching and Learning of Traditional Inuit Drum
Dances in Arviat, Nunavut  71
*Mary Piercey*

SIX  **Looking Back at Choral Music Education in Canada:**
A Narrative Perspective  89
*Carol Beynon*

SEVEN  **Re-Membering Bands in North America:**
Gendered Paradoxes and Potentialities  101
*Elizabeth Gould*

EIGHT  **Community Music Making:**
Challenging the Stereotypes of Conventional Music Education  123
*Kari Veblen*

NINE  **Still Wary after All These Years:**
Popular Music and the School Music Curriculum  135
*June Countryman*

TEN  **E-Teaching and Learning in Music Education:**
A Case Study of Newfoundland and Labrador  147
*Andrea Rose, Alex Hickey, and Andrew Mercer*

ELEVEN  **Focusing on Critical Practice and Insights in the Music
Teacher Education Curriculum**  165
*Betty Anne Younker*

TWELVE  **Marching to the World Beats:**
Globalization in the Context of Canadian Music Education  181
*Carol Beynon, Kari Veblen, and David J. Elliott*

THIRTEEN  **Epistemological Spinning:**
What Do We Really Know about Music Education in Canada?  193
*Carol Beynon, Kari Veblen, and Elizabeth Anne Kinsella*

About the Authors  205
Index  211

# Foreword:
# Questioning Traditional Teaching and Learning in Canadian Music Education

*R. Murray Schafer*

I have no idea how the world should be educated. Each culture has its own targets for citizenship and develops a curriculum to meet those objectives. Those who disagree with the objectives will have a rough time in school. I spent years in school trying to get out. It seemed to me that so much of education was devoted to answering questions that no one had asked while the real questions slid by unanswered. Plato taught that there was an answer to every question. Socrates taught that there was a question to every answer, but that was something my teachers didn't seem to want to deal with. For that reason I never completed my education, but instead set out to travel the world and educate myself. Unfortunately, as Ivan Illich pointed out, the effect of universal education is to make the autodidact unemployable.

It was only after many years of travelling — first as a sailor, then as a journalist, a broadcaster, and a composer — that I began to question seriously why my life at school had been so futile. The failure of the music program concerned me in particular because I had musical talent — I played the piano and sang in a choir — and had eventually adopted music as my vocation.

When the Canadian Music Centre initiated the John Adaskin Music Program, in which composers were invited to visit schools to work with children and young people, I was one of the first to apply. After visiting several schools, I could see clearly what was missing: creativity. In art classes original paintings were produced and in literature original stories and poems were written; but the music scene was dominated by the concert band or the jazz band playing classical arrangements of music that wasn't even written in Canada, let alone within the school itself.

During this period (the 1960s), a wave of international activity was aimed at encouraging creativity in music education. The Manhattanville Music Project was active in the United States, and in England composers like John Paynter, George Self, and Peter Maxwell Davies had penetrated classrooms and were writing music both for and with young musicians. I shared their ideas and wrote a series of little books about my own experiences. The books were descriptive, not prescriptive. You can't tell people *how* to become creative, but you can reveal the excitement of creative activity and hope that it may encourage them to try something on their own. Allowing children to become creative does not require genius: it requires humility.

Above my desk I wrote some maxims to heel myself in line:

1. The first practical step in any educational reform is to take it.
2. In education, failures are more important than successes. There is nothing so dismal as a success story.
3. Teach on the verge of peril.
4. There are no more teachers. There is just a community of learners.
5. Do not design a philosophy of education for others. Design one for yourself. A few others may wish to share it with you.
6. For the five-year-old, art is life and life is art. For the six-year-old, life is life and art is art. This first year in school is a watershed in the child's history: a trauma.
7. The old approach: Teacher has information; student has empty head. Teacher's objective: To push information into student's empty head. Observations: At outset teacher is a fathead; at conclusion student is a fathead.
8. A class should be an hour of a thousand discoveries. For this to happen, the teacher and the student should first discover one another.
9. Why is it that the only people who never matriculate from their own courses are teachers?
10. Always teach provisionally: Only God knows for sure.

When I began to think about these matters in the 1970s, it seemed that a revolution was just around the corner; however, it didn't happen. Instead music education programs in Canada and the United States pioneered backward. My own work in music education moved into other countries and cultures, namely South America and Japan. In South America there was no money for music so teachers had to use their imaginations. "Tomorrow, I want each of you to bring an interesting sound to class," I would say, and the next day a whole flood of sound and noise-makers would fill the room. This became our orchestra, and we produced free improvisations, rondos, and fugues with what we had just as easily as with violins and clarinets — better, probably, because we were unconcerned about the safety of expensive instruments.

In Japan the word for music is *ongaku*, and it means simply "beautiful sounds." Everything — from the singing of birds, the splashing of water, the chirping of crickets, and conventional music — can be *ongaku*, and this opens the soundscape and gives our ears a completely new field to investigate.

Sometimes I think that music programs in Canada are crippled by affluence. How many times have I entered a classroom to have the proud teacher point out all the rooms' possessions: the instruments lined up against the wall, the loudspeakers, the amplifiers, and the CD players. But the problem with flutes, trumpets, and violins is that all you can do is to learn to play them, and that takes years. As a result, a very expensive music education program has been erected in the form of a triangle: the children are enrolled in the program at the base and the apex is the professional performer (or the teacher) or, in a very few cases, the genius who will make the school famous.

"Show Uncle Murray your flute," my brother's wife said to her daughter, just entering high school. She brought it out and took it out of the box.

"Can you play it?" I asked.

"Not yet." And she left the music program a year later.

Too many parents and students have been fooled into believing that if it looks expensive, the music program must be good. And those who don't learn to master those expensive tools will slip down to the category of consumers who simply help the recording industries get richer. That, I think, is the problem music education faces in Canada today.

Can we learn to do more with less? I think so, and there are many people in various countries who are demonstrating how this might be accomplished. The examinations of new approaches to music education in this very book illustrate this potential for change.

In one of my pieces for young players (*Minimusic*), I included the line: "MUSIC IS NOT TO BE LISTENED TO. MUSIC IS LISTENING TO US." That is, the perfect world is listening to the imperfect world and is inviting us to go further, delve deeper, and reach higher in creating the music of the future.

# Preface and Acknowledgements

There are a number of research publications that investigate various aspects of music education, ranging from philosophies of music education to analyses of the tiniest components of the discipline. While at a first glance this manuscript may seem to be just another "research in music education" publication, it is significantly different in a number of ways. First and foremost, it is the first and only collection of papers we are aware of that addresses the phenomenon of music education in Canada as inclusively as possible. Second, the authors represented in this publication are recognized as Canada's leading researchers in music education; they also represent music educators from the eastern-most point of Canada in Newfoundland to the western points of Vancouver Island, from the southern regions surrounding the Great Lakes and the United States border to the northern regions of Yukon and Nunavut. Finally, in each of the papers, the Canadian authors address one topic through a critical, but uniquely Canadian, lens. That is not to say that the content of these chapters is irrelevant to the rest of the world. What we mean is that Canadian music educators — professional and academic, musicians, and students — need not read this book and try to synthesize the content to our Canadian context, as is so often required with music education research. Canada is a vast country with a relatively sparse and clustered population. This book attempts to bring the huge and varied expanse of the current state of Canadian music education, as presented in the following integrated chapters, into some kind of focus. Like the optics in cameras, our minds can only perceive a finite number of aspects in focus at one time, and while it might be easier to look at only a tiny portion of the whole picture, there is also a need to take the big picture into account.

## Organization of the Book

Renowned Canadian composer, philosopher, and music educator R. Murray Schafer sets the stage for this book in his provocative Foreword that questions the very essence of formalized music education practices. His comments and challenges provide a sonorous opening for the subsequent chapters. They resonate loudly and challenge readers to consider music education in a totally different light than has been experienced in the last one hundred years up to the present day.

The book begins with Betty Hanley's (University of Victoria) exploration of the very roots of music education in Canada; it then moves to an overview of music education across the country. Ben Bolden (University of Victoria) provides a cross-country checkup of mainstream music education practices as reported in a national survey; Patricia Shand (University of Toronto) gives a description, overview, and analysis of Canadian-composed music as it is used in Canadian classrooms. Other chapters report on a number of the most intriguing challenges and questions facing music education today both within specific regions and across Canada, such as accessibility to music education as noted by June Countryman (University of Prince Edward Island) who writes about the chronic, pervading wariness about studying popular and alternative musics; and Andrea Rose (Memorial University of Newfoundland) and colleagues, who share some insights into Newfoundland's experiences with teaching music via distance education. Elizabeth Gould (University of Toronto) tackles the mainstay and bastion of music education in Canadian schools — the band — from the perspective of feminist research. The topics not only are provocative, timely, and interesting, but they also challenge us as music educators to consider and to delve into the complexities of our discipline.

This publication is not intended to provide answers but to prompt further questions and dialogue as we continue to critically examine the reality of music education in Canada. Such questions include:

- What are the realistic conditions for the production of music education in Canada given that the current findings in these chapters illuminate more concerns and problems as auspicious conclusions?
- Can music education be autonomous as a subject discipline in schools and communities? Should it be?

• How does one disentangle the varied intents and meanings of process and product in music education from the various societal perspectives of music — from music as an expensive frill subject that adds variety to the curriculum through basically useless information, to music education that supports the development of the creative mind in pupils, an activity that leads to a productive and creative future for the economy?

We invite you to contemplate these questions through your reading of this volume. And we also invite you to go to and interact with this publication's companion e-book, entitled *From Sea to Sea: Perspectives on Music Education in Canada*. The e-book can be found at http://ir.lib.uwo.ca/musiceducationebooks/1/ and contains chapters that expand upon and serve as source information for the ideas in this book, as well as reflections on these issues from national and international researchers, community music workers, and music educators ranging from those who are in training, to current practitioners, to retirees. It also contains several other complete chapters that critically discuss issues in Canadian music education that are outside of the purview of this book. Please visit the e-book and join in the dialogue.

Both of these volumes are intended as snapshot views of music education in Canada between 2000 and 2011. We express our sincere appreciation to you for reading this collection and we welcome your comments and insights. We would love to hear from readers; we can be reached by email at beynon@uwo.ca and kveblen@uwo.ca.

## Acknowledgements

This publication is a result of the contributions of many people and organizations. We extend our sincere appreciation to the Canadian Social Sciences and Humanities Research Council for their support through a SSHRC Research Cluster Grant #857-2005-0017, which has enabled us not only to develop the materials for this book, but also to continue the work we began by setting up music education research clusters and networks across Canada. We gratefully acknowledge the contributions and colleagueship of Dr. Mary Kennedy (University of Victoria), Dr. Wayne Bowman (Brandon University), Dr. Louise Mathieu (Université de Laval), Doyenne Anne Lowe (Université de Moncton), and Dr. Andrea Rose (Memorial University of Newfoundland). We would also like to thank the International Society for Music Education, Canadian Music Educators Association (CMEA), and the Coalition for Music Education in Canada for their partnership in fulfilling our research and networking goals as part of the SSHRC Research Cluster grant.

The entire Canadian Music Educators' Association Board of Directors provided encouragement and sponsorship for this project from its inception and over its entirety. We offer our sincere thanks to each and every CMEA Board member for your faith in us, especially Dr. Betty Hanley, professor emeritus of the University of Victoria, who so willingly acted as a mentor throughout this project.

A great deal of credit must go to the University of Western Ontario and our graduate research assistants who have followed this project through with us:

- Stephanie Horsley, who entered into the editing process with us when we needed an extra pair of hands to pull everything together into a cohesive whole.
- André-Louis Heywood, who provided primary administrative support in communicating with colleagues and preparing print materials, and who was our official videographer and photographer.
- Uresha DeAlwiss, who acted as assistant editor, correspondent, APA specialist, organizer, and the person who kept us smiling with her delightful sense of humour when we got tired.

— Carol Beynon and Kari Veblen

# ONE

# The "Roots" of Canadian Music Education:
# Expanding our Understanding

*Betty Hanley*

"Roots"? What's in a word? I initially thought it would be relatively easy to identify the roots of Canadian music education: there would be French, English, and Aboriginal roots. Simple. Green and Vogan (1991) had already written a comprehensive history of Canadian music education from its inception until 1967, so I just needed to select the pertinent information and, voilà!

Then I began to think about what the word "roots" encompasses: the source upon which something is supported or rests; the bottom or real basis; a discussion of one's social, cultural, or ethnic origins or background. Alas, the topic was becoming more complex than I had first thought.[1]

Next, there was the little matter of what is meant by "music education." Are we just talking about what happens in schools? Green and Vogan (1991) addressed this issue in the prologue to their authoritative book *Music Education in Canada: A Historical Account.* In the seventeenth century, Canadian music education occurred informally in homes, churches, and communities. Green and Vogan concluded that, even after the nineteenth-century emergence of formal music education in public schooling, "it would be remiss ... to represent a historical review that did not recognize the role and contribution of private teachers, church organists, choir leaders, and other community musicians" (p. xv). That is, the phrase "music education" could then and can still now mean many things, from learning at your mother's knee, to learning in private lessons, to learning in school class-rooms. While I limit my discussion mainly to music education in public (formal) schooling, my conclusions might well apply to all forms of music education.

There is also the question of when the roots of Canadian music educa-tion begin and when they end. The traditional starting place has been the sixteenth-century arrival of Europeans. The roots of the European heritage reach back, however, at least to ancient Greek civilization. Furthermore, Europeans were colonizers of an already inhabited country. How did our Aboriginal peoples contribute to the roots of Canadian music education? The same question could be asked about Canadians of non-European heritages who immigrated to Canada. Indeed, the word "roots" is a meta-phor for an organic development in which the past, present, and future are interwoven. The historical nature of this chapter necessarily places the focus on the past, while both acknowledging the connection between the past, the present, and the future, and recognizing that new root systems grow over time.

The most obvious place to seek the roots of Canadian music education would be in its early history. Have the roots already been identified? Before addressing this question it would be worthwhile to review how the history of music education in Canada has been told relative to a process that I see as consisting of three phases:

- Phase 1: Individuals or organizations collect primary data about local or provincial events in archives, documents (cf. Buckley, 1988; Gardi, 1998), published books (Woodford, 1983; McIntosh, 1989), disserta-tions (Trowsdale, 1962; Brault, 1977), and journal articles.
- Phase 2: Historians use this documentation to provide a more com-prehensive picture of the events and people (Kallman, 1960; Green & Vogan, 1991; Bray, Green, & Vogan, 1992).
- Phase 3: Other historians undertake inquiries and interpret the data to show how "education must reflect the civilization it represents" (Tellstrom, 1971, p. vii) or answer research questions (Rainbow & Froehlich, 1987).

To date, most of the work in Canada has been in the first two phases, in data collection and in developing a narrative of events and important people. Although there are excellent examples of Phase 3 studies from other countries (Tellstrom, 1971; Rainbow, 1989; Pitts, 2000), little has been accomplished in this area in Canada.[2] There is a vast richness of new understanding to be found in posing new questions about the past and in going beyond the traditional setting forth of "facts." As Rainbow and Frohlich (1987) explained, "too often...studies end up being mere stories of what happened, without providing any critical evaluation of the happenings" (p. 118). Have the roots of Canadian music education already been uncovered? In my view, no.

Rather than attempting to identify *the* roots of Canadian music education, with an incomplete understanding of what such a task might entail, this chapter begins by first reporting on Phase 2, which largely consists of descriptions of past events (facts) and the contributions of individuals and organizations (people). Then the focus will shift to suggest a third phase, where multiple ways of locating the roots of music education in Canadian schools become possible. These roots can be located culturally and socially; politically; and philosophically and psychologically (i.e., in educational thought).

These locations are not mutually exclusive; the issues do cross these (somewhat artificial) boundaries. Yet each location has a particular focus that warrants further examination. I begin, then, with an overview of the work accomplished in Phase 2: the historical narrative that locates Canada's music education roots in events and in what people do.

## Roots in Events and in What People Do

Green and Vogan's (1991) *Music Education in Canada: A Historical Account* is a seminal book that synthesizes a vast amount of primary source data. The approach used is that of conventional historical narrative—the telling of events and the identification of influential individuals. One caveat is necessary: history, revisionists remind us, is always a selection and interpretation of the "facts." In Phase 2, although the process of selection and interpretation is not made explicit, it is nevertheless present. The authors have selected *the* pertinent facts and are trying to tell *the* objective (truthful) narrative (from their point of view).

In their substantive book, Green and Vogan attempted to "recognize local and regional differences while at the same time viewing music education as a national movement" (p. xvi), thus perpetuating the quintessential Canadian compromise. To accomplish their bold undertaking, Green and Vogan examined reports, speeches, minutes, archives, newspaper articles and editorials, bulletins, letters, periodicals, books (see for example, Kallman, 1960; McIntosh, 1989), music textbooks (see, for example, Cringan, 1888, 1889, 1898; Tufts & Holt, 1883), thirty-five theses, and eighteen dissertations (the latter two categories between 1936 and 1989). What is interesting about this summary is the amount of primary data that is available but not necessarily easily accessible, the small number of published works, and the relatively few historical studies conducted in higher education (only eighteen dissertations over fifty-three years). Most astonishing of all is the fact that it was not until 124 years after Confederation that a comprehensive history of music education in Canada was written.[3]

Green and Vogan wrote of "emerging patterns" (rather than roots) in Quebec, the Atlantic provinces (Nova Scotia, New Brunswick, Prince Edward Island, and, subsequently, Newfoundland, to reflect its later entry into the Confederation), Ontario, and the west (Manitoba, British Columbia, Saskatchewan, and Alberta). Their approach was to lay the facts before the reader in a chronological, but recursive, manner as they related to each region or topic. Therefore, we read of such documented events as the arrival of the Jesuits in 1626 and their efforts to provide instruction in liturgical chant to Huron boys and young Frenchmen; the establishment in Montreal of a music school for English-speaking Protestants by Charles Watts in 1789; the foundation of a Handel and Haydn Society in St. John's in 1838; the hiring of private singing teacher Jacob B. Norton in 1867 Halifax to "train children in the schools to sing" (p. 25); the arrival of Mennonites and their choral tradition in Manitoba in the 1870s; the publication by Henry Sefton in 1871 of an adaptation of a text by Hullah for use in Ontario schools; the appointment of John Jessop as the first superintendent of education in British Columbia in 1872; the introduction of music in the public elementary schools of the Montreal Catholic School Commission in 1873; the Cringan/Holt debate over the merits of the Hullah versus Curwen approaches to sight-singing that began in the 1890s; the establishment of the first summer school of music in Toronto in 1887; and the formation of the Canadian Music Educators Association in 1959.

The roots of Canadian music education can be extrapolated from this sampling of events. For Green and Vogan, the historical roots that underpin the development of contemporary Canadian music education were inextricably linked with geographical considerations (east and west) and two official languages (English and French), and included religious schools and worship, national and regional tensions, private music teaching, community music, immigration and ethnic traditions, the politics of schooling (including who should teach music) and the formation of political alliances, teacher training, and methodological controversies.

But are the roots of Canadian music education to be found in these issues? Perhaps. Having our story told is a very important step. But what does the story mean? Will the reader recognize the implied interpretation of the "facts"?

Events are not the only consideration in *Music Education in Canada*. People lived the events and "[m]any believe that the past (and future) survival of music education depended (and depends) on the energy and will of individual music teachers" (Morton, 1996, p. 49). This view is evident throughout Green and Vogan's book. The efforts of individuals such as Charles Hutton (1861–1949), Rj Staples (1904–72), Roy Fenwick (1889–1970), Ethel Kinley (1887–1967), Alexander Cringan (1860–1931), and George Little (1920–95), who were all committed to the advancement of music education, are recognized but not aggrandized (as befits the Canadian ethos) by Green and Vogan. Speaking of these individuals and other like-minded music education leaders, the authors claimed, "music education has survived bureaucracies, apathies, and other adversities, primarily because of outstanding musicians and teachers devoted to a common cause" (p. xvi).

Since Green and Vogan, other contributions to a historical narrative focused on events and people have continued to be written, but not in great abundance; examples include a scattering of theses and dissertations (Morton, 1996; Wasiak, 1996; Thomas, 1998; Howey, 2003); Vogan's historical vignettes, appearing as a regular feature in the *Canadian Music Educator* (2000–3);[4] the occasional biography of a music educator (D'Alton, 1997; Harris, 1998); and interviews with music educators, available online at http://www.cmea.ca (cf. Franklin Churchley by Hanley, 2005). Given the magnitude of what has already been accomplished, it would be convenient to conclude that all has been said: the story has been told. I do not, however, find this conclusion defensible. Now that we have examined people and events as a source for the "roots" of Canadian music education, it is time to proceed to Phase 3 and contemplate a number of additional approaches that would suggest there is more to music education history and its roots than events and people. A discussion of this new phase could provide a direction for relevant, contemporary, historical research in the coming years. In considering Phase 3, I weave between the past and present to illustrate the significance and richness of examining history through a variety of acknowledged lenses.

## Cultural and Social Roots

Writing of the need to see music education as operating in a larger context, Rainbow and Froehlich (1987) claimed "the social and cultural history of the time is therefore imperative for any good historian in music education" (p. 110). In what I am calling the *sociocultural approach* to music education history, social and cultural history not only provide a background for understanding, but are acknowledged as the basis for historical interpretation. The

cultures that have shaped the lives and beliefs of Canadian music education form the basis for historical narratives and, potentially, can clarify
the roots of Canadian music education. By culture, I refer to "the values
the members of a given group hold, the languages they speak, the symbols
they revere, the norms they follow, and the material goods they create from
tools to clothing" (Giddens, Duneier, & Appelbaum, 2003, p. 55).

The cultural roots of Canadian music education could be situated
broadly in the values and practices of European and Aboriginal peoples. Of
course, these two categories are simplistic; they mask diversity within each
broad culture. For example, early Europeans included French and English
settlers, as well as Irish, Ukrainian, German, and Scottish immigrants.
These settlers brought strong Protestant, Orthodox, Catholic, Menno-
nite, and Quaker beliefs. Their reasons for coming to Canada varied, and
included economic gain, famine, wars, converting the "heathen," loyalty,
persecution, and adventure. They represented different classes of people
with different values about education and the role of music in their lives
and, in time, its desirability in the schools.

Our traditional story has not given a voice to many possible contributors to Canadian culture and music education. For example, the Aboriginal
peoples of Canada represent a diverse group including the northwest coast
nations (Haida, Tsmishian, Wakashan, and Salishan language families);
Athapaskan, Plains, and Eastern Woodlands (Algonquian and Iroquoian
language families); and Inuit (Kallman & Potvin, 1992, pp. 923–935).
They, too, had traditions of passing on their music heritage, when they
were allowed to do so by the colonial, and later federal, government. How
have these peoples impacted Canadian music education, if at all? Green
and Vogan (1991) mention the Métis[5] only once, in the context of the Grey
Nuns' mission work with Indians and Métis and the capacity for music
to nurture "religious and educational aspirations" (p. 76). In addition to
all of these differing groups of people were Canadians of non-European
heritage.[6] How have the latter contributed to Canadian music education,
if at all?

What is sadly missing from our historical accounts is a recognition of
the potential impact of Aboriginal peoples and people of non-European
ancestry on music education, as well as the impact of European values and
practice on Canadians, including those of non-European ancestry. Also
missing is the influence of what Hugh MacLennan (1946) called the two
solitudes — Quebec and English Canada — in the formation and development of music education in Canada.[7] While aspects of culture have been
acknowledged in the history of Canadian music education, we need to go

beyond the narrative of events and people to examine the deeper meaning of the cultural roots that have contributed to contemporary Canadian music education.

One fine example of history that examines the social function of culture is found in Harris's (1998) ethnographic biography of Elizabeth Murray (1917–96). Harris examined Murray's educational contributions to and leadership in music education both in Nova Scotia schools and in her community. Harris wrote that Murray "focused on the educational contexts in which she worked, the way her beliefs and attitudes developed, and how they affected others who became involved in her numerous projects" (p. 7). In writing this biography, Harris explained that she had to "omit many intriguing facts and incidents" (p. 6) in order to address her research questions. Indeed, Harris explained that Murray's story "deals primarily with educational ideas and actions, rather than the intimate details of a life" (p. 7). The concluding chapter, "Opening Spaces in the Imagination: An Assessment," demonstrates the cultural values of a specific time and place:

> Betty [Elizabeth Murray], by example rather than words alone, challenged such organizational markers as hierarchical leadership, upward mobility of career, and competitive individuals. She promoted, on the other hand, the value of people working together; the importance of the arts in building community; an awareness that learning was not just for career purposes, but for "life"; and the fact that finding "the possible" in everyone was a goal well worth the undertaking. (p. 156)

Elizabeth Murray's life illustrates the cultural values of community and service.[8] This type of exploration of cultural roots as they relate to the social functions of different musical communities enriches our understanding of people and events by placing them in a broader context.

It is evident in looking at the music education literature that there is a growing interest in the sociology of music education, one place where culture is studied.[9] The concept of democracy, and our too-frequent failure to live up to democratic ideals, provides an example of the merits of examining cultural roots from a sociological perspective. Canada is a democratic country, but do our cultural roots support or thwart democratic ideals? In *Democracy and Music Education*, Woodford (2005) discussed democratic ideals as expounded by Dewey and, more recently, thinkers like John Ralston Saul and Janice Gross Stein; a study of the roots of democracy can lead to important insights about music education. Woodford states:

Throughout much of the twentieth century, North American music educators aspired to democratic ideals. Influenced by Dewey and the early Progressive Education Movement, they became convinced that all children, not just the gifted, could benefit from musical instruction, and that the social function of music education in the schools was primarily avocational rather than vocational. (p. 8)

Examining the roots of Canadian music education through a democratic lens leads to questions such as "who had access to early music education?" and "how did this availability impact on the progress of music education in Canada?" There is no doubt that, in the past, formal music education was for the privileged and sometimes the gifted, and we continue to live with the consequences of this notion when we contend with the idea that music is a "frill."

Part of the cultural discourse involves observing whose music has been studied. Music in the early years of our history included classical music (the music of the upper and wealthier classes), religious music (including Gregorian chant, Methodist hymns, and Gospel music), and all the rest (folk music, traditional songs, and popular songs).[10] How did schools deal with this diversity? What music was included? Why? Is Woodford (2005) correct in claiming that, in attempting to please all factions, music educators had to invent "a kind of quasi-classical music that was intelligible to the masses and to those in authority yet 'could be taken as classical'" (p. 13), a "polite music" that was inoffensive? Surely, music content has helped shape and nurture the roots of Canadian music education. The choice of past repertoire leads the discussion to a closely related topic — an examination of political roots.

**Political Roots**

Traditionally, politics "concerns the means whereby power is used to affect the scope and content of governmental activities" (Giddens, Duneier, & Appelbaum, 2003, p. 394). In this sense, politics refers to what occurs in formal, organized institutions. Arguably, politics and power are not the favourite topics of Canadian music educators. Indeed, Canadian music educators, unlike their American colleagues, have generally been reluctant to become involved in the political arena.[11] Perhaps we are reflecting the belief system of the formalist, modernist view of music we inherited in our own formal music education in universities and conservatories. As Norris (1989) wrote: "Music holds out the seductive ideal of a language purged of all merely temporal concerns, a language that could best live up to its own responsibilities by rejecting every claim upon the artist's political conscience" (p. 7). This formalist thinking has exerted a strong hold on music education. Elliott (2001), commenting on Reimer's view of aesthetic music education, explained what he considers to be its destructive, formalist features. For Reimer, Elliott claimed, "listening for relationships between musical patterns and meanings of a religious, moral, social, cultural, historical, political, practical or otherwise non-structural nature is to listen 'non-musically'" (p. 36). In contrast, Elliott insisted on the importance of "a *multidimensional* concept of musical works and of music's values — 'music' conceived broadly, as a matter of works, practices, communities, social events, and so forth" (p. 30). Until recently, music educators as a profession have transferred learned formalist beliefs about music to music education based on the assumption that music and music education are above sordid, worldly affairs. In this, once again, mainstream music education has been firmly rooted in European classical aesthetic ideals.

One consequence of our avoidance of politics has been that music education, as delivered by qualified teachers, has received little recognition and earned no voice in decision making at the national level. We do not even have *access* to the decision makers. "The Good, the Bad, and the Ugly — Arts Partnerships in Canadian Elementary Schools" (Hanley, 2003) provides examples of the exclusion of arts education associations from national dialogue and policy making (pp. 16–17). The good news is that the apolitical stance fostered by a formalist view of music education has been slowly shifting as postmodern thinking permeates our lives and challenges our deep-seated beliefs.[12] Unfortunately, while we are becoming more aware of the "discontinuity between political purpose and our actual music education practice,"

> today's music educators ... remain ambivalent about the coupling of democracy and music education. While the democratic purpose of public schooling is usually acknowledged by them, autocratic educational models and methods continue to prevail in music teacher education programs and in public school music programs. (Woodford, 2005, p. xi)

In spite of our resistance, as a profession we are becoming more sensitive to issues of empowerment, rights, and multiple narratives, and we are beginning to see beyond the confines of our own classrooms and rehearsal venues. This trend is emerging both in classrooms and in the music education literature.[13]

What is needed to move forward? An identification of the political roots of Canadian music education would include an examination of national, provincial, and local government decision making (policy) and action (implementation) as related to music education. While royal commissions, curriculum documents, evaluations, grants, teacher salaries, and hiring practices of music teachers and administrators are mentioned in current historical writing, the story of music education and its relation to provincial and national governments has yet to be written. Political power and its impact on music education are, however, being examined in other countries. Pitts (2000), for example, acknowledged the importance of politics in her history of secondary-school music in British schools: "Politics and power are now inextricably linked in Britain" (p. 1). Looking at the process of change, Pitts selected data that identified "significant changes in the development of music education in order to gain insight upon its musical and social purpose for different generations" (p. 7). Similarly, Heimonen (2005) has explored the relationship between Finnish law and access to music education. What are the historical political roots of these issues?

A study of the political roots of Canadian music education must also examine the formation and development of provincial and national music education associations (MEAs), their capacity for exerting influence where important educational decisions are made, and their relationships with other professional education organizations. For example, in a recent look at American music education, Mark and Gary (1992) devoted a section of their book to the "political, cultural, and musical conditions and events" (p. vii) that shaped music education in the first seventy-five years of the United States. One whole chapter discusses the New England roots of American music education, and other chapters trace the growth of professional educational organizations.

Although there has been an attempt to examine the history of Canadian provincial MEAs in Newfoundland (McLennon, 2000), Ontario (Brault, 1977), and Saskatchewan (Kaplan, 1993), national organizations have received little or no attention to date, with one exception. In a master's thesis focusing on advocacy initiatives, Horsley (2005) traced the historical developments of the Canadian Music Educators Association, the Coalition for Music Education in Canada, and the National Symposium on Arts Education. In her work, she acknowledged the political implications of decisions made:

> CMEA did originally consider the universal/cultural dichotomy that plagues those dealing with Canadian public education. For example, the importance of achieving a unified and universal national voice through recruiting and retaining as many members from as many provinces as possible in order to advocate the importance of music

education was stressed from the very first days of the CMEA's creation. But CMEA also hoped to create a forum wherein music educators from across the country could communicate and solve problems
within their own provinces regarding funding, class time, credit for
music at the secondary level, and administrational and community
support. (p. 32)

What are the political roots of Canadian music education? And how
do they differ regionally, provincially, and nationally? We need not limit
the discussion to the government. It would be interesting to inquire into
the historical impact of the policies and activities of cultural agencies
such as the Canada Council (CC) and the Canadian Conference of the
Arts (CCA), organizations that do have at least some political clout on
Canadian music education. Similarly, how have the policies of national
and provincial governments, national teacher organizations such as the
Canadian Teachers' Federation (CTF), international organizations such
as UNESCO, and — especially — the Council of Ministers of Education
Canada, influenced the development of Canadian music education? What
are the interests of arts organizations in music education? What assumptions have formed the basis for political interventions and what have been
the consequences?

An examination of political roots must also address the origins of advocacy initiatives by teachers, administrators, parents, and arts organizations. There are two Canadian examples that address this issue. In her
dissertation, Morton (1996) provided a critical, historical analysis of music
education advocacy and placed the latter's roots in "utilitarian and aesthetic philosophical intent" and "allegiances to progressive or traditional
philosophies of education" (p. 25). Horsley (2005) examined advocacy initiatives undertaken by the Canadian Music Educators Association (CMEA,
1959–), the Coalition for Music Education in Canada (CMEC, 1992–),
and the National Symposium for Arts Education (NSAE, 1997–2004). In
doing so, she traced the historical developments of each group and critically examined their roles in shaping advocacy efforts, exploring the root
causes of the initiatives. One of Horsley's main strategies was an analysis
of the philosophical beliefs guiding the advocacy initiatives undertaken by
each association.

Political roots do not simply refer to government ministries and professional associations; they also refer to the power existing in relationships. Whereas most music teachers think of curriculum as value-neutral
(whether as a document, as implemented, or as experienced), some contemporary educational thinkers consider curriculum itself to be political

because its implementation typically reproduces the ideas and culture of the dominant class (Apple, 1990). Who determines what will be taught? Whose values will be respected? Whose music will be heard? Who decides? When one considers issues of globalization, the Internet, and multicultural societies such as Canada, consideration of these issues cannot be avoided in a discussion about music education. These same questions and political issues, however, are not new to music education; they have had an unrecognized impact on music education since its earliest days.

Charlene Morton's (1996) work provides a strong example of a Canadian study that uses a political lens. Looking at the feminized (marginalized) position of music in the curriculum and surrounding advocacy initiatives, Morton (1996) sought "not so much to present new historical research per se but to situate the long-standing problem of music education's fragile position in curricula and to examine how this position has been interpreted and addressed" (p. 24). One of her objectives was to look at "a larger socio-political context that challenges mainstream interpretations of knowing" (p. 11). In presenting her case, Morton examined the roots and development of six rationales (advocacy arguments) for music education in Canada and commented on a rather "consistent assortment of rationales" surrounding utilitarian or aesthetic arguments that music educators adapted to "the educational aims of the day" (p. 25). They were:

1. music education as a moral mission,
2. music education for enjoyment and emotional outlet,
3. music education to support a leisure culture versus as an intellectual pursuit,
4. music education to promote nationhood,
5. music education as aesthetic education and as developing an intelligence, and
6. music education in support of the music industry and managed diversity. (pp. 25–37)

The underlying premise in each case is that music is seen as a frill in the curriculum. Morton concluded "the history of school music reveals that its marginal status has not substantially improved since music was introduced as a curricular subject" (p. 47).

Many issues can be seen as political, including those associated with the politics of gender, race, age, ethics, and religion. Each of the identified issues has roots in our historical past. Woodford (2005) defined political engagement in a way that democratizes the concept: "Music educators like to think that they are above politics, but politics just refers to the ways people engage in collective decision making" (p. xii). Contributing a different approach to Morton's explanation for music education's marginalization, he explained why music educators must attend to political thought (and action):

> Unless music teachers contribute to public conversations about the nature and purpose of education in general and music education in particular, thereby asserting and establishing their political legitimacy, they will continue to be marginalized and excluded from educational decision making at the government level. (p. xi)

Woodford further claimed that music education in Canada was "both conservative and class-based" (p. 13), issues that have not yet been addressed in historical writing about Canadian music education. The political roots of Canadian music education have barely begun to be identified.

### Roots in Educational Thought (Philosophy and Psychology)

While educational thought[14] is evident to some degree in all histories of music education, some writers use the lens of educational thought explicitly as a way to organize their understanding of historical events. The purpose and goals of education could be studied as they relate to general education, helping us to see a bigger picture and reducing the isolation of music education, or just to music education. I prefer the former approach because of the need to strengthen our links with our education colleagues. So I begin with the question "What does general education history have to contribute to this discussion?"

One answer comes from Gutek (1995), who "revealed [his] emphasis on the roles that key persons have exercised in contributing to and shaping our educational experience" (p. ix) and also explained that "by examining the prevailing thoughts of an age, one can discover its patterns of education" (p. 11). In *A History of the Western Educational Experience*, Gutek discusses the thoughts that contributed to (among others) the Reformation, the Enlightenment, republicanism, revolution, ideology, Marxism, and social Darwinism, as well as the impact of these ideas on education in general. His narrative shows education to be, at times, a reflection of society and, at other times, a contributor to social change.

What have music educators contributed to our understanding of educational thought? Three examples are presented—English, American, and Canadian. Rainbow (1989) performed a service for music education similar to Gutek's: "Although the eventual concern was with the English scene—and essentially with music's place in general education" (preface), Rainbow connected ideas and music education, referring to primary sources he collected over a ten-year period. The titles of his chapters show the focus on educational thought: The New Thought, The Age of Decline, The Age of Ideas, The Age of Reform, and The Age of Rival Systems. It is easy to see that the broader cultural and social contexts and educational thought formed the basis for Rainbow's discussion of music education. Rainbow ended his historical narrative in the 1970s, acknowledging that it was becoming too difficult for him to remain objective when writing about contemporary practice:

> There comes a point…when the narrator's voice represents an intrusion; when it becomes too difficult for him to suspend personal views and prejudices. At that point it is his duty to retire and allow the reader to pursue the investigation for himself. That point, if not already passed, has now been reached. (p. 341)

The honesty of these words and the attempt to remain objective are admirable qualities required of all researchers.

Tellstrom (1971), an American historian, built on the data collection of music education historians such as Birge (1928, 1966); on education history; on primary sources (including music textbooks); and on education principles in order to produce a book intended to help music educators recognize innovative methods as the emerging result of changes to major principles rather than formulas to be accepted or rejected. His book is organized so that each section outlines the "evolution and establishment of a major educational movement" and discusses how these thoughts influenced music education. Major principles included the tradition of humanism, the advent of the Enlightenment, an epoch of utility, and child-centred education. The educational thought emphasized by Tellstrom relied most heavily, not surprisingly given the year of publication, on psychological principles.

Green and Vogan (1991) mention trends in educational thought but do not provide substantive discussion of these philosophical ideas. For example, while discussing school music in the Ryerson years, they write:

> The spirit of Pestalozzi's educational theories, which had spread throughout parts of Europe, Britain, and the United States, held great promise for Egerton Ryerson, the first superintendent of education in Canada West. The idea that education could develop the moral nature of the person and could be directed to the whole of society motivated Ryerson toward the ambitious task of producing a master plan for the public school system. (p. 48)

Pestalozzi is mentioned, as is the direct impact his ideas had on Ryerson and his associates across Canada. The reader, however, is referred to a footnote that identifies Rainbow's 1967 book *The Land without Music* for a discussion of the theories (p. 448).

The search for the roots of Canadian music education must lead to a consideration of the purpose of music education. A logical place to look for this purpose is in the philosophy of music education. Since the first edition of *A Philosophy of Music Education* (Reimer, 1970), and particularly in the last two decades, music education philosophy has been assuming an increasingly important voice in music education. Unfortunately, the philosophical roots of Canadian music education have typically received passing mention or are implied in traditional historical accounts. Morton (1996) identified utilitarian and aesthetic philosophical intents as root issues in Canadian music education (p. 25). Are these intents addressed in historical accounts of Canadian music education? Some form of utilitarianism figures prominently in Green and Vogan (1991), although the word does not appear in the index. "Aesthetic education" does appear in the index in connection with the American 1967 Tanglewood Symposium and the development of aesthetic sensitivity. A second page reference is supplied in the index, but to a page on which I could find no mention of the word "aesthetic." The few references to aesthetic education are not surprising because the term came into common use only in the 1970s; nevertheless, some reference to what could be loosely called aesthetic education, with a focus on self-expression and the aesthetically beautiful (rather than Reimer's focus on the expressive qualities of music), can be uncovered in Green and Vogan's book. Green and Vogan, of course, did not set out to discuss philosophical roots.

Even the kinds of music programs we have offered are based on belief systems. Woodford (2005) reminds us that the origins of our performance-based classes are, after all, "found in autocratic institutions such as the military, church, or aristocracy" (p. 28). There is a need for more in-depth examinations of the philosophical roots of Canadian music education and its relation to educational thought.

## Historical Roots: Unexplored Paths
Where are the roots of Canadian music education?[15] In my examination of events and people, social and cultural thoughts, political issues, and educational thought, I have shown that there is more than one way to conceptualize the "roots" of an endeavour. The research question determines where the researcher will look, what data will be sought and collected, and how it will be interpreted. History is not monolithic. The answers to ques-

tions, even age-old questions, may change as the past is reassessed in the light of contemporary interests. If the purpose of history is "to illuminate the past in order to provide the perspective in time and place that we need to make reflective decisions on the educational choices that face us today" (Gutek, 1995, p. ix), then music educators need to realize that history is not fixed. Instead, it is a product of the storytellers, of their social and cultural background, and of their political and educational thought. *Caveat lector.*

The goal of this chapter has not been to identify *the* roots of music education in Canada. This is not because the task is unimportant, because the task is, in fact, very important. However, such a vast topic is perhaps too ambitious and too important to be addressed so quickly. It is instead more necessary to determine what we still need to know about the history of Canadian music education before we can claim to determine the very roots of the discipline. We also need to acknowledge the impermanent status of "roots," as these are subject to reinterpretation, as well as to multi-interpretations.[16] Therefore, this chapter asked questions rather than provide answers. Too much work remains to be done in Phase 3 types of historical research for any authoritative claims to be made at this time. Too many complex factors contributing to the fabric of history have yet to be examined. If you were hoping that all would be revealed, that the roots of Canadian music education would be laid before you, you will have been disappointed. Nonetheless, while reading this chapter you may have identified themes that should be explored in future historical research. Even radical interpretations can provoke a thoughtful review of our antecedents and engage us in significant dialogue to promote greater understanding.

It is my hope that this meta-analysis of the process of writing music education history will provide Canadian music education historians with a research agenda for the coming decades — beginning with the "roots" of Canadian music education. Of particular interest is whether Canadian music education is a clone of that in the United States or if its underlying assumptions are distinctive (personal communication, Wayne Bowman, May 29, 2005). A Phase 3 examination of "roots" could begin to identify the characteristics that are unique to Canadian music education.

Schools do not exist in a vacuum; neither does music education. Partnerships with ministries of education, ministries of culture, other cultural agencies, and colleagues in general education continually provide new sources of information. Music education provided outside the schools is also an important part of the story. Addressing cultural, political, philosophical, and psychological questions and their interactions, while using accurate information about events and people, can shed better light on the roots of Canadian music education, thus providing a means of understanding the present and of informing our future.[17]

## Notes

1 Relying on common usage, I distinguish between roots and foundations, with the former referring to origins and the latter, more broadly, to "the many significant matters that affect music instruction" (Abeles, Hoffer, & Klotman, 1994, p. xiii).

2 Notable exceptions occur in chapter 2 of Charlene Morton's (1996) dissertation *The "Status Problem": The Feminized Location of School Music and the Burden of Justification* and Stephanie Horsley's (2005) master's thesis, *Music Education Advocacy Efforts of CMEA, CMEC and the NSEA,* which are discussed below.

3 Bray, Green, and Vogan (1992) summarized this information in their entry on "School Music" in the *Encyclopedia of Music in Canada,* 2nd ed.

4 Volumes 42(1) through 45(1).

5 Métis are "any persons who have mixed Indian and European ancestry and who do not have Indian status" (Whidden, 1992, p. 851).

6 Canadians of non-European heritage were less visible until the Canadian Multiculturalism Act (Bill C-93) was adopted by Parliament in July 1988.

7 See John Ralston Saul's (1997) *Reflections of a Siamese Twin: Canada at the End of the Twentieth Century,* especially pages 55–80, for a discussion of solitude and isolation. From an anglophone perspective, I could point out the "Alouette" syndrome, where, for a good part of the twentieth century, a few token songs, including "Alouette," represented French culture in English-language songbooks.

8 Elizabeth Murray's name does not appear in the 1992 *Encyclopedia of Music in Canada.* How many important contributors to music education in Canada await discovery?

9 For examples of examinations of music education from a sociological perspective, see Rideout (1997), *On the Sociology of Music Education*); Green (1997), *Music, Gender, Education*; Small (1998), *Musicking*; DeNora (2000), *Music in Everyday Life*; and Green (2002), *How Popular Musicians Learn.*

10 Alastair Glegg, an education historian at the University of Victoria who kindly provided feedback on my paper, reminded me of this important point.

11 Advocacy initiatives are, perhaps, the exception and may be the way of drawing more music educators into political action. Green and Vogan (1991) do include a chapter on politics and public relations in Ontario, but the political aspects have mostly to do with establishing new programs and trail blazing. Provincial MEAs have admittedly been, historically, more politically involved in educational matters but are not necessarily powerful. Today, however, national educational initiatives are under way (such as the Pan-Canadian Science Project and standardized testing in "core" subjects), and provincial partnerships such as the Western Canadian Protocol for Collaboration in Basic Education (http://www.wncp.ca/general/wpagreement.html), the Atlantic Canada Framework (http://camet-camef.ca/default.asp?mn=1.2), and Learning Through the Arts (LTTA) (http://www.ltta.ca) will require music educators to become politically aware and involved nationally as well as provincially and locally.

12 For an examination of postmodern thought see David Harvey's (1990) *The Condition of Postmodernity,* and for postmodernism and music Judy Lochhead and Joseph Auner's (2002) *Postmodern Music: Postmodern Thought.* For an argument in defence of liberalism and a criticism of postmodernism, see Paul Woodford's (2005) *Democracy and Music Education.*

13 Paul Woodford's (2005) *Democracy and Music Education,* while American in its focus, does include some "Canadian content" and clearly addresses the importance of politics in music education.

14 Here, "educational thought" refers to the philosophical and psychological ideas that initiate and change practice.

15 This question reminds me of history assignments that asked students to list *the* three causes of the Second World War.

16 Nevertheless, as Margaret MacMillan (2008) wrote, "there is an irreducible core to the story of the past. What happened and in what order?" (p. 38).

17 I thank Wayne Bowman, Amanda Montgomery, Charlene Morton, and Paul Woodford for reading a draft of this paper and providing thoughtful feedback. Any remaining errors are mine alone.

## References

Abeles, H. F., Hoffer, C. R., & Klotman, R. H. (1994). *Foundations of music education* (2nd ed.). New York: Schirmer Books.

Apple, M. (1990). *Ideology and curriculum* (2nd ed.). New York: Routledge & Kegan Paul.

Birge, E. B. (1928, 1966). *History of public school music in the United States.* Washington, DC: Music Educators National Conference.

Brault, D. (1977). *A history of the Ontario Music Educators' Association (1919–1974)* (Unpublished doctoral dissertation). University of Rochester, New York.

Bray, K., Green, J. P., & Vogan, N. F. (1992). School music. In H. Kallman & G. Potvin (Eds.), *Encyclopedia of music in Canada* (2nd ed.) (pp. 1190–1199). Toronto: University of Toronto Press.

Buckley, M. M. (1988). *Music education in Alberta, 1884–1945: History and development.* Unpublished manuscript, available from Library and Archives Canada.

Cringan, A. T. (1888). *The Canadian music course.* Toronto: Canada Publishing.

Cringan, A. T. (1889). *The teacher's handbook of the tonic sol-fa system.* Toronto: Canada Publishing.

Cringan, A. T. (1898). *The educational music course.* Toronto: Canada Publishing.

D'Alton, J. P. (1997). *Edward Johnson and music education in Canada* (Unpublished master's thesis). University of Guelph, Guelph, ON.

DeNora, T. (2000). *Music in everyday life.* Cambridge, UK: Cambridge University Press.

Elliott, D. J. (2001). Modernity, postmodernity, and music education philosophy. *Research Studies in Music Education, 17,* 32–41.

Gardi, L. J. (1998). *The history of music education in London and Middlesex County Roman Catholic Separate School Board, 1858–1994* (Unpublished master's thesis). The University of Western Ontario, London, ON.

Giddens, A., Duneier, M., & Appelbaum, R. P. (2003). *Introduction to sociology* (4th ed.). New York: W. W. Norton & Company.

Green, J. P., & Vogan, N .F. (1991). *Music education in Canada: A historical account.* Toronto: University of Toronto Press.

Green, L. (1997). *Music, gender, education.* Cambridge, UK: Cambridge University Press.

Green, L. (2002). *How popular musicians learn.* Aldershot, Hampshire: Ashgate.

Gutek, G. L. (1995). *A history of the Western educational experience* (2nd ed.). Prospect Heights, IL: Waveland Press.

Hanley, B. (2003). The good, the bad, and the ugly — Arts partnerships in Canadian elementary schools. *Arts Education Policy Review, 104*(6), 11–20.

Hanley, B. (2005). *Franklin E. Churchley: Gentleman, scholar, teacher.* Retrieved from http:// cmea.ca/images/PDF/churchley.pdf.

Harris, C. E. (1998). *A sense of themselves: Elizabeth Murray's leadership in school and community.* Halifax, NS: Fernwood Publishing.

Harvey, D. (1990). *The condition of postmodernity.* Cambridge, MA: Blackwell.

Heimonen, M. (2005). *Justifying the right to music education.* Presented at the Philosophy of Music Education International Symposium 6, University of Hamburg, Germany, May 18–21.

Horsley, S. (2005). *Music education advocacy efforts of CMEA, CMEC and the NSAE* (Unpublished master's thesis). The University of Western Ontario, London, ON.

Howey, R. J. (2003). A history of music in the Edmonton (Alberta) Public School System, 1882–1949. *Dissertation Abstracts International, 64*(9), 3229.

Kallmann, H. (1960). *A history of music in Canada, 1534–1914.* Toronto: University of Toronto Press.

Kallman, H., & Potvin, G. (Eds.). (1992). *Encyclopedia of music in Canada* (2nd ed.). Toronto: University of Toronto Press.

Kaplan, D. L. (1993). *Oh no not another meeting: A fond look at the Saskatchewan Music Educators Association, 1957–1993.* Retrieved from http://www.music educationonline.org/smea/smeanews1.html.

Kolstee, A., Baudry, N., Witmer, R., Peacock, K., & Cavanaugh, B. D. (1992). Native North Americans in Canada. In H. Kallman, G. Potvin, & K. Winters (Eds.), *Encyclopedia of music in Canada* (2nd ed.) (pp. 923–935). Toronto: University of Toronto Press.

Lochhead, J., & Auner, J. (Eds.). (2002). *Postmodern music: Postmodern thought.* New York: Routledge.

MacLennan, H. (1946). *Two solitudes.* London: Cresset Press.

MacMillan, M. (2008). *The uses and abuses of history.* Toronto: Penguin Canada.

Mark, M. L., & Gary, C. T. (1992). *A history of American music education.* New York: Schirmer Books.

McIntosh, R. D. (1989). *History of music in British Columbia, 1850–1950.* Victoria, BC: Sono Nis Press.

McLennon, S. R. (2000). *The Music Special Interest Council of the Newfoundland and Labrador's Teacher Association: An historical perspective of its impact on the development of music education in Newfoundland and Labrador* (Unpublished master's thesis). The University of Western Ontario, London, ON.

Morton, C. A. (1996). *The "status problem": The feminized location of school music and the burden of justification* (Unpublished doctoral dissertation). University of Toronto, Toronto, ON.

Norris, C. (Ed.). (1989). *Music and the politics of culture.* London: Lawrence & Wishart.

Pitts, S. (2000). *A century of change in music education.* Aldershot, Hampshire: Ashgate.

Rainbow, B. (1989). *Music in educational thought & practice: A survey from 800 BC.* Aberystwyth, Wales: Boethius Press.

Rainbow, E. L., & Froelich, H. C. (1987). *Research in music education: An introduction to systematic inquiry.* New York: Schirmer Books.

Reimer, B. (1970). *A philosophy of music education.* Englewood Cliffs, NJ: Prentice-Hall, Inc.

Rideout, R. (Ed.). (1997). *On the sociology of music education.* Norman, OK: University of Oklahoma.

Saul, J. R. (1997). *Reflections of a Siamese twin: Canada at the end of the twentieth century.* Toronto: Penguin Books.

Small, C. (1998). *Musicking.* Hanover, NH: Wesleyan University Press.

Tellstrom, A. T. (1971). *Music in American education: Past and present.* New York: Holt, Rinehart and Winston.

Thomas, S. L. (1998). Kenneth I. Bray: His contribution to music education (Ontario). *Masters Abstracts International, 37*(2), 404.

Trowsdale, G. C. (1962). *A history of public school music in Ontario* (Unpublished doctoral dissertation). University of Toronto, Toronto, ON.

Tufts, J., & Holt, H. (1883). *The normal music course.* Boston: Silver Burdett.

Vogan, N. F. (2000). Stories from our past: Alice Harrison: Pioneer music educator and inspiration. *Canadian Music Educator, 42*(1), 22.

Vogan, N. F. (2001). The annual spring concert. *Canadian Music Educator, 42*(3), 6.

Vogan, N. F. (2002). Influential Manitoba music educator: Ethel A. Kinley. *Canadian Music Educator, 44*(3), 5.

Wasiak, E. B. (1996). The historical development of school bands in Saskatchewan: A study of four selected divisions. *Dissertation Abstracts International, 57*(10), 4302.

Whidden, L. (1992). Métis. In H. Kallman & G. Potvin (Eds.), *Encyclopedia of music in Canada* (2nd ed.) (pp. 851–852). Toronto: University of Toronto Press.

Woodford, P. G. (1983). *Charles Hutton: "Newfoundland's greatest musician and dramatist," 1861–1949.* St. John's, NF: Creative Printers and Publishers.

Woodford, P. G. (2005). *Democracy and music education: Liberalism, ethics, and the politics of practice.* Bloomington, IN: Indiana University Press.

TWO

# Cross-Country Checkup:
# A Survey of Music Education
# in Canada's Schools

*Benjamin Bolden*

## Introduction

Canada is a huge and diverse nation, and trying to summarize music education across this vast country in one chapter might seem an impossible
task, yet still one worth attempting. Music education colleagues from
across the country facilitated the writing of this summary chapter by providing written accounts of various aspects of school music education in
their provinces and territories.[1] These music educators submitted reports
describing music teaching and learning issues, activities, and concerns in
their respective regions. Although they were disparate accounts of music
education, a number of consistent themes arose, which resulted in the for-
mulation of six guiding questions that provide a general sense of the issues
surrounding music education in Canadian schools in the early twenty-first
century. These are:

1. What music education curriculum is mandated in Canada's schools?
2. What factors inhibit students from experiencing music education in
   schools?
3. Who teaches music in Canadian schools?

4. How are music teachers trained?
5. How are music teachers supported?
6. What music education initiatives and activities can we celebrate?

## 1. What Music Education Curriculum Is Mandated in Canada's Schools?

Paradoxically, the music education that regional curriculum guidelines *intend* for young Canadians to experience in schools across the country is more or less the same from coast to coast to coast: general music classes are mandatory for elementary students and emphasize singing, with some possibility of mallet instrument, recorder, or ukulele playing. Middle-school students (who are often allowed to choose whether or not to take music classes) play band, and sometimes string, instruments. For second-ary school students, music is strictly optional and is most likely to involve a performance emphasis, particularly of the instrumental or choral variety.

More recent provincial curriculum documents tend to provide guide-lines for more diverse music programs, particularly at the secondary level. Composition and technology-oriented courses, for example, are outlined in both Ontario and British Columbia curriculum guidelines. In Alberta, high schools may offer locally developed music courses, such as marching band, vocal jazz, instrumental jazz, and chamber ensemble. Similarly, in Newfoundland and Labrador, music educators across the province are able to develop and offer local music courses such as musical theatre and media and technology, and schools may offer elective credit courses ranging from a general music course, called "Experiencing Music," to "Applied Music" to "Ensemble Performance." In addition, the Newfoundland and Labrador provincial curriculum document encourages the development of perfor-mance skills on traditional instruments such as fiddle, accordion, and tin whistle. In Nova Scotia, senior-level music courses provide unique oppor-tunities for students to carry out in-depth explorations of specific topics within the music making process. Music 12 (the final year of elective music instruction) is based on a "project approach" so that students may apply their music learning in authentic contexts; teachers select from a range of projects lasting from three days to three months.

Conversely, elsewhere in the country mandated music education cur-riculum guidelines remain narrowly focused. In Prince Edward Island, beyond the elementary level, provincial government guidelines focus solely on instrumental music, without any mention of general music or choral music at intermediate or senior levels. In Manitoba the curricu-lum document is outdated. However, as Bowman identifies in chapter 4 of this book, for many secondary music teachers in the province, band music receives most of the curriculum emphasis, with other areas only receiving scant attention.

Bowman's suggestion that the provincially prescribed curriculum document in Manitoba has not, in fact, greatly influenced what happens in the province's school music programs may well be applicable to the rest of the country. Concerning Ontario and the secondary arts curriculum guidelines released in 2000 and 2001, Willingham and Cutler (2007) explained, "innovative teachers were not slaves to the curriculum. In order for teachers to maintain their own values and beliefs about what is important for music students to study, outcomes have been clustered, layered, and linked, or even ignored" (p. 7). Such musings beg the question: *Are* curriculum documents significantly impacting music education in Canadian schools?

Another recent trend in curriculum emphasis, more prevalent in the younger grades but creeping upward, has been government and administrative encouragement to integrate music with other subject areas, particularly visual art, drama, and dance. As seen particularly in Saskatchewan, the government website and curriculum documents from the Ministry of Education promote an arts-based curriculum rather than a music education curriculum (Bayley, 2007). Music educators have been wary of this shift and resistant to the notion that music education is well served by lumping it in with the other arts. In Ontario, for example, many felt uncomfortable with 1998 elementary curriculum changes that compacted dance, drama, music, and visual arts into one document (Willingham & Cutler, 2007), albeit with separate sections for each subject. The insidious implication that a trained music educator could or should teach in other arts areas, or conversely that a drama, visual art, or dance educator could or should be responsible for a student's music education, has not sat well. There is also legitimate concern that music, relegated to a mere portion of an arts package, will lose ground to the other arts in the interminable battle for status, resources, and — most significantly — time. As Bowman points out in chapter 4, Winnipeg schools schedule between 90 and 120 minutes per week for music, which is higher than the time allotted to other arts subjects.

### What Factors Inhibit Students from Experiencing Music Education in Schools?

Despite the best intentions of the authors of curriculum documents, the music education that young Canadians actually experience within each province or territory varies considerably from district to district and from school to school. Particularly in rural and isolated areas, many schools are simply not able to offer music programs. Less than 50 percent of the high schools in Alberta, for instance, offer any music credits at all (Dust & Montgomery, 2007). This is largely a result of a scarcity of music teachers, who seem to be much more readily available in urban centres. In Toronto, for instance, in 2005 there were seventy-two music specialists wanting to teach music full-time but who did not have positions (Willingham & Cutler, 2007). Another reason why music tends to happen less in rural schools was identified by Anderson and Tupman (2007), who reported that 60 percent of school music programs in British Columbia occur outside regular school hours. As a result, the many students in rural areas who must catch a bus right after school find it difficult to participate in the program. In British Columbia the lack of music teachers is exacerbated by some who elect to teach subjects other than music "because it is just too hard to teach music in the current political, educational, and fiscal realities of the profession ... many potential music teachers are deciding that music teaching is not a sustainable or healthy profession to pursue" (Anderson & Tupman, 2007, p. 4). The one exception to the varying access to music education in Canada is Prince Edward Island. There, "instrumental music education is now accessible to every high school student in the province" (Griffin, 2007, p. 7), and specialists educate students in *all* the province's schools.

Music programs cannot run without teachers, but they are also doomed without political and administrative support. More and more curricular possibilities, combined with a dominant emphasis on literacy and numeracy and often reinforced by government standardized testing, have caused many to feel there is less and less room for music in the school day. Some administrators simply choose to let music go. In the 1990s, the Ontario Conservative government made sweeping changes to the way the province's schools operated. Results saw 32 percent fewer music teachers in elementary schools and an increased reliance on school-based fundraising to support music and the arts in both elementary and secondary schools (Willingham & Cutler, 2007).

Another significant factor inhibiting Canadian students from experiencing music education in schools is student attrition. While at the elementary level it may be political or administrative will that squeezes music out, in middle and secondary schools, when music becomes optional, students opt out. Across the country, secondary students are required to take only one arts credit in order to graduate, or sometimes none at all (although Newfoundland and Labrador requires two). Even when music is available as an elective, the vast majority of Canadian high school students simply choose not to enrol. Less than 10 percent of the high school students in Alberta, for example, received music education at school during the 2003–4 school year (Dust & Montgomery, 2007). In Ontario only 10–12 percent of high school students take music (Willingham & Cutler, 2007). In New Brunswick, less than 1 percent of francophone Grade 11 and 12 students are enrolled in school music (Lowe & Grashel, 2007).

Why *do* so many Canadian students choose not to enrol in school music? Certainly the demands on a student's timetable are significant; the breadth and specificity of courses required for graduation often make it problematic to allot space for music. In addition, it is not always possible for students to enrol in music courses, even if they have an interest. Music education programs usually depend on "long-term, sequential under-standing and development of performance skills to a reasonable standard" (Anderson & Tupman, 2007, p. 6). This implies that a student must have the right prerequisites to be successful in music; she cannot simply decide to opt in if, in Grade 12, for example, she realizes she has room in her sched-ule. Dust and Montgomery (2007) suggested this is a significant problem in Alberta, where instrumental music (i.e., band) may simply be too elit-ist for the majority of high school students — too many hurdles must be overcome before one can join. An increase in general music offerings and guitar classes, they proposed, may attract more students to music classes in Alberta schools than programs that exclusively offer band. Other reasons for opting out of school music were identified in a survey of music teachers in the Yukon Territory. While some teachers commented on negative peer pressure experienced by students taking music, others indicated that the traditional nature of the band programs on offer did little to attract the non-white community (Beynon & Bell, 2007).

Student enrolment in music programs is also diminishing simply because, in certain provinces, there are fewer students in schools. This is particularly true in British Columbia, but also in Newfoundland and Lab-rador, where student enrolment declined from a peak of 162,818 in 1971 to 79,439 in 2004 (Adams & Rose, 2007). This issue is compounded by the fact that traditional music education programs in schools are particularly poorly suited to survive diminishing numbers. Programs oriented around band need large numbers of students — thirty-five at least — for meaning-ful music making in this context. In Newfoundland and Labrador, there is a high proportion of small schools; 25 percent of schools in the province have a total student population fewer than 100 and 45 percent have fewer than 200 students (Adams & Rose, 2007). In schools of this size, running a band program would be problematic at best. In an innovative bid to pro-vide music education to isolated learners in the province, a general music program, "Experiencing Music," is now offered over the Internet through the Centre for Distance Learning and Innovation.

In some parts of the country, music teachers have sought innovative ways to keep programs alive. In Ontario, for instance, music teachers combat diminishing enrolment by giving credit for ensemble work and continuing to seek creative ways of timetabling or by encouraging students to continue to participate in music programs through non-credit (extracurricular) involvement. In francophone New Brunswick, despite low enrolment in music education classes at the secondary school level, many students participate in extracurricular activities such as concert band, jazz band, and choir (Lowe & Grashel, 2007).

It is important to point out that, unlike in the rest of the country, secondary school music in Manitoba is thriving — and it is the band programs that are drawing the students in. A survey conducted by the Manitoba Band Association found that of the 80,000 students in Grades 4–12 who had the option, almost one-third (31.3 percent) were enrolled in band in 2002. Significantly, band not only is doing well in Manitoba but is on an upward trajectory: between 1997 and 2002 both the number of schools offering band and the number of students engaged in band increased.

### Who Teaches Music in Canadian Schools?

Those concerned with music education seem most satisfied that there is sound music instruction happening in schools when the teachers responsible for teaching music are music *specialists*.[2] As Dust and Montgomery (2007) point out, when non-specialist teachers are responsible for delivering the music curriculum, a lack of both confidence and content knowledge will likely result in that curriculum being shortchanged.

In Prince Edward Island, there are music specialists in all schools (Griffin, 2007); but this is not the norm in Canadian provinces and territories, especially in rural areas. In Alberta, for example, less than one-third of elementary schools employ music specialists (Dust & Montgomery, 2007). Although a preference that students be guided in learning about music by teachers who specialize in doing so is understandable, music specialists are not always available. What are the alternatives when there are no specialists to teach music? In Newfoundland and Labrador the music curriculum is designed to be taught by music specialists with the acknowledgement that it is appropriate for non-specialist classroom teachers (generalists) to deliver the program when necessary (e.g., in small and/or isolated communities) (Adams & Rose, 2007). A Yukon music teacher, responding to a survey conducted by Beynon and Bell (2007), suggested specialists might accommodate the lack of specialists in the territory by going beyond their teaching roles to act as resource teachers to non-specialists:

The schools that have music programs are doing well, but there are many schools without music programs. I would like to see music offered in all schools — if not available through a music specialist, at least they should have support and programs available to classroom teachers to help them deliver a music program. I see myself and other music specialists as resources to teachers and schools that do not have music programs. If we can help all schools to see the need for music and the value of music. (p. 4)

Similarly, an Ontario teacher responding to a survey cited by Willingham and Cutler (2007) offered the following:

Sadly, for non-music specialist teachers, they are overwhelmed with the many other (and mostly considered "more important") teaching subjects in literacy and numeracy. It is very difficult to ask them to try to devote more time to learning more on a subject that for most is considered "less important.".... In my school, I try to connect with the classroom music teachers after I have been to a conference and give them some new ideas that I think they would like. (p. 11)

Is it feasible for music specialists to support non-specialists in music-teaching roles? What are the ramifications? Will such additional demands on the specialists exacerbate the already significant incidence of music-teacher burnout? Will administrators and policy makers place even less importance on bringing music specialists into schools? Or, as suggested above, will a little support from the specialists help to foster a climate of greater understanding and appreciation of music and lead to more generous support of music specialists and a more dedicated effort to bring them into schools?

In some regions in Canada, even when music specialists are available, getting students into schools and keeping them there can be problematic. In anglophone Quebec schools, specialist music teachers are often squeezed out to make way for government-mandated French as a Second Language (FSL) instruction. Some schools seek to overcome this either–or predicament by hiring teachers who can teach music in French, thereby satisfying the French-language requirement while simultaneously providing students with music learning opportunities. Finding such teachers, however, is challenging, as the music specialists must not only speak the language but also be familiar with sufficient French-language music repertoire and terminology (Russel, 2007). In British Columbia strong teacher unions, promoting the egalitarian perspective that a teacher is a teacher is a teacher, do not allow the hiring or retention of music specialists over non-specialists; therefore it is sometimes difficult for schools to hire or to hold on to a music teacher, particularly as school populations shrink (Anderson & Tupman, 2007).

Given the considerable emphasis music education advocates place on the importance of having music specialists in schools, it makes sense to examine what the designation actually means. In Manitoba's elementary schools, most musical instruction is delivered by specialists rather than generalists. While acknowledging the value of music specialists, Bowman (2007) points out that what the term music "specialist" actually implies is ambiguous:

> Teachers become specialists by virtue of teaching assignment, not training. There is no official difference in presumed professional expertise between (1) an individual with a music performance degree followed by a Bachelor of Education degree, (2) an individual without a music degree but with considerable musical interest, and (3) an individual with extensive formal training in the discipline of music education. (p. 4)

Bowman's implication is significant: the assertion that a specialist is teaching music carries no guarantee of a quality music education and that the effective teaching of music requires more than a musical background or even musical expertise. Favaro (2007) echoed this sentiment when discussing a predicament in Nova Scotia: Currently, only one university in the province — Acadia — offers music *education* as a degree program. There are *music* programs at Dalhousie University and St. Francis Xavier University, but they offer little or no instruction in methodology. Many graduates of these programs go on to pursue an education degree and seek employment as specialist music teachers, but the lack of skill development in music education can present serious challenges in the delivery of music curriculum.

Concern regarding specialists with plenty of music but questionable *music education* background may be paralleled by concern for those who have plenty of education but questionable *music* background. It is possible, for example, to be admitted into some Ontario faculties of education and train to become a certified "music specialist" with only two undergraduate courses in music (other faculties demand a much more rigorous slate of undergraduate courses). In addition, the Ontario College of Teachers administers a post-certification Additional Qualifications (AQ) program, provided through various faculties of education, which allows teachers without *any* music training to take a three-session course that designates them a music specialist.

Clearly, the role of music specialists is significant in Canadian music education. It is less clear what it means to be a music specialist. In closing this section, perhaps it is helpful to ponder the following from Willingham and Cutler (2007):

> Teachers can be successful and effective in teaching music without all of the formal training, but this is not often the case. Instead, the students fail to reach their creative and artistic potential in a learning situation where the teacher is unable to fully deliver a properly developed and delivered music program. On the other hand, simply having full specialist qualifications does not ensure success in teaching. Teachers are needed who bring a balance of *competence, confidence,* and *courage,* all supported by a strong *calling* to teach children and young people, in order to have healthy and vibrant music in our schools. (p. 12)

### How Are Music Teachers Trained?

In Canada, music educators generally receive certification after completing a two-part program: a four-year undergraduate university degree focused on music and housed within a faculty or school of music, followed by an additional one- to two-year post-degree university program focused on education and housed within a faculty of education. The amount of music *education* coursework that is involved in the first portion of this teacher preparation experience — the undergraduate Bachelor of Music degree — varies considerably. For undergraduate music students at the University of Victoria, for example, who choose to focus on music education, more than one-quarter of the coursework required to graduate directly addresses music education concerns — philosophical, psychological, sociological, methodological, instructional, and curricular. Students proceed from such a program to a post-degree education program and thence to music teaching positions with considerable music education background, awareness, and understanding. It is also possible, however, to enter some post-degree (consecutive) music education programs from a music degree that required no music education coursework whatsoever (see, for example, admission requirements for the music teacher education program at the Ontario Institute for Studies in Education). It follows, then, that new music teachers may begin their careers with negligible background, awareness, or understanding of music education issues and concerns.

Bowman (2007), speaking specifically about Manitoba but identifying a significant issue throughout the country, raises an additional concern:

> The first-degree plus second-degree structure fails to address the integration of content and method. In fact, it works against it in many ways. The music curricula in Schools of Music are based extensively on considerations like the development of musical performance skills, together with significant knowledge in the areas of conventional ("classical") music history and music theory. Admissions and recruiting are based on considerations other than music education; and curricula yield room for music education concerns grudgingly, if at all. The predominant result of socialization is an identity as a musician, not as a music educator. In Faculties of Education, geared as they are to the creation of a general "educator" identity, there is similar resistance to the incorporation of music education courses. As a result, music education enjoys a place of significance in neither Schools of Music nor in Faculties of Education, the former regarding it as Education's concern, and the latter regarding it as Music's. (p. 11)

Under this institutional model, then, music education tends to be marginalized in both portions of the consecutive-degree teacher preparation structure; while the music educators are the poorer cousins of the performance-focused musicians in music faculties, the music educators in education faculties are resented for resisting the less-specialized designation of "educator."

In some provinces, as an alternative to the consecutive teacher preparation process, concurrent programs are available and provide a more integrated teacher preparation experience. For example, L'Université de Moncton — the only French-language university in New Brunswick — offers a five-year combined BMus/BEd program (recently developed and implemented in January 2006), as does Memorial University in Newfoundland and Labrador. At the University of Prince Edward Island the five-year Bachelor of Music Education degree, offered by the Faculty of Music, qualifies students for a Prince Edward Island Teaching Certificate.

### How Are Music Teachers Supported?

Currently, across the country, there seems to be little professional support provided to music teachers. At one time, school districts hired one or more music education consultants; however, there are now few left to support teachers in schools. Funding for these positions, or more specifically the political will behind it, appears to be drying up. A recent restructuring of the English sector of the provincial department of education in New Brunswick eliminated several consultant positions, including the one for fine arts and music. In British Columbia most of the music and arts district staff positions have been cut. Likewise, in Ontario many central resource staff positions have been cut, with the result that boards of education no longer offer regular professional development opportunities for music teachers. Of the seven school districts in Nova Scotia, only one — the Cape Breton–Victoria Regional School Board — employs a full-time arts education consultant. As Favaro (2007) pointed out, this absence of music leadership and advocacy can negatively impact schedules, budgets, resources, and hiring practices. "More significantly," he writes, "it creates a sense of isolation for music educators and it seems to be decreasing overall morale" (p. 6).

One way in which school music educators have been positively connected is through Canada's music education associations (MEAs), which have played a hugely significant role in supporting music teachers and in helping to combat the perennial issue of music teacher isolation. Below, for illustrative purposes, is a quick overview of some of the country's MEAs, though most provinces and territories have their own version of these valuable organizations.

Active since 1960, the Newfoundland and Labrador Music Special Interest Council — previously known as the Music Council of the Newfoundland Teachers' Association — is one of twenty special-interest councils of the Newfoundland and Labrador Teachers' Association. Its purpose is "to keep teachers informed of curriculum changes, to assist in the professional development of its members, and to share innovative approaches to teaching" (Adams & Rose, 2007, p. 8). The council provides professional support to its members through curriculum resources, tutorials, teaching references, lesson links, and discussion forums available to its members.

The Nova Scotia Music Educators' Association holds a conference each year that is well attended by teachers from both New Brunswick and Nova Scotia. New Brunswick does not have a provincial organization of English-speaking school music teachers, creating a void for ongoing professional development for its English music educators in the province. Some teachers fill the gap by belonging to the Nova Scotia Music Educators Association and attending their conferences, or other regional workshops in Orff, Kodály, and/or various aspects of instrumental instruction. However, "there is still a need for a locally-based professional organization that can be responsive to the needs of teachers in New Brunswick itself" (Vogan, 2007, p. 7).

The Ontario Music Educators' Association supports teachers with a quarterly journal, annual conference, and various regional "Toolkit" workshop days. In Manitoba the Manitoba Music Educators' Association primarily supports elementary music, while secondary teachers tend to be more involved with either the Manitoba Choral Association (MCA) or the Manitoba Band Association (MBA).

The British Columbia Music Educators' Association (BCMEA), active since 1959, is similarly structured as a specialist association within the BC Teachers' Federation. It supports a broad range of music education areas throughout the province with an active network of Local Specialist Music Teacher Associations, a quarterly journal, and an annual conference. Sadly, the organization is finding it progressively more difficult to find teachers to take on leadership roles, and the BCMEA annual conference numbers are decreasing. "At one time there used to be 1,000 teachers attending...now there are fewer than half that many in a good year" (Anderson & Tupman, 2007, p. 6). The Yukon Music Educators' Association consists of sixteen elementary and secondary music teachers who meet regularly for idea sharing, collegial learning, and group support.

In addition to comprehensive music educators', band, choral, and registered music teacher associations, many provinces benefit from active Orff and Kodály organizations that provide significant support to music educators. As Bowman (2007) pointed out, however, given their inherent devotion to particular methodologies, these organizations also have the potential to provoke division and fragmentation among music educators.

## What Music Education Initiatives and Activities Can We Celebrate?

Despite the shortcomings of music education in Canada, there is also much to celebrate. Among the reports from Canada's various provinces and territories, a handful of shining lights warrant mention here. In Whitehorse, Yukon Territory, secondary school music teachers work to bring students from across the city together. The Whitehorse All-City Senior Concert Band consists of senior-level students from the territory's three secondary schools, from Yukon College, and from the community. Co-directed by the music teachers from F. H. Collins and Porter Creek secondary schools, the band allows students to see first-hand the concept of "lifelong learning" and participation in music. Also in Whitehorse, high school students who are currently in "out of school" programs may continue studying music by attending a class every Wednesday evening. This evening class allows them to keep up with the required curriculum so that they may re-enter the regular music classes when they return to school (Beynon & Bell, 2007).

In Nunavut Mary Piercey's choir, Arviat Imngitingit, made up of students from Qitiqliq High School and adults from the community, specializes in the recently revived traditional Inuit music originating from the Kivalliq region of Nunavut. The singers excel in traditional throat singing, a-ya-ya singing, drum dancing, and contemporary Inuit folk songs and gospel songs sung in Inuktitutl. Global Television and the Aboriginal Peoples Television Network have featured the choir, as well as newspapers such as the *National Post, Evening Telegram, Southern Gazette, Kivalliq News,* and *News North* (see chapter 5 in this volume).

In francophone New Brunswick, despite very low secondary-level enrolment in music classes, extracurricular choirs and bands are thriving; "Les Jeunes Chanteurs d'Acadie, a community youth choir composed of students from schools in the Moncton area, has been recognized in Canada and abroad for the superior quality of their vocal performance" (Lowe & Grashel, 2007, p. 4). Another successful New Brunswick performing organization is the New Brunswick Youth Orchestra. Although there are very few opportunities for the two language groups in the province to make music together, this ensemble draws both anglophone and francophone musicians. It performs several concerts throughout the school year in communities across the province and has performed as far afield as Italy and Carnegie Hall in New York City (Vogan, 2007).

Shallaway, the Newfoundland and Labrador Youth in Chorus (formerly the Newfoundland Symphony Youth Choir), is a community-based cultural organization consisting of 220 young musicians between the ages of eight and eighteen:

> Shallaway's primary vision is to value, promote, and transmit Newfoundland and Labrador's distinctively rich culture. In terms of music education leadership, the Shallaway's Scholarship and Mentorship Program provides scholarships, mentored leadership, and collaborative experiences to seven university students and seven secondary students annually. (Adams & Rose, 2007, p. 9)

In the province's capital city, St. John's, the Memorial University lab band provides local Grade 5 students the opportunity to study a wind instrument for one year. The young musicians are supported in their learning by undergraduate, pre-service music education students who are able to apply newly acquired teaching and learning principles to the band ensemble context. Newfoundland and Labrador also has its Learning through the Arts program, which is designed to complement the provincial music curriculum. Supported by partnerships with the corporate community, artists come directly into classrooms to work with students and teachers over an extended period of time. "Their mandate is to serve as agents of change within the schools and to promote collaboration, risk-taking, and continuous learning by teachers and students alike" (Adams & Rose, 2007, p. 6).

In Nova Scotia an innovative project-based secondary curriculum enables students to focus on and richly explore specific topics within the music-making process, including advanced performance, composition, conducting, and sound recording. Students who take Advanced Music 11 and Advanced Music 12 benefit from special funding that facilitates the development of mentorship programs involving professionals in the field. The students themselves are required to forge community links with appropriate mentors, thus taking ownership for their learning (Favoro, 2007).

In Prince Edward Island, a high-school-level program entitled Styles of Popular Music has been created and initiated as a local pilot, breaking free from provincial secondary curriculum guidelines that are focused on instrumental music (i.e., band) (Griffin, 2007). Donagh Regional School also offers musical instruction beyond the ubiquitous instrumental band program. Building on a rich tradition of Celtic music in small island communities, a fiddling program was approved for Grades 7 to 9 in 2002 and has since grown to involve children in upper elementary grades as well (V. Allen-Cook, personal communication, June 17, 2005, cited in Griffin, 2007). As Griffin points out, this "integration of community music into the school context is an example of a vibrant partnership between school and community. In this geographical area, maintaining the historical traditions of Irish music has been an integral component of the relationship between school and community culture" (p. 5).

## Summary
As mentioned in the introduction, this chapter was guided and structured by six questions that provided a general sense of the issues surrounding music education in Canadian schools in the early twenty-first century. I return to them now in this summary.

### *What Music Education Curriculum Is Mandated in Canada's Schools?*
In most regions of the country, music education curriculum guidelines are in place, outlining rich and varied music education experiences for Canadian students; but although there are some nods to popular music and attention to our diverse cultures, traditional Eurocentric music still seems to prevail. A trend evident in various parts of the country is an impetus to integrate music with other subjects and, in particular, with the other arts. More recently developed curriculum guidelines, particularly for senior grades, reflect a burgeoning desire to broaden the scope of traditional school music experiences. The extent to which government curriculum guidelines actually have an impact on what goes on in music classrooms, however, is not clear and warrants skepticism.

### What Factors Inhibit Students from Experiencing Music Education in Schools?

Despite the best intentions of those behind the curriculum documents, a number of factors currently inhibit students from experiencing music education in Canadian schools. Particularly in rural and isolated areas across this vast country, many schools are simply not able to offer music programs. This is largely a result of a scarcity of music teachers, who seem to be much more readily available in urban centres. Increasingly available curricular possibilities, combined with a dominating emphasis on literacy and numeracy often reinforced by government standardized testing, cause policy makers, administrators, teachers, parents, and students alike to feel there is less and less room for music in the school day. Sadly, in middle and secondary schools, when music becomes optional, students often opt out. Even when music is available, the vast majority of Canadian high school students simply choose not to enrol.

### Who Teaches Music in Canadian Schools?

In order to maximize the quality of the music education that students experience, there appears to be consensus among music educators that music should be taught by "specialists." However, music specialists are not always available. Is it appropriate for non-specialist classroom teachers to deliver the music program if there is no one else to teach it? Some suggest specialists might act as resource teachers to non-specialists. Is this desirable? In certain regions in Canada, even when music specialists are available, it can be problematic getting them into schools and keeping them there. An increasingly prevalent ethos in teacher federations resists the notion that one teacher should be valued over another for any reason other than seniority. As a result, school administrators face growing challenges in hiring or retaining music specialists over non-specialist teachers. Parenthetically, in any discussion of music specialists, it is important to recognize that the designation "specialist" represents teachers with an extremely broad and diverse range of music and music education backgrounds, not only from one part of the country to the next, but even within regions.

### How Are Music Teachers Trained?

While music teacher training in Canada generally consists of an undergraduate degree in music followed by a further degree in education, there is considerable variation in the nature and scope of the coursework involved from one program to the next, particularly in the first-degree portion. Analysis of music teacher preparation programs often results in the identification of one of two principal, and sometimes conflicting, concerns:

(1) that the music portion of the training is inadequate, and (2) that the music *education* portion of the training is inadequate. Another concern with music teacher preparation identifies that, in both portions of the consecutive degree structure, music educators tend to be marginalized: they have lower status than the performance majors in music faculties, and they are too specialized to fit in with the general educators at the faculties of education.

*How Are Music Teachers Supported?*

Currently, with fewer and fewer music consultants in place across the country, music education associations play an increasingly significant role in supporting in-service music teachers with journals, conferences, curriculum resources, workshops, discussion forums, and other professional development opportunities. In addition to comprehensive music educators' associations, many regions benefit additionally from active band, choral, Orff, and Kodály organizations.

*What Music Education Initiatives and Activities Can We Celebrate?*

While Canadian music education has room for improvement, it also has much to celebrate. Performing organizations in all corners of the country, housed both in schools and in the community, continue to bring young people together to enrich lives with music. Music curricula designed at all levels, from provincial governments to neighbourhood schools and classrooms, demonstrate innovation and a powerful desire to meet the changing needs of students and to connect meaningfully with local communities. We continue to achieve so much, while we strive for so much more.

## Notes

1  The original reports from the authors can be found in an e-book housed by the University of Western Ontario. Please see K. K. Veblen & C. A. Beynon (Eds.), From Sea to Sea: Music Education in Canada: What Is the State of the Art? http://ir.lib.uwo.ca/musiceducationbooks/1/.

2  The often enigmatic definition of music "specialist" in the Canadian context is discussed below.

## References

Adams, K. & Rose, A. (2007). Music education in Newfoundland and Labrador. In K. K. Veblen & C. A. Beynon (Eds.), *From sea to sea: Perspectives on music education in Canada: What is the state of the art?* (pp. 1–21). E-book. Retrieved from http://ir.lib.uwo.ca/musiceducationbooks/1/.

Anderson, A. & Tupman, D. F. (2007). Music education in British Columbia. In K. K. Veblen & C. A. Beynon (Eds.), *From sea to sea: Perspectives on music education in Canada: What is the state of the art?* (pp. 1–11). E-book. Retrieved from http://ir.lib.uwo.ca/musiceducationbooks/1/.

Bayley, J. G. (2007). Music education in Saskatchewan: An outsider's perspective. In K. K. Veblen & C. A. Beynon (Eds.), *From sea to sea: Perspectives on music education in Canada: What is the state of the art?* (pp. 1–9). E-book. Retrieved from http://ir.lib.uwo.ca/musiceducationebooks/1/.

Beynon, C. & Bell, R. (2007). Music education in the Yukon: State of the art. In K. K. Veblen & C. A. Beynon (Eds.), *From sea to sea: Perspectives on music education in Canada: What is the state of the art?* (pp. 1–10). E-book. Retrieved from http://ir.lib.uwo.ca/musiceducationebooks/1/.

Willingham, L., & Cutler, J. (2007). Music education in Ontario: Snapshots on a long and winding road. In K. K. Veblen & C. A. Beynon (Eds.), *From sea to sea: Perspectives on music education in Canada: What is the state of the art?* (pp. 1–20). E-book. Retrieved from http://ir.lib.uwo.ca/musiceducationebooks/1/.

Dust, T. J. & Montgomery A. P. (2007). Music education in Alberta: The contribution of school music programs. In K. K. Veblen & C. A. Beynon (Eds.), *From sea to sea: Perspectives on music education in Canada: What is the state of the art?* (pp. 1–11). E-book. Retrieved from http://ir.lib.uwo.ca/musiceducationebooks/1/.

Favaro, E. W. (2007). Music education in Nova Scotia. In K. K. Veblen & C. A. Beynon (Eds.), *From sea to sea: Perspectives on music education in Canada: What is the state of the art?* (pp. 1–8). E-book. Retrieved from http://ir.lib.uwo.ca/musiceducationebooks/1/.

Griffin, S. M. (2007). Music education in Prince Edward Island: A view beyond the bridge. In K. K. Veblen & C. A. Beynon (Eds.), *From sea to sea: Perspectives on music education in Canada: What is the state of the art?* (pp. 1–12). E-book. Retrieved from http://ir.lib.uwo.ca/musiceducationebooks/1/.

Lowe, A. & Grashel, J. (2007). State of the art of music education in the francophone schools of New Brunswick. In K. K. Veblen & C. A. Beynon (Eds.), *From sea to sea: Perspectives on music education in Canada: What is the state of the art?* (pp. 1–12 ). E-book. Retrieved from http://ir.lib.uwo.ca/musiceducationebooks/1/.

Mathieu, L., Moreno, M. T., Peters V., & Vilar, M. (2007). La situation de l'enseignement musical dans le milieu scolaire du Québec. In K. K. Veblen & C. A. Beynon (Eds.), *From sea to sea: Perspectives on music education in Canada: What is the state of the art?* (pp. 1–25). E-book. Retrieved from http://ir.lib.uwo.ca/musiceducationebooks/1/.

Russell, J. (2007). The domino effect: Quebec's language legislation and its effect on music teacher education in the anglophone sector. In K. K. Veblen & C. A. Beynon (Eds.), *From sea to sea: Perspectives on music education in Canada: What is the state of the art?* (pp. 1–8). E-book. Retrieved from http://ir.lib.uwo.ca/musiceducationebooks/1/.

Vogan, N. (2007). The present state of music education in the English schools of New Brunswick. In K. K. Veblen & C. A. Beynon (Eds.), *From sea to sea: Perspectives on music education in Canada: What is the state of the art?* (pp. 1–12). E-book. Retrieved from http://ir.lib.uwo.ca/musiceducationebooks/1/.

# THREE

# Canadian Music in Music Education: "Sounds Like Canada"

*Patricia Martin Shand*

The first systematic efforts to promote Canadian music in education were made by the Canadian Music Centre (CMC), which began to develop a Graded Educational Music Plan in 1961. This plan, initially conceived and developed by John Adaskin (CMC Executive Secretary), sought to achieve 25 percent Canadian content in music education (Adaskin, 1963, p. 10). In 1965, the plan was renamed the John Adaskin Project, and in 1973 the Canadian Music Educators' Association (CMEA) joined CMC to co-sponsor the project.

Over the years, many local, provincial, and national organizations have sought to promote the use of Canadian music in education. This promotional work has had various aims: (1) to acquaint educators with Canadian music suitable for student performers; (2) to promote publication of Canadian repertoire for student use; (3) to encourage Canadian composers to add to the repertoire of music for student performers; (4) to provide teachers with resource materials to assist them in teaching Canadian music; and (5) to provide opportunities for students to perform and listen to Canadian music and to undertake compositional work.

Promotional efforts on behalf of Canadian music in education continue today. For example, the Association of Canadian Choral Communities

(ACCC) has undertaken an ambitious project designed to produce a series of guides to Canadian choral music that is suitable for both school and community use. The first phase of the project was a guide to choral music by BC composers — prepared by the BC Choral Federation (BCCF) in partnership with the John Adaskin Project — and published in 2004 (Szabo & St. Dennis, 2004). It includes assessments of twenty-five choral works by BC composers, each assessed by a choral specialist according to his or her experience rehearsing and performing that particular composition. To facilitate this project, Szabo and St. Dennis, on behalf of BCCF, developed a choral assessment form based on formats previously employed in the preparation of John Adaskin Project guidelists. The form was made available to choral specialists in print and electronic formats. Eight choral directors, working in a variety of school and community contexts, submitted assessments of works by BC composers. In the final publication, musical, technical, and pedagogical aspects of each piece are described, and details are provided concerning the publisher, date of publication, price, accompaniment, author and language of the text, voicing, duration, level of difficulty, recommended grade level(s), and performance suggestions.

Phase Two of the choral project has focused on music by Ontario composers. Following the BC research methodology, Rodger Beatty of Brock University worked with the Ontario Music Educators' Association (OMEA) and the John Adaskin Project to prepare a guide to choral music by Ontario composers. *Published Choral Compositions by Ontario Composers* contains analyses of twenty choral works recommended by thirteen choral teachers/conductors. The guide is posted electronically on the OMEA website, and Beatty plans to update it as additional analyses are received (Beatty, 2010).

Another current venture is the Canadian Wind Band Repertoire Project, which was established in 2003 to promote the performance of Canadian band music and to encourage the creation of new repertoire. The first product of the project was an article in *Canadian Winds* assessing sixteen recommended Canadian band compositions (Grant, Kinder, & Reynolds, 2004). For each piece, the authors provide information on level of difficulty (ranging from Grade 1 to Grade 6), duration, and availability of score and parts. There is a short description of each piece that provides useful information on technical challenges, musical characteristics, and pedagogical value. Biographical details on each composer are also included, plus information on recordings, if they are available. The authors emphasize that there are

benefits inherent in promoting the culture of one's own country, including the nurturing of artists and the development of a strong national self-image. ... Even though our own country has produced some fine wind-band music, this repertoire tends to be overshadowed by American and European influences. We need to become better at embracing the efforts of our Canadian composers and promoting their music. (Grant, Kinder, & Reynolds, 2004, p. 31)

An outgrowth of the Canadian Wind Band Repertoire Project was an OMEA 2004 conference workshop on Canadian band music, presented by Jeff Reynolds with the University of Toronto Wind Ensemble. Lynn Tucker, an experienced teacher and PhD student at the University of Toronto, participated in the OMEA conference workshop and provided the following comments:

I observed Jeff Reynolds' presentation from a unique perspective. Not only was I a teacher, but also a performer with the Wind Ensemble. I was amazed at how accessible the music was. As a band director, sitting in a music store examining reams of scores can be tedious. And most of that music is American. Having access to a live performance of Canadian music was such a treat! Much of it I had never heard of, but most of it was of excellent quality. Jeff presented material suitable for beginner through to advanced students, and certainly made me believe that accessing this music is not so hard at all. I believe we should be playing more of our own music. It was a valuable presentation — very informative for the band director.

Promotional efforts on behalf of Canadian music in education have been valuable, but the question remains as to whether or not those efforts have borne fruit. Research studies sponsored by the University of Toronto Canadian Music Education Research Centre and the John Adaskin Project have explored this question as it relates to elementary and secondary school music curricula. The studies asked two questions: (1) To what extent have the various promotional efforts to increase Canadian content in music education been successful? and (2) Has John Adaskin's aim of 25 percent Canadian content been achieved?

The first step toward answering these questions began with an analysis of the content of music curriculum documents produced by provincial ministries of education (Bartel & Shand, 1995) and by local boards of education in Ontario (Shand & Bartel, 1998). In 1997–98, Lori Dolloff joined the research team addressing this question, and data was collected on the music and other curricular materials used in thirteen southern Ontario elementary and secondary school music programs (Shand, Bartel, & Dolloff,

**Table 3.1** *Comparison of All Categories of Canadian Content in School Instruction*

|  | Reported School Programs | |
|  | Canadian Content | Non-Canadian Content |
| --- | --- | --- |
| Individual pieces | 295  (21.8%) | 1058  (78.2%) |
| Music books | 148  (32.2%) | 311  (67.8%) |
| Reference books | 23  (18.9%) | 99  (81.1%) |
| Film/video | 8  (34.8%) | 15  (65.2%) |
| Recordings | 43  (26.5%) | 119  (73.5%) |
| Kits | 5  (16.1%) | 26  (83.9%) |
| Miscellaneous | 4  (18.2%) | 18  (81.8%) |
| **Total** | **526  (24.2%)** | **1646  (75.8%)** |

1999). Then the project was extended to include data on music programs in schools across Canada (Bartel, Dolloff, & Shand, 1999). Data collection regarding the music and other curricular materials that elementary and secondary school teachers were using has continued, and a rich amount of information from all types and levels of music programs has been obtained. What follows is a brief summary of the information obtained from ninety-seven school music programs across Canada from 1997 to 2005.[1]

This discussion focuses on one research question: what proportion of music and musical materials being used for study and performance in Canadian schools is of Canadian origin? Table 3.1 shows that 24.2 percent of all the music curricular materials documented during the research were Canadian — just slightly less than Adaskin's goal of 25 percent Canadian content, while 21.8 percent of the individual pieces were Canadian. The reported use of Canadian music books, films and videos, and recordings surpassed Adaskin's target (32.2 percent. 34.8 percent, and 26.5 percent, respectively). The use of Canadian reference books, kits, and miscellaneous materials (18.9 percent, 16.1 percent, and 18.2 percent, respectively) was, however, below Adaskin's 25 percent target.

These figures are presented as examples of practice in ninety-seven school music programs, but one must be warned against generalizing from such a small sample that was not systematically stratified; volunteers provided the detailed information on curricular materials in use.[2]

The research focused not only on what teachers *do*, but also on teachers' *reasons* for making their curricular choices. Therefore, surveyed teachers were asked several questions about their use of curricular materials, the results of which are discussed below. Ninety teachers completed the brief surveys.

In answering the question "When choosing music for teaching/performing in your school, do you intentionally include Canadian music (folk and/or composed)?" teachers were asked to respond on a scale from one (never) to five (frequently). All teachers answered positively concerning their choice of Canadian music, resulting in an average score of 3.7 on the five-point rating scale. When asked, "How important do you think it is for Canadian schools to use Canadian music (folk and/or composed)?" teachers were again asked to respond on a five-point rating scale, from a score of one (not important) to five (very important). The teachers indicated that they valued the inclusion of Canadian music in the classroom (an average score of 4.3). It is interesting to note that the teachers ranked the *importance* of Canadian music higher than their personal *choice* level. *Practice* seems to fall behind *theory*.

These results led to a new direction in research, as the attitudes and beliefs behind the teachers' curricular choices require investigation. To date, follow-up interviews have been conducted with nineteen teachers. The qualitative data obtained supplemented the quantitative data and provided a fuller (though admittedly still very incomplete) picture of Canadian music in education. For example, when asked, "Why do you include Canadian music in your curriculum?" the teachers gave a variety of responses. Most of the teachers mentioned the importance of making students aware of Canadian culture and of their Canadian cultural heritage. One high school teacher wrote:

> I have used Canadian pieces to develop a sense of ownership, a sense of belonging to a tradition, a pride in sharing a common land, history and stories, moods, heroes. Including material of one's homeland deepens a sense of self and how one fits into the picture.

Linked with the general need to make students aware of Canadian culture was concern among teachers about the importance of supporting Canadian composers. For example, an elementary teacher wrote:

> As a Canadian, I think it is vital to sing the repertoire that represents our incredible heritage in Canada. For our heritage to flourish and continue for future generations, we must support, encourage and pass on the music written by Canadian composers. Our children should be proud of and experience our living heritage in Canada.

Several teachers emphasized the importance of supporting local composers and of making students aware that there are composers active in their own communities. For example, an elementary music specialist reported that she intentionally teaches the music of local composers because there may be opportunities for her students to meet these composers. She feels it is important for students to realize that some composers are alive and active in communities, and to be aware that some people have careers as composers. Some children who would not have otherwise considered composition to be a viable career path might rethink their futures as a result of this exposure. A Toronto-area high school teacher wrote:

> I think a sense of community is important and I introduce my kids to the music of Toronto for this purpose. I guess working as a musician for 15 years in Toronto has made me very grateful for what we have right here, which is some of the finest music and musicians anywhere. I bring Toronto musicians into my school. We listen to their music and we play some of the music of Toronto musicians.

Some teachers mentioned that studying the music of Canadian composers helps to encourage students in their own creative work. An elementary teacher reported that her students do their own composing and arranging. The study of Canadian composers helps validate what the students do. They can feel the excitement and passion of living composers. A high school instrumental teacher reported that she likes "to showcase a student's composition" as part of the music program. Some teachers indicated that they teach Canadian music because of its high quality. For example, an experienced high school choral specialist reported teaching Canadian music because "It's good. Quality of the repertoire is important." Several teachers simply indicated that they teach Canadian music because they and their students enjoy it. For example, a high school band teacher wrote "our music is distinctive. I like it," while a secondary school choral teacher reported that "the students enjoy it and make a connection to it."

Only two respondents reported administrative reasons for teaching Canadian music. One teacher noted that "administration usually likes to see some Canadian content," while another teacher stated "the Ontario Ministry of Education guidelines require us to look at different cultures, especially Canadian music." Music teachers make important decisions about curricular content, and those decisions reflect their own values and interests. Their comments reveal much about their own beliefs and feelings of Canadian identity.

The research to date has provided information about the Canadian music used in performance programs in schools, about Canadian recordings and videos used in listening programs, and about Canadian reference books and workbooks used in teaching music theory and analysis. Some of the in-depth teacher interviews have resulted in comments about students' creative work in the classroom and about composers' work in schools.

The roles of Canadian composers in education have varied considerably over time and place. In some cases, composers have been commissioned to write music for student performers without being directly involved with teachers and students. In other (generally, more successful) cases, composers have worked with teachers and student performers to write pieces for school use, and this collaboration has been to the mutual benefit of composers, teachers, and students. In other cases, composers have visited schools, focusing on listening and analytical approaches, and on introducing students to a variety of recorded Canadian compositions. In still other cases, composers have worked with teachers and students in classrooms, assisting students in creative activities, and guiding the students as they compose their own music.

Ben Bolden, who draws upon his experience involving students in compositional activities, commented at the 2005 Pan-Canadian Music Education Symposium:

> Various initiatives have sent professional composers into classrooms, to work with students and teachers in creative music-making activities. While these programs have garnered praise, they have not led to a significantly increased sustained level of creative music-making in schools — teachers tend to return to the more familiar performance-based activities when the creative "experts" leave. In my research, I have involved pre-service music educators in creative activities and explored their attitudes to this work. The results were encouraging — most participants were successful in the composing exercises, and recognized multiple advantages of participation. One can only hope such pre-service creative music-making experiences will inspire young music educators to make similar opportunities available to their own students in the future.

Bolden's emphasis on the importance of pre-service music teacher education is reinforced by Nancy Dawe, an experienced teacher educator who investigated factors affecting pre-service music teachers' attitudes to teaching Canadian music:

The primary purpose of my study was to examine the Canadian content of a music teacher education program through the perspectives of three undergraduate music education majors. I sought to discover what these students perceived to be the Canadian content that was being taught, and *how* it was being taught. Materials alone do not ensure adequate Canadian music instruction — the attitudes, philosophy and pedagogy attached to these materials establish the nature and quality of instruction. I was also curious to discover the students' attitudes toward and values placed on Canadian content in music teacher education curriculum and elementary school music curriculum. The three undergraduates were asked to reflect on their experiences with Canadian music and to consider how they may use Canadian music in their future programs. I discovered that the students' attitudes towards Canadian content were closely connected to their philosophies of music education and their personal experiences with Canadian music. Teacher education programs can play a role in helping pre-service teachers define their identities as Canadian music educators. Building awareness of Canadian repertoire and resources is essential, but it is not enough. Pre-service teachers must first be conscious of their own identities, of how they position themselves within Canada's diverse cultural landscape. (see Dawe, 2005, p. 39)

In recent years, the number of post-secondary educational institutions offering courses in Canadian music has increased, but as Robin Elliott has noted (2003), these courses tend to be specialized courses that contribute to the "ghettoization" of Canadian music. He advocated the inclusion of Canadian music in required undergraduate music survey courses both to provide a broader view of the history of Canadian music and to position Canadian music in the mainstream of music history. He warned against simply including "a few token Canadian pieces in place of (or in addition to) works by U.S. composers in the section on the twentieth century," and argued that this approach "sends the message that music arrived only recently in this country, and thus exists outside of (or at best at the very end of) the chronological progression of history" (p. 202). Elliott recommended a broader inclusion of Canadian music in survey courses, reflecting more fully Canada's historical musical development. Such changes could have a positive impact on future teachers' knowledge of and attitudes to Canadian music. Elliott advocates for the inclusion of Canadian music at all levels of the educational system:

It is important to teach and study Canadian music because it not only provides deeply satisfying artistic, intellectual, and emotional rewards, but also encourages inclusiveness and a sense of belonging in students. Now, this is not going to happen unless the students are introduced to a very broad spectrum of Canadian music, including First Nations music, traditional and classical idioms, popular music and jazz, and the music of the many ethnic groups who have made Canada their home. This way, students (and indeed teachers) can learn a lot about how music helps to shape our identity, or rather identities, as Canadians. Music class should be a place where a concept of "Canadian" that values inclusiveness can be embraced, thus enabling teacher and student to explore the potential for fulfillment in music that we all bear within us. (quoted in Shand, 2002)

Beyond the public schools and universities, Canadian music is used in private studios, conservatories, and student performance ensembles in the community, as well as in festivals, concerts, and religious institutions. And much is happening in the media to assist teachers and to enrich the life of Canada. Recordings of Canadian music are increasingly available, and valuable online resources have been developed to provide information about Canadian music. Through the media, Canadian music can reach a large audience. I note, for example, McGill University professor Eleanor Stubley's work on a film of Canadian composer Jean Coulthard's composition *The Pines of Emily Carr*.[3] The film's effective use of photographs and Carr's paintings of BC landscapes enriched the musical presentation. Stubley describes her work on the film as "part of a larger outreach movement that sees music education as addressing all age groups and that sees the notion of 'Canadian' within the broader context of arts more generally" (personal communication, May 9, 2005).

Diversity and variety characterize Canadian music, Canadian music education, and indeed Canada itself. There is no simple answer to the question "What is the current status of Canadian music in education?" There is considerable variation from one geographic region of Canada to another and, indeed, from one community to another. Furthermore, the status of Canadian music in music education varies from place to place and from person to person. While a great deal of time and energy has gone into the promotion of Canadian music in music education, much remains to be done in the future. While the challenges are great, the rewards may be greater if Canadians are given more opportunities to experience the sounds of Canada — music that evokes, illuminates, and defines our regional and national character.

## Notes

1 For further information on the research procedures for data collection, content analysis, and data analysis, readers should see Bartel, Dolloff, & Shand (1999).

2 During the ongoing study, databases of the Canadian and non-Canadian materials reported as "in use" have been developed. This information provides a rich resource for further study.

3 *The Pines of Emily Carr* was shown as an episode of CBC TV's *Opening Night* (February 3, 2005).

## References

Adaskin, J. (1963). CMC has a story. *Music across Canada, 1*(1), 8–10.

Bartel, L., Dolloff, L., & Shand, P. M. (1999). Canadian content in school music curricula: A research update. *Canadian Journal of Research in Music Education, 40*(4), 13–20.

Bartel, L. R., & Shand, P. M. (1995). Canadian music in the school curriculum: Illusion or reality? In T. McGee (Ed.), *Taking a stand: Essays in honour of John Beckwith* (pp. 125–145). Toronto: University of Toronto Press.

Beatty, R. J. (2010). A new Canadian choral resource. *The Canadian Music Educator, 52*(2), 11–12.

Bolden, B. (2004). Students composing: Examining the experience. *The Canadian Music Educator, 45*(4), 20–27.

Dawe, N. (2005). Canadian music content in music teacher education: A student perspective. Unpublished paper, Graduate Department of Music, University of Toronto. A revised version of this paper was awarded first prize in the 2005 CMEA Dr. Franklin Churchley Graduate National Student Essay Competition and was published in *The Canadian Music Educator, 47*(2), 39–43.

Elliott, R. (2003). Cancon and the canon. *Canadian University Music Review, 23*(1–2), 201–213.

Grant, D., Kinder, K., & Reynolds, J. (2004). Canadian wind-band repertoire. *Canadian Winds, 3*(1), 31–35.

Shand, P. (2002). Teaching and studying Canadian music. *The Canadian Music Educator, 44*(2), 7.

Shand, P. M. & Bartel, L. R. (1998). Canadian content in music curriculum: Policy and practice. In B. Roberts (Ed.), *Connect, combine, communicate* (pp. 89–107). Sydney, NS: University College of Cape Breton Press.

Shand, P., Bartel, L., & Dolloff, L. (1999). Canadian content in elementary and secondary school music curricula. In B. Hanley (Ed.), *Leadership, advocacy, communication: A vision for arts education in Canada* (pp. 81–92). Victoria, BC: Canadian Music Educators' Association.

Szabo, M., & St. Dennis, I. (2004). *Choral works by Canadian composers: A selective guidelist. Published choral compositions by BC Composers.* BC Choral Federation.

# FOUR

# Manitoba's Success Story: What Constitutes Successful Music Education in the Twenty-First Century?

*Wayne D. Bowman*

## Introduction

In 2005, the Coalition for Music Education in Canada (CMEC) reported, province by province, the findings of a national survey it conducted on music education. Manitoba stood out as a leader in delivering quality music programs in its schools: an indication that the collective efforts of Manitoba's music education community were meeting with considerable success. Gratifying and affirming though these observations were — and laudable though the achievements of Manitoba music educators are — I am not quite so sanguine about the current state and future trajectories of the discipline. In this chapter I explore a few reasons why.

In brief, what constitutes success in music education depends on one's understanding of the needs the profession exists to serve; and those needs are not things to which we typically devote a great deal of critical thought. Music is good, we appear to believe, and accordingly any and all music instruction is good — the more the better. The trouble is that neither music nor music education is inherently good. The value of music and the success of music education depend on the ends they serve: the life-wide and life-long differences they make; the ways they enrich and transform people's lives; the human needs they discernibly serve long after students have left school. What constitutes a quality program or successful instruction cannot be gauged solely or even primarily by criteria internal to school music instruction, as if music education somehow reaches its culmination or expires upon graduation, as if our instructional obligation to students is met in the skills and knowledge we transmit. We have worked tirelessly to fine-tune and advocate what we're currently doing, which is pretty much what we've done for decades. But while we have achieved noteworthy success, we have not asked whether or how our efforts serve the emerging and changing needs of a twenty-first-century Canadian society. And as a result, I submit, the successes we celebrate are quite fragile and our programs quite vulnerable. We have claimed success for music education without critically considering the criteria by which musical and educational successes will be gauged in a twenty-first century whose values, priorities, and musical practices diverge substantially from those with which we are familiar. The sustainability of music education is ultimately at issue.

In this chapter, I will comment briefly on the current state of Manitoba music education as illustrated in its elementary general music and school band programs. I will pass over important endeavours like the growing presence of guitar instruction — and even Manitoba's rich choral tradition — not because they are insignificant but simply to keep the chapter relatively concise. I single out Manitoba's elementary programs and instrumental music programs, in other words, to explore issues, challenges, and concerns that apply inclusively to all of school music's disciplinary specialties — and, I suspect, to music education well beyond Manitoba's provincial boundaries.

## General (Elementary) Music Education
### Time and Expertise
Manitoba music educators have worked diligently and effectively to ensure that musical instruction is available to all elementary-school-aged students. At K-8 levels 10 percent of the school day (about 30 minutes) is supposed to be devoted to the arts, and in a majority of school divisions something like half that time is dedicated to music. Students in Winnipeg schools typically receive between 90 and 120 minutes of music per week. Historically (though, as we shall see, there is reason to believe this is changing) music has been favoured in comparison to the other arts. It is an often-cited point of pride that most elementary music instruction is delivered by "specialists" as opposed to "generalists" or, perhaps more accurately, teachers without extensive musical training. As we will see, though, the meaning of claims to "specialist" status is not entirely clear.

While pride in the extent and quality of musical instruction in Winnipeg schools is justified, considerable unevenness exists across the province. In particular, claims about instructional time and musical expertise cannot be sustained for more rural Manitoba, the one-third of Manitoba's population that resides outside Winnipeg's perimeter highway. Moreover, because what is presumed to count as musical instruction is ill defined, there is a tendency where funding is tight or where music education is poorly understood to equate mere musical activity or exposure with instruction, or to assume that the musical component of the arts requirement is adequately addressed in extracurricular engagements, concerts, assemblies, or by supposedly integrating art into general classroom activity. Musical instruction is thereby reduced to musical exposure, that is, to "time allocated to music." Furthermore, because music's place under the "arts" umbrella is not specified in policy documents, one can claim to have met provincial guidelines with little or no actual instructional time by qualified music educators. The distinction between exposure or activity and instruction is not drawn; nor is the place of musical education within arts instruction specified.

If music education specialists were exclusively charged with delivering instruction, these might be minor concerns. But there exists no provincially recognized definition of what counts as music education expertise, and, as a result, virtually any teacher may be charged with delivering musical instruction. This, coupled with the possibility of designating an extraordinarily broad range of arts activities or music-related activities, means that there is no effective standard for music education time allocation or instruction other than a loosely consensual one. Additionally, music positions (especially in rural areas) are often designated fractionally. In such cases, music educators must choose between teaching outside their area of expertise or accepting what amounts to unstable, part-time employment. These considerations often impede hiring and retaining music education specialists.

To complicate matters still further, musical expertise is widely equated with music education expertise. The province does not certify music education specialists, or even music specialists: rather, it certifies teachers who are presumed capable teachers in virtually any area. Thus, teachers of music become specialists by virtue of teaching assignment, not training. There are no formally acknowledged differences, then, among (1) individuals with extensive formal training in the professional discipline of music education; (2) individuals with music performance degrees followed by generic bachelor of education training; (3) individuals with musical performing experience outside the context of degree-granting programs; and (4) individuals whose qualifications consist solely of musical interest.

With no officially recognized difference between specialists and non-specialists, their respective roles in music education are not differentiated. There is little consideration of how specialist and non-specialist roles articulate with or complement each other. Nor, for that matter, is there any clear policy addressing how the musical efforts of community partners (musicians or musical interest groups without music educator training) relate to those of qualified music education professionals.

In short, while there is validity in the claim that elementary music education in Manitoba tends to be delivered by individuals with relatively strong musical training, two significant caveats must be acknowledged: (1) these claims are true primarily in Winnipeg, and (2) the claim to specialist delivery often equates musical training with music education expertise, which is an assumption music education professionals might rightly resist. If one assumes that music education differs significantly from mere exposure or activity, and if one further assumes that music education expertise involves more than musical expertise, claims to the amount and specialization of musical instruction in Manitoba schools must be equivocal. In actual practice, instructional time and instructor expertise are often circumvented.

## Curriculum

There is considerable variation across the province when it comes to adherence to the provisions of its early-years music curriculum. That may be partly because the predecessor to the current curriculum, which dated from the heyday of "aesthetic" education (the 1970s), was overly prescriptive and not terribly useful as a guide for innovative musical or instructional practice. As well, its vague claims to the aesthetic value of musical study were easily disregarded, serving purposes of advocacy and self-affirmation rather than providing concrete guidance for renewable, culturally relevant instructional practice. The old curriculum's lack of currency created potentially fertile ground for innovation, since no one appeared particularly concerned that official documents be followed. However, effective innovations require music curriculum theory, the allocation of adequate time and resources, and mechanisms for the diffusion of innovative practices — none of which were particularly extensive. Instead of widespread innovation and renewal, then, an aging curriculum resulted in stagnation: in the entrenchment of practices that had outlived their usefulness and social relevance. The basis for instructional practice, in other words, was often more habitual than intentional. Such habits remain powerful influences, despite curricular revisions.

These problems have been exacerbated by the troubling elimination of music coordinators, those individuals whose responsibilities should be devoted to facilitating curricular diffusion and renewal and to helping nurture collaboration and common direction among music educators. Indeed, if one were to set out to de-professionalize music education one of the surest strategies would be to undermine coordination and communication, filling individual music educators' time with instructional obligations and administrivia, and assuring that music is not effectively represented at the table when budgetary and other priorities are discussed at administrative/district levels.

The vacuum created by years of curricular inactivity in early-years music education in Manitoba was filled primarily by methodology. Brand-name instructional methodologies — the presumed means to educational ends — became ends in themselves. Such "methodolatry," as it is often called, came to supplant critical consideration of the ends and aims of music education, the ways these evolve over time, and the ways they vary with the educational needs and priorities of diverse communities. At the elementary level, Orff or Kodály proficiency (and the accumulation of "levels" by teachers) became increasingly equated with music education expertise, to the extent that educators who are differently or more broadly prepared are often deemed less qualified. Such doctrinaire orientations have led to unhealthy divisions within the field and pose obstacles to the creation of new methods tailored to changing circumstances and to diverse musical needs and interests.

After years of expressed concern by early-years music educators over the age of the "old" curriculum, a new one has been recently developed and is currently being rolled out. Whether it is better or more effective in guiding or informing instructional practice than the old remains to be seen; however, habitual actions and assumptions die hard. It is doubtful that meaningful change will be accomplished without dramatic changes to the instructional methodologies and educational aims with which music teachers have become comfortable.

An equally serious set of concerns stems from the conflation of music curriculum revision with curricular revision efforts in "the arts" more generally. In their enthusiastic endorsements of collective virtues of the arts, music educators have sometimes lost sight of the potential for changes in the arts curriculum to reconfigure music's place within that curriculum — to lead to the demise rather than enhancement of music education in the province. My concern is that a justified interest in musical curriculum revision became part of the broader agenda devoted to enhancing the status of the arts, inclusively. Since we have seen the unfortunate results of such efforts elsewhere, it will be important to monitor future developments carefully.[1]

In short, years of curricular neglect and a lack of attention to curricular interpretation and application have led to misunderstandings about the dynamic nature of curriculum and about the fluid and elastic relationship between formal guidelines and professional practice. Many seem to regard curriculum documents as prescriptive devices for assuring standardization and uniformity, while others dismiss them as irrelevant. Care must be taken lest interests in curricular uniformity suppress diversity and impede necessary change.

One further outgrowth of the state of affairs discussed above — where professional knowledge is reduced to method, and local responsibility for ongoing curricular adaptation is neglected — is the absence of meaningful linkage between early, middle, and senior years instruction. The coherence and continuity that should exist between various levels of a carefully and sequentially devised curriculum are not evident in Manitoba. This has been a significant problem for decades, and has been exacerbated by political divisions that impede dialogue across disciplinary lines. These same divisions are evident in professional development efforts (both pre-service and in-service) that accept and perpetuate the discreteness of elementary, secondary, general, choral, and instrumental musical concerns — to the detriment of the broader conception of music education that should unify them. The tendency of elementary music educators to teach skills and concepts without carefully considering the instructional needs and practices of secondary music programs, and of secondary music educators to re-teach things already addressed in elementary years (for example, systems of teaching rhythm and counting), create serious inefficiencies of the kind that structured curricula are supposed to alleviate. Students can hardly be blamed for finding the resulting practices frustrating.

## Certification and Professional Development

Since the late 1980s, teacher certification in Manitoba has been based on successful completion of a bachelor's degree followed by a two-year (sixty credit hours) bachelor of education "after degree." To become certified, in other words, one completes two bachelor's degrees. The music or music education content of the first degree may range from negligible to substantial, while the BEd includes no coursework in music and relatively little in music education. The BEd is designed to create generalist teachers, *not* music education specialists. The distinctiveness of musical development and of music education are not widely acknowledged in educational circles: a problem exacerbated by the administrative penchant for flexibility of instructional assignments. There exists little support for the training and certification of music education specialists.[2] Accordingly, beginning music teachers typically enter the field with relatively modest preparation in the foundational concerns distinctive (or unique) to music education: philosophical, psychological, sociological, ethical, and curricular.

Among the unintended results of this approach is intensive training of prospective music teachers as elementary music teachers, choir directors, or instrumental (i.e., band) directors rather than as music educators. Such narrow streaming is rationalized in various ways, such as (1) the obvious differences in the skills required in each of these areas, (2) the problems associated with postsecondary curricular crowding, and (3) the presumed difficulty of engaging novice teachers meaningfully in more abstract considerations. Another unfortunate, if unintended, result is a massive front-loading of professional development.[3] Students often enter the field with six years of university studies behind them, usually accompanied by significant debts. There are no requirements and few incentives to pursue substantial studies in music education after entry to practice. Indeed, disincentives abound.

One of the major casualties of this system is music education's professional disciplinary identity. Music teachers identify as practitioners of this or that methodology, in this or that instructional setting. They belong to special interest groups that reinforce and perpetuate disciplinary divisions. The foundational concerns that should undergird, unite, and direct the field are largely neglected.

The first-degree plus second-degree structure fails to address the integration of content and method. In fact, it works against it in many ways. Postsecondary music curricula are devoted primarily to the development of professionally oriented performance skills, supplemented by studies of music history and music theory.[4] Music students are recruited, admitted, and socialized primarily as musicians rather than as music educators. Geared to the creation of a general "educator" identity, faculties of education are similarly reluctant to incorporate music education courses. As a result, music education enjoys a place of prominence neither in schools of music nor in faculties of education: the former regard music education as education's concern, while the latter see it as music's. The voice of music education in pre-service preparation is often marginal and muted, while opportunities for meaningful, sustained in-service professional development that might redress this concern are impeded by a system that neither prioritizes nor facilitates graduate studies.

The direct results of this situation for elementary music education are that (1) both pre-service and in-service training are devoted primarily to developing methodological proficiency, and (2) elementary music instruction is a relatively minor concern within the broader domain of music education — often to the detriment of both the profession and the students it exists to serve. One of the things made clear by the emerging research literature on early childhood development and music is the profound importance of high-quality musical experience and instruction in the early years. Unfortunately, the lion's share of available resources goes elsewhere.

*Evaluation*

As observed at the beginning of this chapter, consensus is that Manitoba is doing a good job with elementary music education. Judged in quantitative terms (the amount of time devoted to instruction, the number of students receiving it, and the specifically musical preparation of most teachers, at least in Winnipeg), and comparatively (in light of circumstances in many other provinces), this view is largely justified. Still, there are those who would argue that preoccupation with conventional concerns like music literacy and musical performance has meant the neglect of things like musical uses of technology, cultural diversity, multicultural music education, musical composition, and interdisciplinary musical pursuits. While recent revisions to the early-years music curriculum seek to address these concerns, it remains to be seen whether revised curriculum documents can offset the inertia of habitual instructional practice, or whether advances can be made in these areas without jeopardizing conventional concern for literacy and performance. Even the updated curriculum guides leave unresolved the most perplexing of curricular problems: *Of all the things that should be taught, what (given finite time and resources) must be taught?*

Outstanding programs abound in Manitoba's elementary schools.[5] But on average and province-wide, the situation may be less rosy. In the early 1980s (ancient history, to be sure) a Grade 5 provincial music assessment yielded troubling results, among them: (1) Grade 5 students were, on average, satisfactorily meeting the objectives set for Grade 1 students; (2) there was not a significant correlation between allotted instructional time and student achievement; (3) the strongest correlation to achievement was student involvement in private, out-of-school lessons; and (4) formal evaluation, when and if it occurred, was seldom undertaken by music education specialists — and most often by school principals (Manitoba, 1985).[6] These findings challenged conventional wisdom that curricular objectives were being satisfactorily addressed. It is remarkable that so little use was made of the results of this comprehensive survey, which, in the wrong hands, might well have been taken as grounds for eliminating rather than continuing elementary music instruction in the province. One constructive response would have been curriculum revision, if the items on the assessment (derived from official curriculum documents) were no longer deemed relevant or valid. Another might have been to undertake a different, complementary form of assessment: one designed to address what practitioners believed to be their "real" instructional priorities (again assuming that the assessment's validity was questionable). Still another (also assuming assessment validity) would have been to change instructional practices. None of these responses occurred, nor, fortunately, were the distressing results apparently regarded as problematic by the educational authorities at the time. Since no systematic evaluation has been undertaken in the ensuing thirty years, there is little evidence that things have changed (or, to be fair, that they have not changed). The drift that inevitably occurs in the absence of evaluation may have led to even greater disparity between curricular objectives and outcomes. Without ongoing evaluation, we lack data documenting the effectiveness of elementary music education in the province; and without this data, claims to effectiveness or ineffectiveness of elementary music education remain largely anecdotal — hardly the foundation one would have expected for recent curriculum revisions.

In short, we have reasonably reliable figures documenting the frequency of music instruction in Manitoba elementary schools. Similarly, we know the extent to which music classes are taught by instructors with formal music training (though again, this is not the same as music education training). However, we are not able to speak unequivocally about the return on these investments, or the criteria by which that return should be gauged. We are unable to address: (1) the disparities between rural and urban programs, (2) the inequalities created by differing assumptions about the nature of "music specialization," and (3) the differing results that stem from dedicated musical instruction and instruction "integrated" into other subject areas.[7] We are also ultimately unable to substantiate claims to the durability or effects of musical learning. Concerns like these require regular, systematic evaluation tailored to the instructional efforts and priorities of local practitioners, evaluation that shows what is and is not working, and evaluation linked carefully to the development of strategies for improvement. This in turn requires professional development of a kind that is not widely available at present; it also requires the provision of time, resources, and supports designed to assure that such vital concerns are not neglected.

The literature on professionalization in teaching suggests that deskilling and intensification are significant deterrents to professional stature. Elementary music educators routinely teach large classes with inadequate preparation time, one of the circumstances that undermine professional

growth and effectiveness. Without systematic evaluation, substantial professional development, or clearly defined standards,[8] professional concerns
like these are reduced to mere political issues.

*In Sum*

Manitoba can be justifiably proud of many of its achievements in school-
based elementary music education. Indeed, its early-years music education
system may be among the healthiest in Canada. The passionate commitment and tireless efforts of those who teach at this level are both inspired
and inspiring. At the same time, unless decisive steps are taken in the areas
discussed above, all this could change overnight. Instructional time and
expertise vary much more widely than they should in a province convinced
of and committed to quality early-years music education. Although the
curriculum has recently been revised, a significant investment in ongoing
professional development would arguably yield more substantial returns,
as would entrusting curriculum design, implementation, evaluation, and
revision to locals, ensuring that they have the skills and resources required
to do these jobs well. In addition, music teacher certification and professional development are conceptualized and executed in ways that do not
serve elementary music specialists particularly well.

Finally, the neglect of evaluation in elementary music education
renders it vulnerable to those who regard the latter as an entertaining
diversion rather than an educational component crucial to a balanced,
sustainable school curriculum. Elementary music education currently
thrives where it does because of a delicate balance between passionate
music teachers' commitment and administrators' belief in music's unique
social and educational benefits to the school community. It struggles,
where it does, because music is seen as an enjoyable diversion or release
from the rigours of schooling, rather than a vital component thereof. For
the most part, and especially in the city of Winnipeg, administrators have
seen elementary music as a high enough priority to warrant allocation
of the resources it requires. In rural areas, the fact that school funding is
tied to enrolments, together with the desire to offer a full complement of
programs, has situated music much more precariously: the trends do not
appear promising.

Put in slightly different terms, elementary music education thrives in
Manitoba where the good will and determination of teachers, administration, and parents insist it must; but there are no guarantees, and this
precarious balance could deteriorate quickly.[9] This is especially the case for
elementary music education because it tends to be regarded as charming but
not necessarily educational (so much so that, please note, any teacher can

teach it). The problem is exacerbated by the fact that it tends to be less visible or "flashy" than the high-profile performing ensembles that predominate at secondary levels.[10] The health of elementary music thus requires special, collective vigilance toward the possibility of erosion — signs of which are already evident in many rural areas. Where elementary programs are neglected, the health of secondary programs is seldom far behind. That is one further reason the health of elementary music programs must become a paramount concern for all who value music education in Manitoba.

## Middle and High School Instrumental Music Education in Manitoba (i.e., Band)

*Facts and Figures*

Thanks to the initiatives of the Manitoba Band Association (MBA), we have more specific information about Manitoba's school band programs than we do about most other areas of school music. MBA conducted surveys of band activity in both 1997 and 2002, the latter including all bands in the province at the time. These surveys provide valuable insight into trends and are quite useful for setting goals for music education in Manitoba.[11] If judged by the number of participants, by the number of schools offering band instruction, and by the extent of support band receives from school administrators, the band movement in Manitoba is quite healthy, arguably among the healthier in North America. Although it is an elective subject (not required for high school graduation), it was a requirement in about one in ten middle schools offering band in 2002. Some 257 schools had band programs in 2002, a reported increase of 13 percent since 1997. Of the 80,000 students in Grades 4–12 to whom band was available, almost one-third were enrolled in band in 2002, a slight increase between 1997 and 2002. In individual schools, the proportion of the student body involved in band ranged from 2 to 100 percent.

According to these surveys, in most school divisions, students began band in Grade 7. Of those, approximately 16 percent remained in band until graduation. The greatest attrition occurred during middle-years instruction (as much as 24 percent per year), but it moderated in senior years, with 8 percent attrition between Senior 3 and Senior 4. Attrition is strongly associated with the introduction of curricular options and choices, and with the requirement that students elect more specialized courses upon entry to senior-years study. Scheduling conflicts are often a major influence on decisions to discontinue participation. With the sole exception of the Western Manitoba region (which has seen moderate declines), both the number of schools offering band and the number of students in band programs increased between 1997 and 2002.

Almost all band students received high school credit for concert band participation: approximately 85 percent received full credit; about 10 percent received half credit; and 3–5 percent received no credit. According to the 2002 survey, jazz band was offered for credit in about 64 percent of schools with band programs (41 percent full credit, 23 percent half), an increase from 44 percent in 1997. It was a non-credit offering in about 15 percent of schools with band programs, and not offered at all in 22 percent, compared with 38 percent in 1997.

In 2002 there were 222 band directors in the province's schools. Although the teaching credit for band instruction varies, most positions were designated 50 to 100 percent of a full teaching load. In larger programs, load credit increased, with a trend toward multiple positions. In smaller programs, load credit decreased. Three-quarters of directors indicated that fundraising was a necessary part of their job, and over half relied on fundraising efforts to subsidize purchases of such essentials as instruments, books, and music. Sixty percent of Manitoba's band programs reported having parent organizations.

*Curriculum*
Manitoba's band curriculum is quite dated. There appear, however, to be relatively few concerns about this state of affairs among band directors — which may raise questions about the perceived role of curriculum guides in the context of performance-based programs. The curriculum frequently consists of the music performed — that is, the "program" is the band — and other emphases in the curriculum guide receive modest attention. It is not clear that curricular revisions currently under way will necessarily change these circumstances.

A jazz curriculum (developed in the US by the International Association for Jazz Education) was adopted by the province in 1998 (Manitoba Education, n.d.). The primary significance of this addition was the introduction of credit for jazz instruction, which had previously been primarily an extracurricular option. The number of jazz bands in Manitoba has increased dramatically in ensuing years. However, relatively few directors have had substantial jazz experience or formal instruction in jazz improvisation, history, theory, and pedagogy. As a result, the distinction between jazz bands and their "stage band" precursors is not always evident; nor is improvisation as prominent a feature as the curriculum stipulates it should be. These concerns may relate more directly to professional development needs than to the curriculum per se, illustrating the fundamental interdependence among curriculum implementation, meaningful and sustained professional development, and effective evaluation.

## Evaluation

Indicators of program effectiveness mostly take the form of enrolment numbers and are supplemented by the informal impressions of administrators and parents as well as by festival adjudications. Although festival participation is optional, it is very widespread and in many instances a clear expectation of the job. Festivals provide valuable opportunities to perform and hear others perform, but it is not clear they serve the educational functions of improving school instruction or enhancing student musicianship. The relative brevity of performance and adjudication time, the need to offer criticism to directors indirectly (through comments to the group which must be "gentle" and constructive), and the optional nature of participation each limit the extent to which these events actually improve music education, their obvious motivational and social values notwithstanding.

Although numbers are useful and important indicators of the health of the band movement in Manitoba — and they can be particularly helpful in fortifying advocacy arguments, persuading administrators of the significance of these endeavours, or winning the many resources they require — we generally lack qualitative indications of success. Of equal concern is the lack of attention to the intended outcomes of band participation, since these are essential to making the case for its broad or enduring educational value. Some would argue that the benefits of participation do not extend beyond graduation — a major (arguably urgent) concern. Nor is attention typically devoted to the relatively small proportion of the student body whose musical needs and interests are addressed through large performing ensembles.

## Professional Development

Most of the concerns about professional development opportunities expressed previously apply equally to instrumental music instruction, in particular the tendency to focus upon instructional techniques and methods to the detriment of more broadly educational considerations — the ends the music education profession ultimately exists to serve. Professional development prepares future teachers to replicate the status quo rather than to transform it or to discern when transformation is needed. Since the band director's instructional role in middle and secondary programs in Manitoba is extensively equated with that of the conductor, advanced studies often take the form of advanced conducting study, to the unfortunate exclusion of broader professional knowledge in such foundational areas as music curriculum theory, philosophy, ethics, psychology, sociology, and evaluation. Furthermore, since directors' roles in concert band and jazz

settings differ quite markedly, professional development devoted to conducting may not serve the advancement of jazz education particularly well.
The most costly casualty of band-centric professional development, however, is awareness of the commonalties that undergird and unite diverse
professional practices in music education. This weakens alliances that are
vital to the future of the field and contributes unfortunately to professional
and curricular fragmentation.

*Organization*

The MBA is a strong advocate for band programs in the province and
deserves a good deal of the credit for the patterns of growth described
above. Although it advocates passionately and tirelessly for band, its contribution to the overall health of music education in the province is somewhat less clear. Rather than arguing this claim at length, I will simply pose
a few rhetorical questions whose careful exploration might provoke much-
needed dialogue: Might the indisputable success of a band movement
undermine the status of music education as a whole? Might the province
have large numbers of highly accomplished bands yet neglect the broader
aims of educating society musically and of providing meaningful, durable
musical education to every student? What values, aims, priorities, and professional obligations do secondary instrumental music educators (band
directors) share with other musical organizations and educators in the
province? How are these being addressed?

*Concerns*

Whether gauged by the number of students involved, by enrolment trends,
or by the number of bands proportional to the province's population, Manitoba's band movement is among the healthiest in the country. The health
of bands and the effectiveness of MBA in helping to create and maintain it
are, however, but one side of the coin. The other is that for many, instrumental music education has come to mean band only. There exist only
pockets of guitar instruction; there is relatively little attention to composition, songwriting, or technologically mediated music; there are very few
divisions in which strings are taught; and there are almost no programs
built around alternative or multicultural instrumental configurations.
While the strength of the band (and jazz band) movement is clearly cause
for celebration, then, it is also cause for concern. Where music education is
equated with jazz and concert bands to the exclusion of other possibilities,
the means of music education become ends in themselves, and innovative alternative practices may be perceived as threats rather than as valuable or necessary complements to conventional school music endeavours.

When that happens, the profession's crucial capacity to respond to changing socio-educational values is seriously compromised, music education's broad educational relevance is obscured, and it becomes increasingly necessary to devote valuable resources to defending the status quo.

In 2005, MBA's executive identified three primary concerns. The first had to do with the status of band programs in small, rural communities. In recent decades the number of applicants for band positions in rural Manitoba has declined steadily. When filled, they are often occupied for only a year or two before the band director moves on, frequently to an urban position. Thus, many small or remote communities become "revolving doors" for band instruction. Others are even less fortunate, with programs being eliminated for want of qualified personnel. These trends require not just careful monitoring but strategic action.

A second concern had to do with the revision of the band curriculum. The worry is that anticipated revisions may fail to recognize, protect, and build upon current strengths, jeopardizing what is working well and has worked well historically. In other words, band programs might fall victim to the well-intended efforts of educationists and bureaucrats who do not represent the fundamental interests and values of existing practices and practitioners. Curriculum revision extends significant opportunities, but it is a delicate process fraught with potential dangers. Given the perceived health of the present situation, the potential benefit of revising the band curriculum must be weighed carefully against possible adverse consequences.

Finally, MBA is interested in mandatory middle-school band programs. It is believed that required band helps address perennial problems in music education like scheduling, course competition, and financial stability. Requiring middle-school band raises important questions about the role of music in the context of general education beyond the early years, questions that have not as yet been collectively addressed by the music education community. It is, however, a clear indication of the esteem in which school music is currently held that required band is even regarded as a serious option. Whether bands are the instructional means best suited to extending music study to the general student body in middle schools is an issue that warrants more careful scrutiny than it has received to this point.

### Toward a Sustainable Music Education
Manitoba music education is, as CMEC's 2005 report concluded, remarkably healthy. Manitoba music education is (as evident in its increasing reliance upon advocacy campaigns) at risk. Which of these claims is accurate? Both of them, I submit. What constitutes success depends upon

one's understanding of the profession's raisons d'être — the ends it exists to serve; and while we owe a great deal to the tireless devotion of Manitoba's music teachers, we have devoted too little attention to the definitive nature and aims of music education. If we ignore the inevitability of change and fail to prepare for it, the health of music education could decline dramatically and suddenly — even amid apparent successes. We are vulnerable because of the narrow and anachronous nature of many of our program offerings; because of our naive faith in curricular or political solutions to issues that stem from deeper, more fundamental musical, professional, and social concerns; because of the ad hoc and frequently piecemeal nature of our efforts; and because of careless subscription to slogans like "learning through the arts," "artists in the schools," and "arts integration." We have single-mindedly embraced professionally oriented performance practices and taken refuge in techniques and methods — the "tricks of the trade" — instead of confronting the more elusive challenges of nurturing musical amateurism, devising our own instructional strategies in response to local needs, and preparing for a musical future that is already vastly different from the one envisioned by our training. We have not ensured that certification practices require professional expertise specific to music education and relevant to our evolving professional needs. Instead of devoting energy to modifying what we do in response to emerging and ever-evolving societal needs, we have embraced advocacy strategies designed to rationalize the status quo, making brash promises on which we are ill-prepared to deliver.[12] The future of music education depends not so much on our ability to convince people of the worth of past or even present practices as on our ability to anticipate and address musical futures that are, strictly speaking, unknowable. Flexibility, strategic diversity, creativity, and collaboration across conventional specialized networks are crucial to a sustainable future. These will require habits very different from those with which we have grown comfortable.

Considerations like these have rather dramatic implications for professional development, in which institutions responsible for music teacher training must assume a leading role. Postsecondary music education curricula are crowded and congested, but not with music education content of the transformative kind envisioned here. Much of the coursework in undergraduate and graduate programs is there for reasons that are historical and political rather than professional. A system devoted to supplementing basic conservatory-oriented musical training (to the end of preparing "music specialists") with generic educational studies (to the end of preparing educational generalists) is not really adequate to the preparation of professional music educators. Nor does the separation of educational "method" from musical "content" support the growing need for pedagogical proficiency among non-school-based musicians.

We need to devote considerably closer attention to the distinctions among professional knowledge in music, education generally, and music education proper. The differences between teaching music and music education — between the development of musical skills or the transmission of musical knowledge on the one hand, and educating musically on the other — are crucial to our understandings of what, how, by whom, and why music education exists, whether within or outside schools.

Manitoba music education is doing what it does very well. Manitoba music educators are a highly committed group for whom "advancing the cause" is a task in which everyone seems prepared to accept a personal share of responsibility. However, assumptions as to what that cause *is* do not receive the kind of scrutiny they require. We acknowledge casually that "music educator" means more than elementary music teaching, or band, or choir, or what have you; but relatively little time or effort is devoted to exploring what that implies for professional identity, professional development, and instructional practice. Music education in the province remains largely an untheorized practice, one devoted to doing what we do, and to garnering the supports deemed necessary for its continuation. Music education's means have become its ends.

There are many reasons for the health, as gauged by conventional standards, of school music in Manitoba. Among them: Manitoba's history as a province of immigrants determined to take responsibility for their own cultural endeavours; the concentration of a large proportion of its population and resources in one geographical area;[13] enlightened school administrators with strong beliefs in the importance of music to the school community; ongoing efforts not just to explain but to demonstrate the ways musical involvements enrich students' lives; the passion and enthusiasm of individual music educators, whose remarkable achievements have helped assure that the public expects and appreciates high-calibre music making; the efforts of special interest groups; a robust system of community festivals and private musical instruction; and many more.

Notably, what do *not* appear to have been contributing factors to this province's music educational health are networks ensuring communication and collaboration among all groups with stakes in the future viability of Manitoba music education. The music education community in Manitoba is highly fragmented. It is intriguing to speculate what might be achieved if we were to coordinate our efforts and bring our resources to bear on shared goals or future directions. The years just ahead will be critical ones for the music education profession in Manitoba, when many of the senior educators whose achievements have led and inspired others take retirement. The need for close collaboration among music's various subdisciplines and organizations has never been more crucial.

What constitutes disciplinary knowledge and expertise in music education is a pressing issue for Manitoba — or at least it should become one. The nature of the music education discipline is not often debated, either in the field generally or by those within the academy whose decisions and actions are crucial to the profession's vitality. The unexamined belief that what is good for music and musicians (or, alternatively, what is good for general education and educators) is good for music education is disturbingly pervasive. The long-term viability of the music education profession would be better served by energetic advocacy for *music education* — with careful attention to what that entails — than it is by the current practice of advocating for the mere presence of music in the schools.

The issues raised in this chapter are deliberately provocative and bound to be misunderstood. It would be irresponsible to gloss over such concerns, however, and my intentions are ultimately constructive. Before wrapping things up, then, let's try a couple of other ways of looking at one of the more important points I have tried to make here. Methods of teaching music and modes of music making are means to the end of music education: they are tools for doing the job of educating musically. We music educators have become quite proficient at maintaining and refining (and defending) certain specialized sets of tools. But the nature of music and the ends of education — that is, the job to whose service music education's tools must be dedicated — are changing and have changed. We don't seem to have noticed that. Music teacher training thus teaches people how to use existing instructional tools efficiently rather than how to modify them, to evaluate their successes and shortcomings, or to create better ones. We are in danger of becoming a well-maintained Commodore 64 in an iPad world.[14] We have become very good over the years at doing what we do — there is no disputing that. But we have not asked ourselves whether (or how) what we're doing is still adequate to the job at hand. We learn and teach the effective use of conventional tools instead of creative or alternative ways of achieving the tasks these tools were designed to execute. Meanwhile, the nature of our "subject" — music, its evolving practices, the ways it promises to enrich human life — has changed dramatically.

Since the ends of music education are historically evolutionary and culturally diverse, so must be the tools by which we pursue them. We have "technicized" music teaching and learning, reducing professional knowledge to efficient adherence to standardized procedures rather than to attention to the ends these procedures were devised to address.

Manitoba music educators must not underestimate the potential fragility of our current circumstances. Strategic, collective, and critically informed action is imperative if the current good fortunes of music education are to serve as a foundation for future prosperity. The precipitous demise of music education in places where it once thrived is a lesson that should be studied carefully if it is not to be replicated in Manitoba, and perhaps elsewhere in Canada. The challenges that lie just ahead will require skills, attitudes, and dispositions that embrace and facilitate change. They will require a broader, more comprehensive vision of music education than the one we have inherited. They will require that we as musician-educators make paramount the habit of changing habits when warranted. None of these challenges exceed our capabilities, but we have not given them the attention and the priority they require.

The choice we face can be simply stated (though the simplicity ends there): shape the future or be shaped by it. The first of these options is clearly the one I favour. It is the professionally responsible course of action. But its success will require a rather different attitude toward current and past practice, and the courage to forgo the comfort of familiar habits. To be clear, this does not mean the wholesale renunciation of current instructional and curricular strategies: that would be irresponsible, to be sure.[15] But it does require that we think about what we do in terms of the discernible differences it makes in people's lives — the ways our instructional actions prepare students to thrive amid change in an uncertain future. There is every reason to be proud of music education's current accomplishments, then, but little reason to believe that these are sufficient to the needs of twenty-first-century society or the basis for a secure professional future.

We urgently need to unite our efforts in a shared vision of a musically vibrant society, a vision that is not only appreciative of exceptional achievements, but passionately dedicated to nurturing a full range of life-long and life-wide musical pursuits — a range far broader than the one that has delivered our current successes.

## Notes

1 An "arts-oriented" examination of current practices in Manitoba schools can be found in Francine Morin (2010).

2 Both Brandon University and the University of Manitoba have "concurrent" or "integrated" programs in which students can complete certification requirements in five rather than six years. These rely on cooperative agreements between faculties that are quite fragile and that generally neglect the disciplinary integrity of music education.

3 By this I mean simply that professional development is, for all practical purposes, a pre-service consideration. In-service professional development is primarily

devoted to brief sessions seeking modest refinements to technical skills initiated during teacher training.

4 Although called "theory," there is little that is theoretical about it. A more apt designation might be "rudiments." And the stories devoted to the history of music seldom venture beyond the boundaries of common-practice European art music. Both music history and music theory focus quite selectively on very narrow ranges of musical practice.

5 Whether these are "programs" or rather the exemplary achievements of individual music teachers is a question I raise in passing, but one that warrants careful consideration.

6 Correlations between student achievement and teacher training or expertise were not among the concerns the assessment was permitted to address.

7 In the words of one rural Manitoba elementary music educator, "integration is killing us."

8 Here I speak of standards with regard to things like teacher time, class size, the definition of instruction (as distinct from activity), and so forth. I do not speak of, nor do I endorse, the development of performance standards for students on any but a local level.

9 The alarming declines in participation in music courses in the state of California between 1999 and 2004 were led by General Music, which plummeted 86 percent during that period. The overall declines in music participation in California amounted to a staggering 47 percent — the largest of any subject area by a factor of four! In short, the decline in music programs was "vastly disproportionate" to all other curricula, the other "arts" included (the "other arts" declined only half as fast as music). That these precipitous declines were led by declines in general music suggests that its welfare may be an important index of the overall health of music education.

10 To compensate, elementary general music programs increasingly resort to "flashy" performances, spectacles of the very kind that comprise secondary music programs.

11 Copies of these reports can be obtained by contacting the Manitoba Band Association through their website at http://www.mbband.org.

12 Although space constraints prevent elaboration here, I would go further: many of these advocacy claims promise things music education *should not* seek to deliver.

13 The "down side" to this state of affairs is, as I have suggested, the temptation for people to attribute what is generally true of Winnipeg to the province as a whole.

14 This, like all comparisons, has its clear limitations; and I have no doubt that my reference to the iPad will itself be quite dated within months of this publication. The broader point, obviously, is that many of the practices comprising school music are no longer linked to thriving musical practices outside the school.

15 Let me make the point even more explicitly: I do not propose that conventional practices be abandoned altogether.

### References

Coalition for Music Education in Canada. (2005). Music education "State of the nation" benchmark study. Retrieved from http://musicmakesus.ca/wp-content/uploads/2010/10/ EnglishMusicReport.pdf.

Manitoba. Curriculum Development and Implementation Branch. (1985). *Manitoba art and music assessment program 1983: Final Report.* Winnipeg: Manitoba Education.

Manitoba Education. (n.d.). *Arts education: Senior 1 to 4 jazz band.* Retrieved from http://www.edu.gov.mb.ca/k12/cur/arts/april98_1.html

Morin F. (2010). A study of arts education in Manitoba schools. *Manitoba Education Research Network 3.* Retrieved from http://www.edu.gov.mb.ca/k12/cur/arts/study/full_doc.pdf.

Turino. T. (2008). *Music as social life: The politics of participation.* Chicago: University of Chicago Press.

# FIVE

# Traditional Indigenous Knowledge:
## An Ethnographic Study of Its Application in the Teaching and Learning of Traditional Inuit Drum Dances in Arviat, Nunavut

*Mary Piercey*

*O n a cold, windy Thursday evening in February 2002, just over seven months since I had first taken the bumpy Calm Air flight from Winnipeg to Arviat, I sat with my choir in a circle in my music classroom at Qitiqliq High School. Eva Aupak, a seventy-year-old Inuk elder and tradition bearer from the community sat to my left and patiently listened to Gara translate my words from English into Inuktitut. Eva was accompanying me in the magical experience of teaching young people to sing. This was her first visit to the school and with the choir. Agreeing that it was important that the youth of Arviat learn traditional Inuit drum dance songs that originate from Arviat, she had left her warm, comfortable home to share her songs with the girls. When she started to sing, I felt excited and proud. I was proud to be the trailblazer that would revive traditional Inuit drum dancing among the Inuit youth of Arviat by facilitating this meeting of elder and young people. It only took moments for that feeling of excitement and pride to turn to trepidation and apprehension. After singing her song several times, Eva looked at the girls and in words that I am ashamed to say I don't understand, spoke to them in a manner that I thought indicated frustration. I glanced at Gara for an explanation of what was happening. She said, "Eva wants to know why we aren't singing with her."*

In 1996, the Royal Commission on Aboriginal Peoples[1] recommended the application of indigenous knowledge[2] and incorporation of tradition in Aboriginal educational policy in Canada (Brant Castellano, 2000). Since then, communities such as Arviat, Nunavut, have responded to the commission's challenge of articulating what traditional indigenous knowledge is and formulating new ways of transmitting it to younger generations. For example, the Arviat District Education Authority[3] hires elders to take senior students "on the land" to participate in caribou hunting exhibitions. Students learn how to "read" the landscape as well as how to track caribou herds, skin hides, and prepare meat. Basic survival skills are taught and learned through lived experience, but song has not yet been taught in these contexts. In this chapter, I discuss the application of indigenous knowledge in music making and music education, specifically in the teaching, learning, and performing of the recently revived traditional Inuit drum dances at Qitiqliq High School in Arviat. I examine the relationship between elders and youth involved in the teaching/learning experience and explore tensions between oral and literate educational approaches.

Walter Ong (1988) discusses the difference between oral cultures and writing cultures and examines the fundamental dissimilarities in the thought processes of the two types of culture. In the context of my specific research, both Inuit elder and youth are from the same "culture," but the elder has participated in an oral tradition throughout her lifetime and her students have been exposed to and have adopted a literate one. The "thought processes" of the two generations are different. Veblen, Beynon, and Odom (2005) advocated the use of pedagogical strategies in teaching music that match the cultural way in which music is transmitted within particular cultural contexts. The present study examines the tensions that arise when this is not initially possible. In this case, the tradition bearer of Inuit music attempted to teach her literate students traditional Inuit songs through oral transmission, in the same fashion she was taught in her youth. This tension has been addressed in other studies as well. For example, Dyc (2002) addressed the tensions between orality and literacy in her study of Navajo language "re"-learning by English-speaking and -writing members of the Navajo nation. However, the "re"-learning of traditional music has never been examined in this way.

Drawing on Abu-Lughod's (1993) theory of "writing against culture," which argues that stressing particular life experiences works against making generalizations about communities, my study of this situation focuses on the particularity of one teenager's musical experiences for the purposes of exploring her specific struggle with traditional methods of learning music. By building a picture of her specific musical teaching and learning situation from discussions, recollections, disagreements, and musical actions, I can make more tangible the effects of resettlement and colonization on educational approaches. More specifically, her stories — and my own observations — illuminate themes about music transmission and function, relationships with elders, cultural erosion, and community cohesion.

## Gara Mamgark

Gara Mamgark, my neighbour and friend, was my informant for this ethnographic study. I first met Gara at Qitiqliq High School in 2001 — I was the music teacher and she was a student. Her mother, Rosie Mamgark, was a teaching assistant at the same school and independently took on the responsibility of showing me the ropes, so to speak. It was not long before I bonded with the Mamgark family and was welcomed into their lives and their home.

Gara is an eighteen-year-old woman born to a semi-traditional family of hunters and gatherers, and raised in the Hamlet of Arviat. Gara and her family are dedicated Catholics; she attends mass every Sunday with her family, sings in the church choir, attends youth groups, and travels with Inuit youth to Catholic summer camps and gatherings. She is actively involved in the musical community. As a member of *Arviat Pilirigatigit* (working together), she hosts a radio request show on Tuesday evenings; she sings in my community choir Arviat Imngitingit (singers), which was established in 2001, and has travelled with the choir to Alberta (to perform for the opening and closing ceremonies of the Arctic Winter Games), Brandon, Manitoba (to perform with the Brandon University Chorale at Rural Forum 2002), and St. John's, Newfoundland (to participate in Festival 500: Sharing the Voices, international choral festival in 2003), and again in 2007 for the Pan-Canadian Symposium on Music Education; she plays the guitar at the Mikilauq Centre (R.C. youth centre) during singalong gatherings for children; and she regularly attends the teen and square dances held on weekends.

A Grade 12 student, Gara is bilingual. Inuktitut is her first language; it is the language of instruction at school from Kindergarten to Grade 3 and the language spoken with friends and family throughout the community. Her second language is English, which is used in school from Grades 4 to

12. Gara's parents are avid hunters; they hunt every weekend and holiday. I often went on hunting expeditions with the Mamgark family and feel that these lengthy excursions, where I talked and interacted with Gara and her family on a very personal level, contributed to the close and comfortable relationship I have with my informant.

## Constructing a Community

Arviat is a rural settlement in the Kivalliq Region of Nunavut, on the south-western part of the Hudson Bay. The 2,500 Caribou Inuit in Arviat are an Inuktitut-speaking group consisting of three distinct bands: the Ahiarmiut (Inland Inuit), Arviamiut (Sea Inuit), and Padlirmiut (Nomadic Inuit),[4] who were resettled there in 1958. Today, Inuit negotiate social diversity within the community in response to massive sociocultural changes since these three distinctive groups were resettled there. These changes include the loss of their semi-nomadic lifestyle, the enhanced role of colonial insti-tutions in their lives, and political reorganization including the establish-ment of Nunavut as Canada's newest territory in 1999.[5] While the three groups of Inuit still protect customs and practices deeply rooted in their respective cultures, they struggle with concerns about cultural erosion and practical issues related to drug abuse, youth support, employment, education, and community cohesion. Today, Inuit children speak English at school, spend limited time on the land, consume TV shows and movies, and create popular music.

Of particular relevance to this study is the fact that, due to the effects of colonization,[6] youth of Arviat now learn through literary-based education in both languages; the oral transmission of histories and songs and other forms of traditional indigenous knowledge has been reintroduced in this modern educational context, but the two modes of learning are inherently at odds.

## Music in Arviat

Arviat is known as the birthplace of renowned Inuit performers Charlie Panigoniak[7] and Susan Aglukark.[8] The community has a strong musical tradition, including an annual four-day Inuumariit (real Inuit) Music Fes-tival where community members demonstrate their musical talents at the Mark Kalluak Hall. There are four churches, each with a large band that includes an organ, bass guitar, electric guitar, acoustic guitar, and scores of singers who actively sing in large church choirs and smaller ensembles. The community hosts a teen dance every Friday night; though called a "teen" dance, it is actually open to people of all ages, and pop music is played. On Saturday nights there is a square dance at which Irish/Scottish music is performed live using accordion, bass guitar, electric guitar, and drum set. Under my direction, there is a new but strong music program at Qitiqliq High School, where students learn to read and write music, to perform music from a multitude of cultures in a variety of languages, and to play an instrument. The local radio station, Arviaqpaluk (the voice of Arviat), plays mostly Inuit gospel songs to a large listening audience.

## Traditional Inuit Drum Dancing

Traditional Inuit drum dancing historically was passed on orally. Drum dancing played a part in almost every gathering, whether it was a celebration of birth, a marriage, the changing of the seasons, a successful hunt, a first kill, a greeting for visitors, to honour someone who had died, or in shamanistic spiritual rituals (Pelinski, 1979; Cavanagh, 1982; Nattiez, 1983; Beaudry, 1978; Charron, 1978). However, it no longer has these functions in contemporary Inuit society. *Pisiit* (plural — personal drum dance songs) are no longer sung to convey indigenous histories and knowledge. Instead, community elders practise drum dancing for tourists and visitors (Pelinski, 1981). When I arrived as the new music teacher in 2001, the general attitude toward these songs by the youth was one of indifference, and not one young person knew any of the traditional drum dance songs.

In the traditional dance, singers — usually women — sat in a circle. Sometimes a man would volunteer to be the first dancer; at other times a group of men sitting behind the singers would coax someone to start. If no one came forward, the women would start singing, usually a personal song (singular — *pisiq*) of a man in attendance, who would then be obligated to dance (Rasmussen, 1999; Marsh, 1987).

Every drum dancing song is a story in itself and is a life experience of the typically male composer. Pat Netser, an Inuk (singular for Inuit) employee with the Department of Education in Arviat stated, "the language of drum dance songs is very poetic; the composer never says things directly, he writes his songs metaphorically" (my summary from a Pisiit Workshop in Baker Lake, Nunavut, 2003). The composers of drum dance songs were usually male and they wrote about their experiences on the land. Traditionally, stories and songs were the primary medium used to convey Aboriginal knowledge;[9] they were used to record a history of the people and to pass it on from one generation to the next. Netser stated, "The men sang their *pisiq* to their wives, who in turn taught the songs to the other women in the camp. At social times, when this song was sung, that man who made the song was supposed to drum dance." She continued: "This was how his story about his hunting experience was told to the rest of the camp and people remembered it."

Netser (2003) explains the use of metaphors in traditional drum dance song and speaks about "agitating the spirits." Such talk about spirits alludes to the use of drum dancing and singing in shamanistic rituals. In a convincing paper, anthropologist Bernard Saladin d'Aunglure (as reported in Nattiez, 1983) has proposed that games and drum dances were performed during the shamanistic period on the occasion of three collective feasts: the spring equinox, the summer solstice, and the winter solstice. In winter,

> these feasts would be a kind of celebration of the reproduction of life in order to hasten the return of the sun, the reproduction of the game and dance and the feast of the hunters celebrating the relationship which unites them.... [At the beginning of spring] the dances may have had the function of hastening the return of the big migratory birds: the geese. At the end of spring, it could coincide with the brooding period, another important moment in the reproduction they encouraged. (p. 90)

This particular piece of information led Nattiez (1983) to hypothesize about the function of drum dances in the past, before the missionaries exerted their influence. He stated the drum dances were traditionally related to shamanism; the Inuit of Arviat practised shamanism before the Christian missionaries arrived there in the 1920s (Rasmussen, 1999; Marsh, 1987).

Pelinski (1981) reports that, during the 1970s, almost no drum dancing or a-ya-ya singing could be seen or heard in the Kivalliq communities of Arviat or Rankin Inlet. He attributes the decline of traditional Inuit singing in these communities to the influence of Christian missionaries and Western cultures.

## Southern Influence

The loss of traditional songs and dances among Inuit youth is just one example of cultural erosion in Arviat. In Arviat today, many institutions are organized in "the southern Canadian way" and Western influences are strong. For this reason, the people of Arviat are concerned about retaining their cultural identity. Presently, schools are modelled after Alberta schools, teachers speak English, educational curricula are written in English, stores and municipal governments are managed by people from southern Canada, and spiritual leaders in the churches are English or French speakers originating from outside of Nunavut. In Carolyn Kenny's (2002) research paper *North American Indian, Métis and Inuit Women Speak about Culture, Education and Work*, one Inuk woman says, "schooling took most of my culture ... our teacher was unilingual English and I was unilingual *Inuktitut*....

For 10 months of the year you lost your daily contact with your culture" (pp. 49–50). Due to this infiltration of and immersion in Western culture, the people of Arviat express the importance of identifying and promoting those significant objects and ideas that strengthen Inuit identity and ensure that traditional indigenous knowledge is passed on to future generations.

In the 1970s, political leaders of the Inuit Tapirisat of Canada (ITC)[10] entered discussions with the federal government of Canada about dividing the Northwest Territories into two separate territories. Discussions and plans continued throughout the 1980s and 1990s. In 1993, the Nunavut Tunngavik Incorporated[11] was established to ensure implementation of the terms of the 1993 Nunavut Lands Claim Agreement. Finally, in 1999, Nunavut became a reality and Inuit were well under way toward defining what it means to be Inuit in a place that belonged to them (Nunavut means "our land" in Inuktitut). Thus, recently, in contrast to the existing Western-style institutions, Inuit institutions in Arviat have been organized in accordance with Inuit ideologies and perspectives. Arviat's institutional structure is unlike most in Canada. The schools, municipal government, and the churches are all organized similar to southern Canadian institutions because they are managed by white people originating from the south of Canada, but Inuit institutions are designed from an Inuit perspective and promote Inuit traditional knowledge. For example, the Inuit Elders Society has an important voice in community decision making, the Inuit Community Justice Committee makes legal decisions regarding first-time offenders, and Arviat Pilirgatigit designs programs that teach traditional cultural knowledge to youth. These institutions are organized and designed with Inuit beliefs and values at the forefront: traditional cultural knowledge; respect for elders and their teachings; respect for the vitality of youth; apprenticeship-style education; and community sharing.

## Traditional Indigenous Knowledge

Speaking up for one's own national identity and advocating an Inuit voice in Canadian political decision making and policy development in Inuit communities paralleled what was happening in Canadian federal government movements. Marlene Brant Castellano,[12] a member of the Mohawk Nation, spent five years as co-director of research with the Royal Commission on Aboriginal Peoples, which produced a 1996 report that identified the affirmation of Aboriginal knowledge as an essential goal of Aboriginal policy. As described earlier, Brant Castellano (2000) states that the Royal Commission defines the sources of knowledge as follows:

> *Traditional Knowledge* has been handed down more or less intact from previous generation. Creation of the world, origin of clans,

encounters between ancestors and spirits of the animals. Wisdom
of elder generations is highly regarded and elders are assigned
major responsibility for teaching the young.
*Empirical Knowledge* is gained through careful observation.
*Revealed Knowledge* is acquired through dreams, visions, and intu-
itions that are understood to be spiritual in origin. (pp. 23–24)

The Royal Commission on Aboriginal Peoples (1996) further states the
characteristics of Aboriginal Knowledge:

*Personal knowledge*: Aboriginal knowledge is rooted in personal
experience and lays no claim to universality.
*Oral transmission*: Oral teachings are necessarily passed on in the
context of a relationship.
*Experiential knowledge*: Knowledge of the physical world, which
forms an essential part of the praxis of inner and outer learning.
*Holistic knowledge*: All of the senses, coupled with openness to intuitive or spiritual insights, are required in order to plumb the depths
of aboriginal knowledge.
*Narrative and metaphor*: Traditionally, stories were the primary
medium used to convey aboriginal knowledge. Stories were used
to record a history of a people, to guide moral choice, and for self-
examination. (pp. 25–31)

Influenced by the Royal Commission's 1996 report, the Department of
Education in Nunavut was mandated to write a new curriculum for Inuit
youth that incorporated traditional indigenous knowledge. In Inuktitut,
this is known as Inuit Qaujimajatuqangit.[13] "The term Inuit Qaujimajatuqangit (IQ) encompasses all aspects of traditional Inuit Culture including values, world-view, language, social organization, knowledge, life skills,
perceptions and expectations. Inuit Qaujimajatuqangit is as much a way of
life as it is sets of information" (Tapardjuk, 1998). The Nunavut government also mandated the creation of Inuit Qaujimajatuqangit Schools. The
development of IQ schools involved extensive consultation with District
Education Authorities, educators, parents, and students about IQ education. It required collaboration with Inuit elders, Inuit organizations, and
the Department of Culture, Language, Elders, and Youth to translate the
core IQ values and beliefs into working models for school improvement.
The government stated that each community must have a vision for how
they want to educate their children. This process is ongoing.

## Application of Traditional Indigenous Knowledge

With a vision to bring Inuit indigenous knowledge into the schools of
Arviat, the Arviat District Education Authority hired me in 2001 as the
music teacher at Qitiqliq High School to implement Inuit Qaujimajatuqangit in the music program. For the purposes of exploring the various
functions and meanings this curriculum has for Gara in this particular
musical context, I examined the relationship between Gara and an elder,
Eva Aupak — from whom she learned songs — in order to explore Gara's
successes and difficulties with the oral educational approach that is a part
of traditional indigenous knowledge.

> On a quiet day toward the end of my first year in the community, I
> asked Gara if she knew any pisiit. She said, "I know a couple of them
> but not very well. Those songs are for the elders. Only elders sing pisiit.
> Nobody else knows them or sings them." We sat in the girls' room at
> Gara's home, and on the wall of this sparsely furnished room was a
> vividly colourful photograph haphazardly thumb-tacked to the faded
> wall. It showed her as a typical teenager, standing proudly next to her
> brother, Yvon, in blue jeans and a hooded sweatshirt. Immediately to
> her left in the photograph was an electronic piano, and he was holding
> an electric guitar. As young people living in Arviat, they were expected
> to participate in religious activities at the Roman Catholic Church and
> to teach children how to play the piano and guitar at the mission-run
> Mikilauq Centre. When I asked her to tell me why only elders sing tra-
> ditional pisiit she said, "Elders know about the old ways but we don't.
> Those songs are boring and I don't know that they are talking about."
> She laughed, and wondered why I was so interested in "those old songs"
> while I wondered and marvelled at the success of the Roman Catholic
> missionaries who first came to Arviat in the 1920s. Only three genera-
> tions later and youth knew nothing about traditional Inuit songs but knew
> literally hundreds of Christian gospel tunes. I had thought that there must
> be some traditional songs in Gara's repertoire, but I was wrong.

The youth of Arviat do not interact often with their elders, and, as a
result, many of the old songs are not being passed on to the youth. In an
attempt to stop this cultural erosion, the Inuit Qaujimajatuqangit mandated
the inclusion of traditional Inuit drum dances in the music classroom. To
this end, Eva Aupak — an elder and tradition bearer — was hired.

If you recall the scene I presented to you at the beginning of this chapter, you will remember the nervousness I felt when Eva came to our music

classroom. Eva was upset because the girls were not singing with her. I glanced around the room to see the girls shifting restlessly in their seats. Many of them were watching the floor, looking ashamed because their elder was upset with them. I thought, "This is not working." Gara and I sat in the empty music room after that hour-long, tense rehearsal with Eva and I asked her what had happened. She explained that Eva wanted the girls to sing along with her but that none of them knew the song yet. She said, "I found it hard to just listen to her. She expected us to join in, but I didn't have the words so I couldn't. But I really wanted to." What Eva thought was disrespect and failure to comply with her wishes was simply the girls' inability to carry out her request. They simply did not know the song and could not sing along without lyrics sheets to aid them.

The next rehearsal, I decided that I would have the girls write out the words while Eva sang them. Having come to class to sing and enjoy the process of music making, the girls sat awkwardly, trying to sing along with Eva as she had instructed them to do once again. When she finished her song, "Qumak Pisia"[14] (see appendix for lyrics, translation, and musical transcription), I leaned over to Gara and asked her to request Eva sing one line at a time so the girls could write the words down. As Gara was carrying out my request in Inuktitut, Eva's facial expressions changed. She replied in Inuktitut, pointed at me, and shook her head. Gara looked in my direction and said, "She says that you are not supposed to write out the words; that's not how it is done." Unsure of what to do next, I sat back and listened to the girls struggle with Eva's requests for the rest of the rehearsal.

The next week, Eva, Gara, and I met before rehearsal. We talked about the importance of passing on traditional Arviat songs to the young people and our collective dreams of having the choir sing the songs at the community hall for social functions. She disclosed her frustration with the girls because they refused to sing. Gara and I emphasized their refusal was not an act of disrespect but rather an inability to sing because they did not have the lyrics to read. After a few moments, Eva declared that the students should write out the words of the *pisia* because she wanted the story of Qumak to continue. The subsequent rehearsals went well — smiles and laughter from Eva and the girls, and participation in singing the *pisia* indicated success.

## Conclusion

In this chapter, I have presented an application of indigenous knowledge in music making in a classroom context by examining the relationship between an elder and a youth. When Gara learned "Qumak Pisia" from Eva, the teaching/learning context was a classroom with a student–teacher ratio of approximately 30 to 1. A personal relationship between Eva and Gara had not been established because there were just too many students and not enough time. Compounding this problem was the issue of oral transmission. The classroom setting is a literate one and the students expected lyrics sheets in order to learn this *pisiq*; without the written lyrics the students became frustrated. Oral transmission, an element of traditional indigenous knowledge, did not work in this situation, and other teaching/learning strategies had to be employed.

Recognizing the classroom setting was different from her own experience of learning traditional *pisiit*, Eva changed her method of teaching to one that matched the students' learning styles, and, after much negotiation, Eva, Gara, and the students achieved some success. Today, Gara and her fellow students know many local and territorial drum dance songs and have represented Nunavut at various festivals and games. Gara does so with pride: "I prefer to wear an *amautiq* (woman's traditional clothing) because it shows people that we are Inuit, not just through our music. It adds more to our music. Just to look at us, you can see we're Inuit and our music just adds to that. They're beautiful, too, what our ancestors wore!"

Eva's work with the students has had a direct impact on the success of my choir Arviat Imngitingit. This choir is made up of students from Qitiqliq High School and adults from the community. It specializes in the recently revived traditional Inuit music originating from the Kivalliq region of Nunavut. The Arviat Imngitingit have become famous for their expertise in traditional Inuit throat singing, a-ya-ya singing, and drum dancing, and they enjoy singing contemporary Inuit folk songs and gospel songs in Inuktitut as well. Several members of Arviat Imngitingit have travelled to Greenland and Alberta to perform for the opening and closing ceremonies of the Arctic Winter Games, and others have travelled to Brandon, Manitoba, to perform with the Brandon University Chorale at Rural Forum 2002. All thirty choristers participated in Festival 500: Sharing the Voices, an international choral festival held in Newfoundland in 2003. The choir has been highlighted in television programs on both Global Television and Aboriginal Peoples' Television Network, as well as in newspapers such as the *National Post, Evening Telegram, Southern Gazette, Kivalliq News,* and *News North*.

I have sought here to "write against culture" by working against generalization. As Abu-Lughod (1993) emphasizes, "by focusing on particular individuals and their changing relationships, one could also subvert the problematic connotations of 'culture': homogeneity, coherence, and timelessness" (p. 14). Individual lives in the classroom are complex and involve more than terms such as "Inuit culture" or "traditional indigenous knowledge" imply. Eva was confronted with choices about how to teach traditional songs, she underwent positive and negative changes in her relationships with students and with me, and she argued about points of view on the oral tradition. In the events I have described, it became evident that she debated her understanding of traditional indigenous knowledge — especially the oral aspect of it — and was prepared to make changes in her teaching style to meet the needs of her students. The reconstruction of Eva's and Gara's arguments about, justifications for, and interpretations of what they and others were doing in the classroom allowed a clearer understanding of how social life proceeds in this particular context. Inuit culture is neither static nor homogeneous; individuals such as Eva and Gara are responding to the shifting powers of cultural negotiation and constituting their futures in the dynamic world in which they live.

Elders who have articulated the importance of traditional indigenous knowledge being taught in Nunavut schools have said that they are not advocating a return to the past but a grounding of education in the strengths of Inuit so that their children will survive and successfully negotiate the world they find themselves in today. Musical creation of traditional drum dances in Arviat has evoked a community connection — a connection between elders and youth and a connection with Inuit history. This ethnographic study clearly shows how music can create and foster community identity, cohesion, and development. In the words of Jaypeetee Arnakak: "We owe it to the world, and especially to ourselves, to articulate who and what we were in the past, who and what we are today, and who and what we want to become in the future" (Curriculum and School Services Division, 2002).

## APPENDIX

### Qumak Pisia

Transcribed from Eva Aupak, Arviat, Nunavut
Words transcribed by Jamie Kablutsiak
Music transcribed by Mary Piercey
Translation by Gara Mamgark

ᓂᕐᖑᑦᑳᕐᒐᓂᒃ ᕿᓄᖅᑐᖅ  (Syllabics)
ᐊᕐᖑᑦ ᒍᑳᐃᕐ
ᐱᕐᓗᑐᕐᖅᑐᖕᓗ
ᐊᕐᖑᑦ ᒍᒥ ᐊᕐᑎ
ᐱᕐᓗᑐᕐᖅᑐᖕᓗ
ᐊᕐᖑᑦ ᒍᑳᐃᕐ-ᐃᕐᕐ-ᐃᕐᕐ-ᐊᕐᖑᑦ ᒍᑳᐃᕐ  ᐊᕐᖑᑦ ᒍᑳᐃᕐ-ᕐᕐᕐ-ᐊᕐᖅᖑᖕ-ᕐᕐᕐ

ᐊᑦᑕ...ᓂᖅᐸᕐᖢᓂᒥᒪ
ᖄᓂᖅᖢᖑ  ᐃᒪ
ᐊᕙᑉᒧᒥᐊᕐᓕ
ᐱᓱᓗᕐᖠᑐᖑ
ᐊᕙᑉᒧᑦᑕᐃᔭᕐ-ᐃ-ᔭ-ᐃ-ᔭ-ᐊᕙᑉᒧᑦᑕᐃᔭᕐ  ᐊᕙᑉᒧᑦᑕᐃᔭᕐ-ᔭᔭᔭ-ᐊᕚᖅᖓ-ᔭᔭᔭᔭ

ᐊᑦᑕ...ᐅᓐᓂᓕᐅᑉᐸ
ᖃᒡᓕᔫᓐᓇᖅᖓᖑ
ᓄᑲᑐᒡᕋᕐᔪᒃ
ᐱᓱᒍᒪᐃᖅᑐᖅ
ᐊᕙᑉᒧᑦᑕᐃᔭᕐ-ᐃ-ᔭ-ᐃ-ᔭ-ᐊᕙᑉᒧᑦᑕᐃᔭᕐ  ᐊᕙᑉᒧᑦᑕᐃᔭᕐ-ᔭᔭᔭ-ᐊᕚᖅᖓ-ᔭᔭᔭᔭ

ᐊᑦᑕ...ᓄᐊᒥ
ᐊᕙᓂ
ᑭᕝᕙᓂᐅᒪ
ᐃᕐᐊᑯᓂᑲ
ᐱᓱᒍᒪᐃᖅᑐᖅ
ᐊᕙᑉᒧᑦᑕᐃᔭᕐ-ᐃ-ᔭ-ᐃ-ᔭ-ᐊᕙᑉᒧᑦᑕᐃᔭᕐ  ᐊᕙᑉᒧᑦᑕᐃᔭᕐ-ᔭᔭᔭ-ᐊᕚᖅᖓ-ᔭᔭᔭᔭ


**Qumak Pisia** (Roman Orothography)
Avapmut taija
Pisululiqtunga
Avapmumiarli
Pisululiqtunga
Avapmut taija -i-ya-i-ya- avapmut taija avapmut taija -ya-ya-ya- avaqnga
    -ya-ya-ya-ya-

A-ya-ya......niqipsaminigima
Qiniqthlunga ima
Avapmumiarli
Pisululiqtunga
Avapmut taija -i-ya-i-ya- avapmut taija avapmut taija -ya-ya-ya- avaqnga
    -ya-ya-ya-ya-

A-ya-ya......unniliuppa
Qagliyunnaqnanga
Nukatugarryuk
Pisugumaiqtuq
Avapmut taija -i-ya-i-ya- avapmut taija avapmut taija -ya-ya-ya- avaqnga
    -ya-ya-ya-ya-

A-ya-ya......nunami
Avani
Kivavanimma
Isuakunili
Pisugumaituq
Avapmut taija -i-ya-i-ya- avapmut taija avapmut taija -ya-ya-ya- avaqnga
  -ya-ya-ya-ya-

**Qumak Pisia** (English Translation)
Over there
I am walking
Over there
I am still walking
over there i-ya-i-ya over there taija-ya-ya over there ya-ya-ya-ya

A-ya-ya....... Serching for the
Food yes
over there
I am walking
over there i-ya-ya over there taija-ya-ya over there ya-ya-ya

A-ya-ya.... or I am looking
for the food yes
over there
over there i-ya-ya over there taija ya-ya over there ya-ya-ya

A-ya-ya.... out on the land
over there
towards the north
on top of the hill
doesn't walk on that hill
over there taija-i-ya over there taija-ya-ya over there ya-ya-ya

## Notes

1  The Royal Commission on Aboriginal Peoples was established in 1991 to carry out
   an independent inquiry into the troubled relationship between Aboriginal peoples,
   the Canadian government, and Canadian society. The commission submitted a
   five-volume report in 1996 that addressed issues of respect for cultural differences
   and recognition of the moral, historical, and legal right of Aboriginal peoples to
   govern their collective lives in ways they freely determine. The commission recommended the participation of Aboriginal people, the application of indigenous
   knowledge, and the incorporation of tradition as the basis for devising policy in
   political relations and governance, land use and economic development, family
   rehabilitation and community development, and health and education.

2   In recent years, Canada's indigenous peoples have articulated their respective
    definitions of indigenous knowledge. In his study *Ways of Knowing: Experience,
    Knowledge, and Power among the Dene Tha*, Jean-Guy Goulet (1998) presents his
    perspective of indigenous knowledge as "ways of knowing that are gained through
    directly experiencing life ways rather than through formal instruction." Louis
    Tapardjuk, an Inuk from Nunavut, defines indigenous knowledge as "that knowl-
    edge that encompasses all aspects of traditional Inuit Culture including values,
    world-view, language, social organization, knowledge, life skills, perceptions and
    expectations." In Inuktitut it is called Inuit Qaujimajatuqangit and is considered
    "as much a way of life as sets of information." Written on behalf of all Aboriginal
    people in Canada, Marlene Brant Castellano's definition of indigenous knowledge
    includes three sources: *Traditional Knowledge*, which has been handed down more
    or less intact from previous generations; *Empirical Knowledge*, which is gained
    through careful observation; and *Revealed Knowledge*, which is acquired through
    dreams, visions, and intuitions that are understood to be spiritual in origin. This
    definition is discussed further below.

3   The Arviat District Education Authority is an elected committee of seven commu-
    nity members that deals with the education of all students within the boundaries of
    the Hamlet of Arviat. This committee must (1) provide education to all students in
    the community; (2) develop and deliver culture-based school programs in accor-
    dance with the requirements of the curriculum and with the advice of education
    staff, parents, and community elders; (3) develop and produce learning resources
    and materials to support the delivery of culture-based school programs and other
    local programs; and (4) monitor, evaluate, and direct the delivery of school pro-
    grams to assure the highest possible education standards in the schools.

4   Arviamiut (people of the bowhead whale) were coastal Caribou Inuit who lived
    near Eskimo Point (now Arviat); Ahiarmiut (people out of the way) were inland-
    ers living along the upper Kazan River near Ennadai Lake; Padlirmiut (people of
    the willow thicket) were inlanders who were nomadic and spent their springs and
    summers in the community of Arviat with the Arviamiut. These groups are now
    living together in Arviat, but members still recognize their ancestral names in
    contemporary living.

5   Nunavut officially became the third territory of Canada on April 1, 1999. It is the
    first self-governing indigenous territory in North America. Eighty-five percent of
    Nunavut's residents are indigenous Inuit. Along with self-rule and control over
    their institutions, the Inuit of Nunavut are combating suicide, reversing assimila-
    tion, and regaining a sense of identity.

6   The Roman Catholic Mission and the Anglican Church Mission were established in
    Arviat (Eskimo Point) in 1924 and 1926 respectively. Missionaries from both denomi-
    nations travelled to Inuit hunting camps to educate children and adults. Classes were
    also taught in the community of Arviat when Inuit were there. Throughout the
    1940s RCMP planes flew to the Inuit camps surrounding Arviat to collect children
    to attend a residential school in Chesterfield Inlet. Unfortunately, the experience of
    being away from families and witnessing or enduring physical and sexual assault
    while attending this school left deep emotional scars. In 1959, the Community
    Federal Day School, offering an English curriculum from Kindergarten to Grade 8,
    opened in Arviat. If students wanted to further their education they went to Sir John
    Franklin Territorial High School in Yellowknife and lived at Akaitcho Hall.

7  Charlie Panigoniak — a singer, songwriter, and guitarist — was born in Chesterfield Inlet, Nunavut. His many songs, composed in a country-folk style, have been written in the Inuktitut language and concern family, friends, and everyday events in his life. He has recorded five albums and, as a popular figure in the north, can be heard regularly on the radio and seen on TV and at festivals.

8  Susan Aglukark is one of Canada's most famous Aboriginal singers. She was born in Churchill, Manitoba, and raised in Arviat, Nunavut, where her father was a Pentecostal minister. The lyrics of her songs on her four albums include personal stories and social commentary on issues such as child abuse, alcoholism, and suicide that have plagued many First Nations communities. Aglukark is an advocate for northern Canadian communities and the people who live there; she also serves as a spokesperson for the RCMP National Alcohol and Drug Awareness Prevention Program and travels to northern communities to connect with Inuit youth.

9  *Aboriginal knowledge* and *Indigenous knowledge* are used interchangeably in this paper.

10  Inuit Tapirisat of Canada (ITC) represents Canada's Inuit on matters of national concern. ITC is the national voice of the Inuit of Canada and addresses issues of vital importance to the preservation of Inuit identity, culture, and way of life. One of the most important responsibilities of ITC is to protect Inuit rights and to ensure that Inuit are properly informed about issues and events that affect their lives, and that processes purporting to address Inuit interests are properly informed by Inuit knowledge, perspectives, and vision.

11  Nunavut Tunngavik Incorporated is a private federal corporation established in 1993 to ensure implementation of the terms of the 1993 Nunavut Lands Claim Agreement. Nunavut Tunngavik Inc. is the successor organization to Tunngavik Federation of Nunavut (1982), which itself succeeded the Inuit Tapirisat of Canada, who placed the original comprehensive claim before the Federal Government of Canada in 1976.

12  Castellano is professor emeritus and former chair of the Department of Native Studies at Trent University. She co-edited a book entitled *Aboriginal Education: Fulfilling the Promise* (2001) with Lynne Davis and Louise Lahache. The book presented research that helped inspire education recommendations for the report by Canada's Royal Commission on Aboriginal Peoples. It focused on empowering models of education that seek to address the needs and dreams of Aboriginal peoples, and also looked at obstacles in the form of government policies and institutional criteria.

13  *Inuit Qaujimajatuqangit (IQ) Curriculum Framework Document* (2005) provides the philosophy and cultural components of an education system embedded in IQ. It puts into action the priorities and principles set out in the government's mandate, *Pinasuaqtavut*. It also makes the links to the *Inuuqatigiit* curriculum and other key foundation documents for education in Nunavut, such as *Ilitaunnikuliriniq Student Assessment in Nunavut Schools, Inuglugijaittuq: Inclusive Education in Nunavut Schools* and *Aajiiqatigiingniq: Language of Instruction Report*.

14  Qumak is the name of the deceased man who wrote and owns this song. I recently discovered through an interview with Mary Thompson that his name is actually spelled *Kuumaup*. *Qumak* is the "government" misspelling of his name, which means "head lice."

# References

Abu-Lughod, L. (1993). *Writing women's worlds: Bedouin stories.* Berkeley: University of California Press.

Arthur B. A. (1995). *Semiotics and cultural criticism: A primer of key concepts.* Thousand Oaks, CA: Sage Publications.

Author. (1996). *Royal commission on aboriginal peoples.* Retrieved from http:// xnet.rrc.mb.ca/library/guides2/onlineref/royaborig.htm.

Beaudry, N. (1978). Toward transcription and analysis of Inuit throat games: Macro-structure. *Ethnomusicology, 22*(2), 261–273.

Brant Castellano, M. (2000). Updating Aboriginal traditions of knowledge. In G. J. Sefa Dei, B. L. Hall, and D. Rosenberg (Eds.), *Indigenous knowledge in global contexts — Multiple readings of our world* (pp. 21–53). Toronto: University of Toronto Press.

Cavanaugh, B. (1982). *Music of the Netsilik Eskimo: A study of stability and change.* Ottawa: National Museums of Canada.

Charron, C. (1978). Toward transcription and analysis of Inuit throat games: Micro-structure. *Ethnomusicology, 22*(2), 245–260.

Curriculum and School Services Division, Department of Education, Government of Nunavut. (2002). *Nunavut Curriculum Framework.* Retrieved from http:// www.ecss.nu.ca/writers/framework/framework.htm.

Dyc, G. (2002). Language learning in the American southwestern borderlands: Navajo speakers and their transition to academic English literacy. *Bilingual Research Journal, 26*(3). Retrieved from http://brj.asu.edu/content/vol26_no3/pdf/art8.pdf.

Goulet, J. (1998). *Ways of knowing: Experience, knowledge, and power among the Dene Tha.* Lincoln: University of Nebraska Press.

Kenny, C. (2002). *North American Indian, Métis and Inuit women speak out about culture, education and work.* Ottawa: Status of Women Canada's Policy Research Fund.

Marsh, D. B. (1987). *Echos from a frozen land.* Edmonton: Hurtig Publishers.

Nattiez, J. (1983). Some aspects of Inuit vocal games. *Ethnomusicology, 27*(3), 457–475.

Netser, P. (2003). Workshop notes.

Ong, W. J. (1988). *Orality and literacy: The technologizing of the word.* London and New York: Routledge.

Pelinski, R. (1979). *Inuit songs from Eskimo Point.* Ottawa: National Museums of Canada.

Pelinski, R. (1981). *La musique des Inuit du Caribou: Cinq perspectives methodologiques.* Montreal: University of Montreal Press.

Rasmussen, K. (1999). *Across Arctic America.* Fairbanks: University of Alaska Press.

Tapardjuk, L. (1998). Report of the Nunavut tradition knowledge conference.

Veblen, K., Beynon, C., & Odom, S. (2005). Drawing on diversity in the arts education classroom: Educating our new teachers. *International Journal of Education and the Arts, 6*(14). Retrieved from http://ijea.asu.edu/v6n14/.

# SIX

# Looking Back on Choral Music Education in Canada: A Narrative Perspective

*Carol Beynon*

To provide a definitive accounting of choral music education in Canada, particularly within the scope of just one chapter, is an impossible task. Such an account would assume that there is a set of data that could be gathered, analyzed, assessed, and reported accurately as an extant body of knowledge. And while there are some researchers who might make an honest attempt to accomplish that task, there is absolutely no means by which one could amass all the relevant and definitive information on this topic. The result of such an attempt would, at best, still be simply one view, and still a subjective interpretation of this topic. That being said, it is important to examine some aspects of choral music education with the understanding that this is one writer's attempt to make sense of a complex phenomenon. What follows in this chapter is a narrative accounting of what I know to be a somewhat accurate and experiential history of choral music education at a local, provincial, and national level in Canada from its earliest inceptions in public education to the end of the first decade of the twenty-first century. Narrative, as a recognized and accepted form of research methodology, has been part of the qualitative research paradigm for the past twenty years (Clandinin & Connolly, 2000); this chapter attempts to provide a different perspective on choral music education in Canada than the norm.

My experience as a singer and choral music educator spans seven decades from the 1950s through to the present, mainly in Ontario. My experiences have been rich and varied: as a singer in church and school choirs in my early and adolescent years with devoted and well-meaning, but not always well-trained, music teachers;[1] as an undergraduate music education and voice major at the University of Western Ontario; as a singer in the elite Faculty Singers at Western; as a student of choral conducting under Professor Deral Johnson; as an elementary and secondary choral music teacher in the public school system; as a competitor in local and international music festivals as singer, chorister, and as conductor with my own choirs under the intense scrutiny of the all-knowing adjudicator; as a teacher of music education in the University of Western Ontario's (UWO) Faculty of Education for twenty-five years; as a choral conductor of the Amabile Boys' and Men's Choirs of London, Canada; as an adjudicator — though certainly not an all-knowing one — of school and community, children's, youth, and adult choirs around the world; and as a lifelong student of learning about music through working with many renowned national and international choral conductors. These experiences have brought me into both formal and informal ways of knowing that have had a profound effect on my life and every life experience I have had. I provide this overview because it is critical that the reader have some sense of the lens through which I view choral music education — as an intense, personal experience, one of the ways in which I make sense of the world, and likely the most significant defining element of who I am as a person.

## Early Choral Music Education in Canada: Singing and the Empire
As an elementary student in a two-room schoolhouse in the late 1950s, I became aware, at least in later years, of the limitations and expectations of public education for the masses. My father, a local farmer, was one of the trustees who hired the teachers for our school; these well-meaning farmers with a Grade 8 education decided who would teach their children and how much they could afford to pay them each year. Our itinerant music teacher travelled many kilometres daily from school to school across the townships. Miss Hall was bigger than life, with dyed black hair and a huge, pleasant singing voice. There were always at least three different grades in one classroom and she taught all of us once a week for about thirty minutes; we sang a variety of songs — some that would be considered quite politically incorrect these days — from the *Highroad of Song* and practised our sight-singing to tonic sol-fa from the *Highroad Sight Singing Series.* My

music education was not limited to the one-per-week-lesson at school. My mother drove my sisters and me into the city each week for piano lessons with the nuns at the convent, and we all had to sing in the junior choir at the local United Church. My parents could barely afford to pay for piano lessons and they sacrificed any luxuries for the family to do so; I am a bit ashamed as I think back to the rather disrespectful arguments I gave my mother when it was time for my daily practice. The ultimate goal in that era was for piano students to pass the Grade VIII Royal Conservatory of Music practical examination and Grade II Rudiments, which could be used in lieu of taking Grade 13 music.

In a predominantly rural society, schooling across Canada was geared to the norms, values, and ideologies of the conservative dominant society, which in turn were influenced heavily by the traditions and norms of the British empire. It was considered a mark of the elite to have musical training; families of United Kingdom heritage who aspired to a better station in life — whatever that meant — often provided piano lessons for their working-class children, especially for their daughters, in order to actively seek means of increasing potential for their children, if not themselves, and to be able to share some morsel of upper-class life. In the 1950s and 1960s, working-class mothers could sit beside upper-class parents at piano recitals and public concerts and share the enjoyment of community concerts with a visiting symphony orchestra or current diva.

While public schooling was intended to develop a literate, well-educated society in Canada, the subversive goals were to inculcate the norms and values of conservative British ideologies and to socialize youth to the norms of the dominant society. The curriculum, textbooks, and even the standardized tests were based on what the British colonizers felt were necessary for the education of the colonies. And while the British immigrant inspectors gradually began to relinquish their hold on totally British practices, the education system continued to emphasize "God Save the Queen," which at that time was more patriotic than "O Canada." The colonized aspired to emulate the colonizers, and were encouraged to do so by the colonizers; this phenomenon lasted well into the 1960s in Canada and only began to change when Canada developed a sense of heightened nationalism, which included launching its own flag and transforming the British North America Act. At the same time, the young one-hundred-year-old country began to focus on becoming more globally competitive in all aspects, but especially economically.

Formal music education programs in schools were clustered mainly in large urban areas such as Toronto and Vancouver, as were the major community and professional music programs of symphony orchestras, bands, semi-professional choirs, and excellent church choirs with trained musical directors, many of whom, incidentally, were trained in the armed forces. Radio shows provided mass entertainment with venues for such choral groups as the Don Wright Chorus Radio Show, the Leslie Bell Singers, and the Earle Terry Singers. With a repertoire based on songs of the empire, many songs supported the war efforts of the past, the glory of the empire, and the songs of the people with special attention to folk songs of the British Isles. There was growing awareness and almost discernible discomfort with the newly developing popular rock music scene. Choral music was a major form of mass public entertainment via half-hour radio broadcasts and shared air space with a number of dramas, comedies, and baseball and hockey games. With the advent of television in the 1950s, mass entertainment changed completely and impacted society in rather significant ways.

The sanctioned textbooks for the schools from British Columbia to Nova Scotia, with the exception of parts of Quebec and New Brunswick, came from British stock. Ministry of Education officials modelled the system on its British counterpart, and most supervisory personnel were still trained in the United Kingdom. University education in Canada was limited to urban centres, and those schools, too, were originally based on British models. If one were to conjure up an image of a professor at the University of Toronto in the 1950s and 1960s, *he* would have thick, white hair and a crisp English accent. So too would the majority of school inspectors and music festival adjudicators.

Although public education was provided for the masses, most students in rural areas never expected to go past Grade 8. Once past those entrance examinations, the fourteen- or fifteen-year-olds were considered to be close to adulthood — in stark contrast to today — and males especially went back to their farms to help or to the industrial-based workforce. Anecdotal reports from current seniors indicate that more Canadian women attended high school than men during the first half of the twentieth century, before they became wives and mothers, and teachers, nurses, and secretaries if they worked outside the home.

### Singing, the Baby Boom, and Modernism
As Canada entered the 1960s, massive changes in thought, deed, and rural-rooted norms and values were taking place as the rural population began to move to the cities. There were emerging shifts from traditional societal values to values of modernism and consumerism. People's traditional belief systems were bombarded, challenged, and affected by the proliferation of the influential mass media, more prosperous times, and a relatively peaceful, stable world. More expansive views of schooling developed and

a Grade 10 education became the norm for all students. The baby boom after the Second World War resulted in an increase in school-aged children and a dramatic increase in the building of new schools. Small rural schools were closed, and large, centralized schools took pupils away from their sheltered communities. Segregated elementary and secondary schools were built, resulting in a building boom across many parts of the country. Compulsory schooling for all children up to age sixteen became the norm and students were bused kilometres across the Canadian countryside. The country was prosperous and confident and educational funding was at an all-time high. Where previously music programs had been evident only in large urban centres, they now were being developed in all secondary schools and in some urban elementary schools. Bands, orchestras, and choirs became the showpieces of schools and communities; the development of larger school boards led to increased financial support to fund the largest school population ever.

Given the holdovers from the days of the empire, it should not surprise anyone to recall that, in many large schools, students entering Grade 9 were given aptitude and intelligence tests to determine what form of music education they would be allowed to study. The brightest were channelled into string orchestral programs, the average student into winds, and, finally, the lowest-scoring were forced to study vocal and/or general music. Perhaps this last statement more accurately than any other sums up the prevailing attitudes toward choral music education in the hierarchy of music subjects in the schools. One could speculate that not much has changed even in the first decade of the twenty-first century.

While specialist instrumental music teachers were hired for each of the secondary school music programs, choral specialists were rarely hired for vocal programs. Itinerant music specialists — those with Grade VIII piano — were hired most frequently for the elementary schools. Large sums of money were spent on developing programs, training specialist teachers, and purchasing instruments, repertoire, and other resources during the late 1960s through to the 1980s. Part of secondary education involved the development of academic, technological, and business programs to suit the needs of different students. Looking back on this, researchers such as Michael Apple (1995; 2003) and Henry Giroux (1997) point out that the academic programs catered to the upper class of society, and business and technology/trades programs were aimed at the middle class, while very little was offered to the working-poor classes, who were never aware of, or shown how to access, education equity for their children.[2] Music programs were no different, and they catered to the elite and middle classes. The collegiate institutes offered quite different programs than the vocational and technological schools; often an orchestral program was offered in the former and a band or general music program in the latter, with both offering extracurricular choirs.

From the 1960s onward, when Canada undertook a firm separation from the monarchy, British influences began to diminish, while American influences began to take precedence as a result of the proliferation of media from the United States. Canadians saw modern society first-hand and in living colour via the predominantly American shows on their television sets. Popular music became the music of choice for general society; the classics took a back seat.

When I was in high school in the 1960s, my closest girlfriend—with whom I always shared a seat on the hour-long bus ride to and from school—asked me why I had not ridden the bus home the previous day. I told her that I had to go for an extra singing lesson because I would be competing in the Kiwanis Music Festival in a few weeks and needed an extra lesson. She looked at me with some anxiety on her face for a few moments and said, "I knew you took music lessons but I thought it was just piano." After some discussion, she suggested that I not tell anyone I was taking singing lessons; it was bad enough that I had joined the high school choir. Our high school choir of twenty-five singers — twenty-two females and three males conducted by a much-loved and respected community music teacher who had little choral music education but much enthusiasm — worked diligently. I recall that our favourite repertoire at the time was the medley from *The Sound of Music*; however, we would never have dared sing for a school auditorium for fear of being laughed off the stage. Our fifty-year-old rural/urban collegiate institute had only General Music, and our teacher had been hired to teach it because she could play the piano. The newly built composite high school on the other side of town, on the other hand, had a band program and the band teacher they hired had a university degree with a major in instrumental music.

Early in the 1970s, I found myself studying music education at university — my parents had decided that one of their four children would go to university and, for some reason I must have been the most compliant in the family in that regard. I remember that I could not decide what to study. My aunt, a teacher, commented that I seemed to excel in music and suggested that music would be obvious choice for a program of study. I enrolled in theory and harmony classes in Grade 13, passed Grade III harmony, Grade VIII piano, and Grade IX voice just in time, and then decided that if I had to go to university, I would rather be a voice major than a piano major. Professor Donald McKellar, faculty member in music education at UWO, who met the incoming applicants during auditions, suggested that I follow the music education stream because my ultimate goal was to become an elementary teacher. Caring faculty at UWO, who were committed to excellence in music education, such as Don McKellar, Deral Johnson, Paul Greene, Ilona Bartalus, Dawson Woodburn, and Peter Clements, offered stimulating educational experiences throughout my years of study. Talented and enthusiastic peers motivated me to study, practise, and perform as well as I could, and to have a good time while away from home for the first time. It would have been difficult not to succeed in that environment. A significant year in teacher education with James White — who provided a solid foundation with which to enter the teacher profession in the early 1970s — followed my BMusA. What followed in the 1970s was a time of enormous change in music education.

I began teaching choral music in elementary and secondary schools at a time when the student population in the educational system was still growing. There seemed to be lots of money for education, and music education programs were expanding dramatically. At the large, urban secondary school where I taught, there was both a solid string program and a band program. The department head decided he would like to have a choir at the school, so he hired me — a trained vocal major — to start an extracurricular choir which would be composed mainly of students from the band and orchestra. As the first choir of twelve grew into a concert choir of about a hundred students, we began to offer choral classes; there were always two or three small classes timetabled, which incidentally are still running some thirty years later. Most of the other schools in the school board were offering band programs and working to develop some choral strength. However most department heads relied on their existing band or string teachers to develop the choral program. Very few administrators saw the need to hire a choral specialist; most could not see what skills a person would need just to have people sing. The performance level of those choirs, without exception, was poor.

In my fourth year of teaching in that system, I attended a music subject council meeting — a monthly meeting of all the high school music teachers in the district to discuss various matters of mutual importance. The topic at that particular meeting was the new timing of the Kiwanis Music Festival and the impact on our school ensembles. The festival was growing from one to two weeks in length and the chair of the music council, who was also a band director at one of the schools, announced that he had been consulted about the timing of events. He had asked that choral classes be held during the first week and the instrumental classes during the second week because it took far longer to develop a band or orchestra for performance than a choir. Anyone, he said, could have a choir ready for competition without much effort, but it took real expertise and work to prepare an instrumental ensemble. As one of the few qualified choral teachers in the group, I was disappointed to watch my band colleagues, who also were conducting their own choirs, agree with him. However, such a sentiment still seems to be the norm — there seems to be no need for a trained specialist to develop a choir because it is perceived that anyone can sing and that it takes no skill to train singers to perform. But that is a subject for greater discussion at another time.

As the baby boomers began to reach adulthood, band programs in high schools became the music subject of choice for the majority of most high schools in Canada, again following in the footsteps of our American neighbours. While there had to be curricular band classes in order to teach students to play the instruments, choirs were often formed on an extracurricular basis with perhaps only one or two small vocal classes included in the curriculum. Birth rates dwindled after the baby boom, and by the mid-1970s there were fewer children attending school. As a result, fewer tax dollars were allocated to support such extravagances as full music programs, or even other arts programs for that matter. Teaching positions became scarce, and dollars for resources even more scarce. Instead of growing and developing further, music programs began to experience a decline in both numbers and favour as concerns began to erupt about the need to raise educational standards. Emphasis began to be placed on spending diminishing tax dollars on essential education in numeracy, literacy, and sciences, not wasting it on the "frill" subjects. Where previously music education had been part of the curriculum to develop educated citizens according to traditional norms of the dominant class, it was now seen by many as an extravagance in a public system where the basics should be the foundation of the educational system. As a result, the weakest of the music programs (i.e., choral music) seemed to take more hits than did the predominant band programs, although they suffered losses as well. In short, a depressed economy, fewer tax dollars, a more conservative curriculum, and decreased birth rates coupled with anxieties about social mores created massive uncertainty in Canadian schooling.

### Singing, the Baby Bust, and Postmodernism

As norms have changed, Canada as a country has emerged as an independent world leader, and the information age has taken precedence over industrialism. Modern life has transformed in ways we never could have imagined. Against the backdrop of constant change and the need to succeed in a global economy, the emphasis in schooling has changed to one of increasing standards in schools, specifically in the core subjects of English, math, and sciences, so that Canadian students compete strongly in international testing. As both resources and support for a liberal education dwindle, a revitalized emphasis on arts education has emerged among former music, drama, and art educators in an attempt to save music, art, and other arts subjects in the curriculum. In the elementary schools in most jurisdictions, the itinerant specialist music teacher rarely exists anymore and the general classroom teacher is expected to provide a sound education in all subjects. The secondary system is also struggling with a crowded curriculum. This curriculum is also under pressure to show that it prepares students for the world of work, in part by meeting the goals set by the Conference Board of Canada — a group of private-sector business leaders, not educators. Music educators are experimenting with new musics and new formats to reflect the increasingly diverse society and the need to attract students to programs, while drawing the attention of those who allot the budgets. There is tension, confusion, and uncertainty among music educators as they attempt to develop music education programs that will suit the educational needs of the student population.

In the middle of all this change, what is happening to choral music programs in the first part of the twenty-first century? Few elementary schools have specialist teachers, and only a small number of pupils have formal music classes on a regular basis in their timetables. Fewer schools have junior or intermediate choirs, other than for special occasions once or twice a year. The decline of choral music can even be seen in the use of "O Canada" in the schools: where it used to be sung by the students, it is now almost always played over the PA system.

In the secondary schools, much like in the elementary schools, few schools have formal choral classes in the curriculum, although a small number of arts schools specialize in various art forms and have specially trained teachers and practising performers. Instrumental specialists, rather than choral specialists, more often than not direct choirs, where they exist at all. Furthermore, where choirs do exist, the student membership does not reflect the diversity of the school; choirs tend to be composed predominantly of white, middle-class students.

Recently I was asked to be the choral adjudicator for a medium-sized community festival in another province. While the format remained the same — each choir took its turn lining up on stage and performing its repertoire under the direction of its conductor — the repertoire was as varied as one could ever imagine: spirituals; the classics of Bach, Mendelssohn, and Brahms; a song attributed to Canada's First Nations peoples; an atonal, dissonant song that seemed to have no sense of melody or rhythm; folk songs from Georgia (a former Soviet Bloc country), El Salvador, Finland,

and Nigeria; songs of freedom, and songs of protest. If nothing else, the songs themselves are changing and conductors are currently choosing repertoires with currency and a postmodern flavour.

**Summary**

Since the advent of public schooling more than a hundred years ago, when singing was seen as a mark of an educated person and was instituted as an integral part of the curriculum in order to socialize and inculcate traditional values and norms, much has changed in the world, in society, and in forms of communication. And in Canada, the traditional songs of the empire have been replaced by popular musics that, at the very least, mock and challenge traditional values. Choral music education, never very strong in the system, has seen change and transformation, but not in a significant enough way to find a place of importance in the educational system. There is a sense that an education that involves singing is a good thing, but that policy makers are not so convinced that it is a necessity. Music education in general, and choral music education specifically, are paid lip service in current public schooling. At the same time, there is a proliferation of outstanding choral organizations for children and youth developing around the world, almost always directed by school teachers who are choral specialists. These community organizations seem to be taking the place of the dwindling choral programs in schools, and, like the school choirs, the participants in the community choirs are not at all representative of the diverse community. These community choral music programs are exploding in number with high levels of performance quality, indicating that the parents in some (i.e., elite) sectors of society in the community who can afford to provide these activities for their children outside of school perceive the value of choral music education with artistic excellence.

What is the future for choral music education? At this point, although we can observe incremental growth in community programs, the future for school programs looks bleak. What kinds of choral music programs are appropriate in this postmodern age? There is no easy or clear answer. And there are more questions to which we do not have answers: What value do choral music programs bring to students in schools? What would we lose in society if there were no choral music programs? What does society gain/lose when choral music, or any music education for that matter, is offered through the community rather than in the schools?

I end this chapter by noting that public schooling is the one (and basically the only) venue where each and every child, regardless of background, geographic location, ability, ethnicity, gender, or any other characteristic has access to the cultural capital[3] that one can gain through music education in general, and choral music in particular. All citizens deserve the power and status that are derived through access to the cultural capital of choral music. Those of us who have lived with that privilege must be the ones to work to ensure its continuation, not just for a select few, but for all.

## Notes

1  For decades the accepted standard of musical training to be a choral music teacher in schools was Grade VIII Royal Conservatory piano.

2  In fact, writers such as Apple and Giroux would posit that schools continue to act as a primary means of stratifying society; they privilege those already privileged and maintain the norms of poor and working-class students, filtering them into working-class education and jobs. Bourdieu's (Bourdieu & Passeron, 1990) work also explains and supports Apple's and Giroux's findings.

3  Bourdieu's concept of cultural capital is worth further investigation. His work with Passeron (1990) discussed how the educational system, which is based on power and dominance, tends to override the real function of education. They would note that the reproduction of culture through education actually plays a key role in the reproduction of the whole social system.

## References

Apple, M. W. (1995). *Education and power.* New York: Routledge.

Apple, M. W. (2003). *The state and the politics of education.* New York: Routledge.

Bourdieu, P., & Passeron, J. C. (1990). *Reproduction in education, society and culture.* London: Sage.

Clandinin, D. J., & Connelly, M. (2000). *Narrative inquiry: Experience and story in qualitative research.* San Francisco: Jossey-Bass.

Giroux, H., & Shanon, P. (Eds.). (1997). *Cultural studies and education: Towards a performative practice.* New York: Routledge.

Giroux, H. (Ed.). (Winter, 1980). Ideology, culture and the hidden curriculum. Special Issue of the *Journal of Education, 162*(1).

# SEVEN

# Re-Membering Bands in North America: Gendered Paradoxes and Potentialities

*Elizabeth Gould*

Bands[1] occupy a paradoxical position in US and Canadian societies. Indeed, bands themselves are paradoxical. On the one hand, the music and pageantry they provide for many ceremonial, civic, and sporting events is integral to the life of the community; on the other, their general influence outside of educational institutions has declined, most notably in Canada. Nevertheless, bands provide exceptionally rewarding musical and social experiences for their members and audiences alike, and remain essential to the project of nation building in Canada as well as in the US. From their beginnings in both countries — performing functional and inspirational music for military troops, striking fear in enemies, and consoling the bereaved — to the present day they continue to play a significant role in bolstering and sustaining the citizenry, shaping the youth who would not only fight the nations' wars, but also lead their nations politically and economically. It is little wonder, then, that school music programs in both countries have embraced concert bands in particular as being integral to their curricula.

Bands were founded as — and in many ways remain — tacitly exclusionary organizations, despite their populist appearance otherwise. Long the purview of white, middle-class men, they are characterized by heterosexuality and hegemonic masculinity[2] deployed in an effort to fend off the effects of Western society's even longer-held bias about the feminizing effects of music (Koza, 1993; La Rue, 1994). The vast majority of band conductors in all types of bands in the US and Canada continue to be men — certainly in the military — but most notably and particularly in postsecondary education. In the US, women currently account for less than 10 percent of all university band directors, a proportion that has increased only slightly in the past twenty years (Block, 1988; McElroy, 1996; McLain, 2000). They fare considerably better in Canada, where women currently hold six out of twenty-four high-profile university band positions. While this represents participation rates more than three times greater than in the US, the overall numbers in Canada are much too small to influence the aggregate. With over 2,000 university band positions in the US alone, the exact number of women conducting bands is unknown (College Music Society, 2008).

In addition to occupations, selection of band instruments also remains persistently — even stubbornly, considering that it is still so much in evidence — segregated by gender. This gender stereotyping of instrument selection has been documented by a large body of research spanning thirty years.[3] Taken as a group, findings suggest that gender associations with musical instruments are pervasive, indeed that musical instruments themselves are gendered. Instruments traditionally associated with bands (trumpet and drums) are consistently identified as masculine, while those with little or no association with bands (violin and harp) are consistently identified as feminine.[4] Moreover, gender associations seem to override all other considerations in instrument choice, and the resulting gender segregation becomes more obvious as students become older, suggesting that "the increasing participation of young women in high school and college bands seems to have served to perpetuate gender-based stereotypes of appropriate instruments" (Zervoudakes & Tanur, 1994, p. 67) rather than alleviate them. Gender-based instrument selection affects musical experiences (double-reed players do not play in marching bands), which may later affect job availability (without marching band experience, double-reed players are not generally considered qualified to conduct high school and university bands) (Hartley, 1995).

The ongoing disproportionately greater participation of men, however, has served to ensure that bands are held in high regard even as band directors struggle to assert the musical legitimacy of the ensembles they conduct.[5] Nevertheless, the well-deserved affection with which both US and Canadian societies extend to bands, as opposed to orchestras for instance,[6] is supported in large part by the association of the former with patriotic and outdoor events that create musical spaces that are overtly heterosexual and masculine. As a result, bands ameliorate in one fell swoop the emasculating and feminizing effects of music specifically on boys, while simultaneously enabling girls to fulfill their roles supporting men's endeavours, thus preserving the "natural" order. This socializing function of bands and its part in nation building in both the US and Canada has been largely ignored.

With this chapter, I explore ways in which gender signifies as sites of desire[7] in Canadian and US university and school bands. Remembering bands through their history in Canada and the US, as well as my own positive and valued school and community band experiences, I examine how they may be re-membered, which is to say, how those participating in bands can be constituted in unexpected and even transgressive ways. A performative construct, gender also implicates sexuality. Because heterosexuality and hegemonic masculinity are not stable or monolithic, I argue that spaces of and for difference are opened which hold potentialities for significations of gender and sexuality in bands that are decidedly not heterosexual and masculine, and potentially inclusive of all groups. Further, I maintain that it is the unique paradoxical positioning of bands relative to society that creates ruptures in heteronormativity and hegemonic masculinity, thus enabling my theoretical construct of *hyper-masculinity*. Rather than *hypermasculinity*, or masculinity that is exaggerated or aberrant in psychological terms, hyper-masculinity (with the hyphen) describes masculinity that is virtual, which is to say, not actual but nevertheless real (Deleuze, 1994). As a virtual construct, hyper-masculinity is not enacted; it is not a behaviour or trait that may be seen or identified. Rather, it is a "site of desire" that opens spaces of and for alternative genders/sexualities which are actual, making bands uniquely situated to provide social and musical space to all members. Beginning with a brief overview of bands in Canada and the US in the context of women's participation, I then describe the role of bands in the nation-building efforts of both countries. Finally, I address paradoxes and potentialities of bands that both destable and enable alternative and even dissident subjectivities.

## Bands in the United States and Canada

The beginnings of the band movement in both the US and Canada may be traced to European military bands (Goldman, 1946; Hazen & Hazen, 1987), which were and continue to be integral to the founding and building of both nations. In Canada, the first documented use of wind instruments occurred in 1535 by a French expeditionary force (Maloney, 1986), while in the US, the first documented performance of a military band did not occur until 1755 in Philadelphia (Camus, 1976). Regimental bands were important to the Continental Army during the American Revolution and were organized in the US military by the end of the eighteenth century. Providing concerts in addition to their military obligations in Canada, British regimental bands became "the backbone of cultural activity" (Kopstein & Pearson, 2002, p. 17). Many British military musicians chose to remain in Canada or returned there after completing their military obligations elsewhere, and became involved in the burgeoning Canadian military band movement. Within two years of Confederation in 1867, the Canadian militia supported forty-six bands.

It is impossible to overestimate the importance of bands in communities across North America during the nineteenth century, when they were organized in virtually every segment of society: bands on the St. Lawrence River and the Thousand Islands region, town bands, circus bands, industrial bands, institutional bands, lodge bands, ethnic bands, women's bands, children's bands, and family bands. Certainly most popular were town bands, which were exceptionally widespread. With their beginnings in towns with garrisons in the first quarter of the century, they could be found in virtually every part of both countries by the end of the century. Originally associated with the local militia, these bands were essentially civilian organizations composed of and directed by men. A notable exception to this was a band formed in 1820 by the religious sect Children of Peace, located in the village of Hope (later Sharon, Ontario) (Maloney, 1986). The band played during religious services, presented monthly concerts, and marched in local village parades as well as for important occasions in Toronto. Their reputation for musical excellence was well known, as they performed a variety of music for events inside and outside of church services. Referred to in some newspaper accounts "as the oldest and best civilian band in [Canada]" (Keillor, 2006, p. 97), perhaps what is most notable about this band is that it is thought to be the first band in North America to include women members, although not for some years after its founding.

Professional touring concerts bands also emerged from the military, particularly in the US. The most notable of these professional bands were John Philip Sousa's band, which he formed in 1892 after leading the US Marine Band for twelve years (Milburn, 1982), and Patrick Gilmore's Grand Boston Band, which performed in London (Ontario) in 1888 (Maloney, 1986). Having emerged at a time when there was little competition for audiences — only four professional orchestras existed in the US as late as 1880 (Fennell, 1961) and another four in Canada by 1900 (Keillor, 2006) — limited means of transportation, and no mass media other than newspapers and radio, these bands were particularly successful until just after the First World War. Given their lingering association with the military, underscored by the uniforms they continued to wear, it is not surprising that they were composed completely of men.

The best-known women's professional touring band in the US was founded and conducted by Helen May Butler as a women's orchestra in 1891–92 (Edwards, 1997). In 1899, she changed the ensemble's instrumentation and created the US Talma Ladies' Military Band. Two years later, the band was known as the Helen May Butler Ladies Brass Band, and it extensively toured the US in the first ten years or so of the twentieth century (Hazen & Hazen, 1987). Indeed, during one thirteen-month period in 1903–4, the band played at least one concert daily. Enormously successful, Butler's band was the only women's band to perform at the 1901 Pan American Exposition in Buffalo, New York. Other notable national performances included: in 1902 the Elks' Fair in Washington, DC, and the Women's Exhibition held at New York City's Madison Square Garden; the 1903 Eagles' Exposition in Baltimore, Maryland; and the St. Louis World's Fair in 1904. The band completed tours in Texas and Colorado in 1908, as well as the Chautauqua circuit,[8] including Kansas, Nebraska, Colorado, and Wyoming in 1909, and Iowa, Illinois, Kansas, and Oklahoma in 1910, when Butler became conductor of the American Ladies' Grand Concert Band, founded by Colonel O. E. Skiff (Edwards, 1997). Although this was the height of the professional and town band movement in the US, with approximately 10,000 bands performing across the North American continent (Hazen & Hazen, 1987), Butler left the band in 1911 and conducted very little during the ensuing years, although she did run unsuccessfully for political office.

In both the US and Canada, community amateur bands remained extremely popular at the turn of the twentieth century. While usually composed exclusively of men, several women's community bands are known to have existed in the US, including the Keota (Iowa) Ladies Band, the Provo (Utah) Ladies Military Band, the Watertown (Minnesota) Ladies Band, and the Ladies Imperial Band of Bozeman, Montana (Sullivan, 2008a). Further, the Maryville (Missouri) Women's Band led the National Women's Party Parade of 1913 in Washington, DC, and is widely regarded as the first women's band to lead a parade in the US capital (Sullivan, 2008). Interest in amateur bands in Canada was generated by keen rivalries developed through a variety of festivals and competitions. Perhaps the leading figure in the Canadian band movement was Charles F. Thiele, who assumed leadership of the Waterloo (Ontario) band in 1919. Born in 1884 during the height of the US band movement, Thiele never served in the military or played in a military band. Instead, he first played in local bands that paraded in the streets of New York City in support of various politicians and other groups (Mellor, 1988). By 1905, however, he had formed his own concert band, in which his wife Louise and daughter Caroline eventually played. Both women became accomplished soloists (cornet and saxophone, respectively).

As the popularity of both professional and amateur bands of all kinds diminished throughout the twentieth century, interest and participation in school bands steadily increased. Indeed, the school band movement gained tremendous impetus following the First World War in the US and the Second World War in Canada. This surge of growth occurred primarily from the backing of instrument manufacturers, which began marketing directly to schools as professional and amateur bands quickly disappeared (Whitehill, 1969). Like the vast majority of professional and town bands, early school bands were conducted almost exclusively by men, many of whom were returning servicemen who had played in or conducted military bands in Europe (Birge 1928; Keene, 1982) and various regimental bands in Canada (Green & Vogan, 1991). The high school girls' band formed in Edmundston (New Brunswick) in the 1930s was an anomaly, as most youth bands in Canada prior to the Second World War were city-wide boys' bands.[9] School bands were formed earlier in the US than in Canada, and girls were typically admitted to them by the beginning of the twentieth century. Despite this, high school girls' bands were formed in communities such as Benton Harbor (Michigan) and Seaside (Oregon) (Sullivan, 2008a), both of which were conducted by men. As late as 1948, Franklin High School in Seattle supported a boys' band (founded in 1938) and a girls' band (University of Washington Libraries, 2008). Both were conducted by the same man. Much earlier in the century, Thiele had formed separate boys' and girls' bands in Rumford (Maine) (Mellor, 1988). The Iowa State Normal School Band, depicted in a 1906 photograph, was similarly conducted by a man (Sullivan, 2008).

With the success of military, professional, and town bands, which is to say adult bands, interest in university bands was high. Established sporadically during the nineteenth and early twentieth centuries, university bands were essentially student groups both organized and conducted by students, the vast majority of whom were men (McCarrell, 1971). Women were generally admitted to them only according to circumstances of the time and each particular institution, a practice that is vividly demonstrated in pictures of the California Polytechnic State University Band (Mark & Patten, 1976). A picture circa 1916 depicts the band seated outside in concert formation. It consists of all women musicians, including the director.

A 1927 picture depicts the band in military uniforms. Only two of the members are women, and the director is a man. In a picture taken just ten years later, the band, standing in marching formation, consists exclusively of men, including the director. Permanent university concert bands, mostly organized between the world wars, were more likely to admit women, but many US university marching bands provided opportunities for women only when the Second World War caused huge enrolment losses in the previously men-only ensembles. While some marching bands admitted women during the war — and excluded them again after the war ended — others chose to disband or discontinue public performances rather than admit women. Still other bands created separate women's bands that were used in conjunction with the depleted men's bands. The women's band at the University of Minnesota, for instance, was used to "highlight particularly important parts of the formations. In no case, however, did the girls [sic] execute any of the exaggerated steps and movements of the men [sic]" (Sperry, 1954, p. 31). Not only did the women perform "ladylike" manoeuvres distinct from those of the men, they also, unlike the men, were required to buy the "feminine" uniforms that they wore for performances.[10] Excluded from university marching bands because of the bands' military association and appearance, and because of fears they would cause disruptions in discipline and would be unable to march uniformly with men due to their size, women endured institutionalized discrimination until 1972 with the passage of Title IX of the US Education Amendments and subsequent enforcement of affirmative action laws. Because marching bands have not enjoyed the same popularity in Canada as they do in the US, the inclusion of women in Canadian university bands generally was not as contentious.

Without question, women participated in bands in North America beginning sometime in the nineteenth century. What is in question is not their (necessarily limited) participation in bands but the nature of that involvement and its necessity. Undeterred by systematic and institutionalized exclusion from most bands in the nineteenth and early twentieth centuries, women formed their own ensembles — except in schools, where men formed girls' and women's bands. Women tended to conduct ensembles in situations where men were not admitted to the sponsoring organization. For example, women's military bands were conducted by women in both the US and Canada, but members of those ensembles were members of military organizations from which men were excluded (Sullivan, 2006, 2007): the Canadian Women's Army Corps and, in the US, the Women's Army Corps, the Marine Corps Women's Reserve, the Coast Guard SPARS, and the Navy WAVES. All of these bands were commissioned during the Second World War and most were deactivated shortly after the war ended (Sullivan, 2008a).[11] This separatism recalls the experiences of women in higher education during the Progressive Era (1890s–1920s).

Although 70 percent of US postsecondary institutions were co-educational, women were not necessarily welcome on campus in classrooms or student organizations, and often consciously separated themselves from men. Regrettably, separatism "did not constitute equality on campus, anymore than it did elsewhere, [but] it gave co-educated women a power base, drew them together to form a community, connected them with older women on and off campus ... helped them to develop leadership skills, and provided forums for discussion of career opportunities" (Gordon, 1990, p. 41). Clearly women's bands — particularly military bands — provided the same opportunities and lifelong relationships for their members, but that did not help women in terms of the larger issues of segregation and discrimination in the military and society generally. The cultural backlash that occurred against "the woman problem" at the beginning of the twentieth century provided university administrators with a convenient excuse to segregate classes and impose quotas on the admission of women. As early as 1900, women comprised nearly half or more than half of the student body at twelve state universities in the US, including California, Illinois, Michigan, and Texas, causing considerable fear that the feminization of these institutions would result in their becoming female seminaries (Woody, 1929; Rosenberg, 1982). This was unacceptable to both "educators and male students [who] made it clear that they would not tolerate equality, even the equality of separate, complementary spheres" (Gordon, 1990, p. 44). Some restrictions placed on the participation of women in higher education in the US at that time, such as admission quotas and restricted access to specific disciplines (for example, women studied social work because they were barred from studying sociology; see Gordon 1990), were not lifted until the 1950s and 1960s.

Universities, however, are essential in the band world of North America. Other than a handful of professional bands worldwide (e.g., Dallas Wind Symphony, Tokyo Kosei Wind Orchestra, Netherlands Wind Ensemble), the most prestigious bands currently are affiliated with universities in North America — and specifically in the US (e.g., Eastman Wind Ensemble, Cincinnati Wind Symphony, Northwestern University Symphonic Wind Ensemble).[12] While women musicians are certainly welcome in these ensembles — and in many school concert bands they often exceed the number of boys or men (Sullivan, 2008) — their conductors continue to be almost exclusively men.[13]

## Nation Building and Bands

Since their beginnings as military ensembles, bands have been integrally implicated in nation building in both the US and Canada. Used first to inspire ardent patriotism in the public and "shock and awe" in troops, bands have fulfilled an essential role in creating national identities and democratic citizens for both countries. Providing free public entertainment often outdoors in parks or public squares, bands literally "fostered democracy" by playing music that could "enrich and improve the common people" (Hazen & Hazen, 1987, p. 11). Not only was the ensemble itself constructed as egalitarian (even as it was exclusionary), its performances were essential to virtually any public ceremony, whether joyous or sorrowful. Performing in a band was thus vested with the power to instill "a sense of citizenship, of belonging to an organization which is considered necessary to the success of public enterprises, of pride and importance in having a part in civic affairs" (Graham, 1951, p. 179). Despite their responsibility to "God and county," the place of bands in North American society is not without tension, specifically because they perform *music*.

Historically associated with emotion, non-cognitive understanding, and the body (McClary, 1994), music is aligned with the feminine in North America. This association, however, manifested itself in complex and contradictory ways in both the US and Canada during the nineteenth and twentieth centuries. As musicians and politicians attempted to establish respective national identities, distinguishing so-called American or Canadian music from European music, concerns were raised about "preserving the moral virtue of the citizenry as the main insurance for the survival of the republic" (Eaklor, 1994, p. 41). While this claim is made specifically in reference to the US, it is not inconsistent with Canadian concerns (Silverman, 1998). Concomitant with and in response to the fears and aspirations of the middle class, a "parlour culture" was cultivated that conflated in a general sense the social functions of women and music. Based on the ideology of separate spheres, which had approached "the level of an obsession" (Eaklor, 1994, p. 40) in the US and was constituted as ideology in both countries linking the private with women and the public with men, this culture typically limited women to making music at home, in private, playing the piano primarily and singing — even when they performed in public. With women participating in every type of band (town, professional, industrial, family) except those composed of active military personnel, even bands could not escape feminization entirely.[14] As an integral aspect of femininity, music, and bands specifically, were essential to the enculturation of the family and, by extension, society and the nation. This was underscored by increased industrialization, which contributed to music's becoming "one of the 'feminized' professions ... associated in circular fashion with both culturally defined feminine qualities and with women as practitioners" (Eaklor, 1994, p. 40–1) that created an "inherent conflict between the 'masculine' public role of the expert and inherited 'feminine' role of the activity" even as music — and bands — were literally "given the 'female' role in American [and Canadian] society ... to contribute to the nation's survival and growth" (p. 43).

One of the central concerns related to this during the Progressive Era and continuing well into the first half of the twentieth century was inculcating morals in youth, which is to say the white middle-class boys who would become the nations' future leaders (Lesko, 2001). Implicated by colonial relations of racism and sexism that marginalized various "others" and specifically and irrationally feared feminization, the concern with morality contributed to gender segregation in education so that boys could be boys and girls would be girls. This was demonstrated most perniciously through imposition of the differentiated curriculum that effectively barred girls from studying subjects other than those related to "Domestic Art and Science," thus preparing "girls and boys for their sex-specific roles as worker and citizen" (Graves, 1998, p. xviii). Promulgated by the gender ideology of "New Liberalism," which was based on social Darwinism in the context of social efficiency, and arguing that only a few individuals in any society are capable of rational thought, vocational education in terms of race and sex roles became the norm in high schools. Thus the way was opened for "The Ascent of the Domesticated Citizen" (Graves, 1998) as the differentiated curricula received by boys and girls directly and specifically addressed the so-called "boy problem" — which of course was actually a girl problem — the problem of too many girls graduating from high schools and going on to attend university. To entice boys to stay in school, the high school curriculum was expanded well beyond its liberal classical curriculum, at which girls had excelled, to include practical courses intended to appeal to boys, while societal resources were directed to inculcating morals that would ensure boys' success. Not surprisingly, boys' bands organized early in the twentieth century played a high-profile role in this endeavour.

Meredith Willson's musical *The Music Man*, of course, speaks directly to this mission. "Ya got trouble!" exclaims con-man-cum-would-be-band-director Harold Hill to the citizens of River City, Iowa. The attack on the unsuspecting community's virtue had arrived in the form of a pool table, and its antidote was to be a boys' band. Ubiquitous in both the US and Canada, boys' bands were endorsed by police departments for much of the first half of the twentieth century and embodied the sentiment (Mellor, 1988), "Teach a boy to blow a horn, and he won't blow a safe."[15] Not only did the bands occupy boys' time and expend boys' energy, they also incorporated discipline and obedience to the conductor, traits not incidentally required of the domesticated or civilized citizen (Lesko, 2001). Team or group activities such as band were preferred in no small part because they subsumed the needs of the individual to the good of the group. The boys' band that emerges at the end of *The Music Man* is a marching band, but not just any marching band. Rather, it is an ensemble of over-sized proportions — 76 trombones and 110 cornets — that saves not only the boys — and not incidentally the girls and their parents — from various forms of depravity, but Harold Hill and his love interest, Marian Paroo, as well.

## Paradoxes and Potentialities

Both men and women are constituted in bands in terms of heterosexuality and its accompanying hegemonic masculinity. This is expressed in terms of desire of the other: men desire women while women desire men. Although heterosexuality is "constructed as a coherent, natural, fixed and stable category; as universal and monolithic…a diversity of meanings and social arrangements [exist] within the category" (Richardson, 1996, p. 2). Most notable of those social arrangements, of course, are gender divisions, or social relations of women and men that privilege men. Based on these relations, heterosexuality for men is about sexual agency enacted on women, the success of which is the means by which they attain manhood. With this success comes "heterosexual entitlement" that in its usual state is characterized by male homosexual panic, because it is often achieved through intense male relationships that are not always easily distinguished from homosexual relationships (Sedgwick, 1990). Such panic, with its attendant misogyny, is well documented among musicians (Brett, 2006). In this context, "heterosexuality is not a balanced (or even unbalanced) institutionalisation of masculinity-and-femininity, it *is* masculinity" (Holland, Ramazanoglu, & Thomson, 1996, p. 145; emphasis added). Women must negotiate how they fit into this construction of hegemonic masculine agency (heterosexuality) such that "for women [heterosexuality] is an identity defined primarily in relation to desire for men and/or the social and economic privileges associated with being the partner of a man, in particular the traditional roles of wife and mother" (Richardson, 1996, p. 2). Consequently, sexuality is always already understood in terms of sociality in that it is both constitutive of and produced by the social, becoming "a central and determining feature of our understanding of social life. The heterosexual couple are the raw material through which society may interpret and imagine itself" (p. 11). This describes, however, only "normal" heterosexuality associated with marriage and family: the white, middle-class, heterosexual couple that upholds and protects the nation (Williams, 1989).

In the context of bands, heterosexual desire is shaped in terms of a "gender regime...of practices that constructs various kinds of masculinity and femininity among [players and conductors], orders them in terms of prestige and power, and constructs a sexual division of labor within the [ensemble]" (Kessler, Ashenden, Connel, & Dowsett, 1985, p. 42). Within bands, it constitutes spaces where femininity, due to the conflation of misogyny and homophobia, is foreclosed. I am not arguing that individuals associated with bands are necessarily misogynist or homophobic (although some are), but that band *cultures* are historically constituted that way (Gould, 2003). Originally, of course, bands existed to entertain or support other activities and presented a singular image as all players wore identical uniforms, whether sitting in concert formation or marching.[16] This made sense not only because bands typically kept military-style uniforms long after all ties to the military were severed, but because historically band members were men. When women were introduced, their presence could be minimized, if not altogether disguised, by uniforms. Thus, uniforms maintain bands' hegemonic masculinity in the context of heterosexuality. Because of its instability, however, heterosexuality — like all social relations — is always constructed, always under construction, making it open to negotiation. Although normative, it is never finished but constantly reiterated, producing an effect of normality (Butler, 1993). The undifferentiated appearance resulting from the uniforms worn by bands contributes to this instability, because the anonymity of uniforms simultaneously creates space for band members free of the discourse of heterosexuality that disciplines women and men as described above in terms of hegemonic masculinity. In other words, uniformity of appearance makes possible forms of desire other than heterosexuality in what I describe as *hyper-masculine space.*[17]

Virtual in the sense that it is real and consequently does exist, hyper-masculine space is not actual in that it cannot be seen, heard, or touched.[18] It is the conceptual space occupied by bands in society, the space in which band members live and perform. What is made actual is not the space, but potential ways of living (as band members) that go beyond and even subvert hegemonic masculinity. I posit *hyper-masculinity* theoretically in sociological contexts in contrast to the psychological state of excessive and aggressive masculinity (hypermasculinity).[19] With the hyphen, hyper-masculinity is constituted by ruptures or disturbances in the discourse of hegemonic masculinity, and is ambiguous in the sense that it and its potential actualizations are always in flux and never stable. Further, it is *hyper-* because it goes beyond hegemonic masculinity, and *-masculine* because it both occurs in the context of hegemonic masculinity and forecloses it. As space exceeding and excluding hegemonic masculinity, hyper-masculinity enables women and non-normative men not to fit themselves into bands, but to fit bands to themselves, and create band subjectivities expressive of their own experience and values. Succinctly, hyper-masculinity is ethical space opening up the problematic field of bands (Deleuze, 1990) to new and unexpected potentials of enacting one's band membered-ness. In many ways, this is largely personal space. Clearly, women and non-normative men band members have done little to change the culture of bands — at least in terms of who conducts them; but cultures change slowly, and resistance from within is crucial to every potentiality of change.

Potentialities of hyper-masculine space exist within band cultures, I believe, because of the unique positioning of bands relative to society. Historically, of course, bands served entirely functional roles in both the military and society that had nothing to do with artistic concerns (Goldman, 1961). It was these very roles, however, that connected them directly to the communities they served. In responding to the material needs and desires of society, bands continue to hold a place characterized less by valour and honour and more by emotional connection and ethical responsibility. These tangible connections make it possible for those participating in bands to feel similarly connected — not so much to each other as band members but to the communities that support them: military, church, business, family, school. As part of everyday life, a function of material reality, bands do not so much uplift as they make real. And in making real, they are situated in terms of power and history, which also causes them to be rife with a multitude of paradoxes that are exactly their strength and what make possible potentialities of difference.

First among these paradoxes, of course, is the overwhelming hegemonic masculinity of bands in relationship to the feminized sphere of music in which they perform. Related to this is the paradox of a so-called egalitarian and populist ensemble that nevertheless consistently and systematically excluded women and for centuries men of colour — practices that in some cases were only suspended under force of law and in other cases (such as with instrument selection and university band conductors) persist to this day. The paradox of heterosexual desire within a masculine homosocial organization, which is to say one composed of individuals whose interests, activities, and social characteristics (for instance, race, sexuality, class in addition to gender) are generally the same, certainly creates confusion and not a small amount of consternation — if not panic. Perhaps most important, however, is the paradox associated with nation building, which simultaneously reinforces and underscores hegemonic masculinity, even in extreme cases, to the point of psychological hyper-masculinity believed necessary for success on the battlefield, while it also assumes the "female role" in society to nurture and sustain. This para-dox exposes all of the tensions plaguing bands around feminization and homosexual panic. Similarly paradoxical, the very tensions that resulted in first rejecting and then "covering up" women simultaneously create gen-der/sexual ambiguities with potentialities to open space for unexpected, incongruent, and contingent articulations of gender/sexuality. Attempts to cover up subjectivities in bands enable ways of living that are otherwise forbidden. For example, some members of what would later be known as the Central High School Kilties all girl drum and bugle corps (Spring-field, Missouri) were forced to drop out of the corps after their first per-formance in 1926 because the kilts they wore exposed their knees, which was considered to be "immodest" (marching on ..., 2009). Nevertheless, the band not only continued performing but is thriving today. A simi-lar brouhaha occurred decades later during the Second World War, when members of the Canadian Women's Army Corps Pipe Band were not per-mitted to wear specially designed uniforms featuring kilts that fell above the knee — as men wear kilts. Considering them to be "incorrect and unac-ceptable" (Cape, 2009, p. 33), Canadian Defence Headquarters objected to women wearing kilts as men wear them. Dressed rather more modestly in white jackets over dark tops, knee-length white skirts, hose, and shoes, the Kitchener Ladies' Band, founded in 1925 by George Ziegler, was touted as "one of the largest and best on the continent" (Uttley, 1937/1975, p. 269) and eventually boasted ninety-two members (Lamb, 1975). During the approximately ten years of its existence, the Kitchener Ladies' Band was immensely popular[20] and well known throughout Canada and in the US. Similarly, Bert Etta Davis became star soloist of the Prairie View Co-Eds, an all-women's dance band organized at historically black Prairie View College (Texas) by Will Henry Bennett in 1943 when members of the Prai-rie View Collegians, the all-men's dance band, left school to fight in the the Second World War. Three years earlier, Davis had auditioned against twenty-seven men and won a coveted spot playing saxophone in the Col-legians but was subsequently barred from performing with the men by the Dean of Women, who asserted her own sense of (im)propriety (Handy, 1981; Tucker, 1999).

It is this most paradoxical relationship of and with difference specif-ically related to gender and sexuality, but also to race and class, which enables significations of gender and sexuality (and race and class) that are *not* necessarily constituted in terms of hegemonic masculinity and hetero-sexuality. Thus we re-member (put together or make whole) bands in ways previously constructed as impossible, and remember (recall or think of) them in terms of multiple and even contradictory configurations. In other words, the paradoxes in which bands are implicated incite potentialities for *all* women and men, as well as *all* girls and boys, to enact new ways of playing in the band and living in the world.

## Notes

1  With the term *band*, I refer most specifically to wind and percussion ensembles that perform in concert and/or marching configurations. As will become clear, however, the term refers generally to almost any grouping of instruments — except those associated with the symphonic orchestra and its chamber derivatives. In this more comprehensive sense, a grouping of fifes and drums constitutes a band, as does a grouping of pipes. Taken to its logical conclusion, any predominantly instrumental grouping that may or may not include winds (but almost always includes percussion when winds are absent) constitutes a band.

2  *Hegemonic* masculinity refers to the type of masculinity that dominates social groups or society; it is a descriptive category only. In relationship to bands, it is usually characterized by valuing sports — particularly high-status activities such as football, basketball, and hockey — and other typically male outdoor activities such as hunting and/or fishing, as well as paternalistic attitudes toward women, and competitiveness within the group (Kessler, Ashenden, Connel, & Dowsett, 1985). It should not be inferred, however, that this category is monolithic or singular, but rather may be more accurately understood as changing and multiple (Connell, 1995).

3  See, for instance, Abeles and Porter (1978), Griswold and Chroback (1981), Coffman and Sehmann (1989), Delzell and Leppla (1992), Fortney, Boyle, and DeCarbo (1993), Zervoudakes and Tanur (1994), Cramer, Million, and Perreault (2002), Sheldon and Price (2005), Hallam, Rogers, and Creech (2008).

4  Flute is arguably an exception to this.

5  Nearly fifty years ago, Allen Britton (1961/1985) made the now-famous observation that band directors are bonded "in a kind of truculent fraternity . . . that participates vitally in the essential business of music education, i.e. teaching music, but that also manages to maintain a certain professional aloofness from the rest of the profession, an aloofness compacted of pride of accomplishment, singleminded attention to the business at hand, and hurt at the criticism" (p. 225).

6  For instance, in Canada, where bands are arguably much less popular than in the US, the webpage *Canadian Community Band and Orchestra Resources* lists 172 community concert bands nation-wide as compared to 52 community orchestras. Other types of community bands that are listed include marching bands, brass bands, and big bands. Community youth orchestras are the only other type of orchestra listed on the site. See http://www.grahamnasby.com/misc/music_local -resources.shtml.

7  The concept "sites of desire" invokes post-structural theory, which holds that everything is situated or located. Things, people, concepts exist only in relationship to a situation or location, which is to say, a "site." This is not a geographic or physical site, but a "politics of location" (Rich, 1986) in which concepts such as desire are contested in terms of "situated knowledges" (Haraway, 1991). I understand desire explicitly in terms of sexuality (desire-for), or more accurately, "the

regime of power-knowledge-pleasure that sustains the discourse of human sexuality" (Foucault, 1978, p. 11), and implicitly in terms of connections (desire-as) producing joyful experimentation (Gould, 2007; see Deleuze & Guattari, 1983).

8  The Chautauqua and Lyceum circuits, founded in the US in 1826, consisted of tours across North America that provided a variety of musical and theatrical entertainment, as well as educational lectures. Louise and Caroline Thiele, wife and daughter of renowned band director Charles Thiele, regularly appeared on the circuits in the US before the family moved to Canada in 1919 (Mellor, 1988). The Chautauqua circuit in Canada was closely linked to Methodist Temperance and operated successfully until 1935 (Keillor, 2006).

9  The still-thriving Edmonton (Alberta) Girls Pipe Band, formed in 1945, is a notable exception.

10  Members of the Kitchener (Ontario) Ladies' Band, a community band formed in 1925, were similarly required to buy their uniforms, while an "annual municipal grant funded the purchase of the *men's* uniforms" (Morrison, 2006, p. 136, emphasis in original). Behaviour expectations for the two ensembles differed as well; for instance, men were permitted to loosen their ties during warm weather while women players "had to adhere to a rigid code" that emphasized "propriety."

11  A notable exception is the US 14th Army Band, Women's Army Corps, which survived until 1976, with all but the last three years conducted by a woman (Kerbey, 2008). Another exception is the Women's Air Force Band (WAF), which was commissioned in 1951, four years after the US Air Force was formed, in order to recruit women, entertain the troops, and perform music at ceremonial functions (Nichols, 2008). Conducted by a woman, the WAF band was deactivated in 1961.

12  Notably, none of these ensembles use the term "band."

13  Mallory Thompson, director of bands at Northwestern University (Illinois), is by far the most notable exception among the most prestigious university bands in the US and Canada.

14  For example, the Ladies G.A.R. Military Band (Utah) was "organized in 1883 by a ladies auxiliary that coexisted with a Union soldiers' veteran organization, the Grand Army of the Republic" (Sullivan, 2008, p. 34).

15  This slogan is attributed to "public school music director" Dr. R. Ritchie Robertson, who coined the phrase in the 1920s (marching on ..., 2009, n.p.). Not only is Richardson credited with "securing community support of the largest Boy Scout Band in the world," he founded in 1926 "the first all girl drum and bugle corps in the United States." Now affiliated with Central High School of Springfield, Missouri, the Kilties Drum and Bugle Corps continues to perform throughout the US.

16  This has changed in the past thirty-five years or so as marching bands now eschew military styles in favour of showier versions that often outfit the percussion section or "pit" in uniforms different from those worn by the rest of the band. Similarly, for most concert band performances today, women almost always wear long black dresses while men wear tuxedos, as they do for orchestra performances.

17  "Hyper-masculinity" is a widely used psychological term associated with emotional insensitivity, stark individualism (Smith, 2005), and risk-taking behaviours (White and Young, 1999). In this context, "hyper" refers to extreme masculinity that is understood to be unhealthy. In addition to "excessive" or "unusually high," however, "hyper-" can also mean "over, above, beyond" (retrieved from http://encarta.msm.com, 2009) in the sense of masculinity that is something more than itself; not an extreme version of itself, but rather, something else entirely.

18  See Gould (2007) for a more complete discussion of Gilles Deleuze's concepts of virtual and actual.
19  In sociology, "hypermasculinity" was probably first used (with a hyphen) by Ashis Nandy (1983). Thomas Scheff (2006) theorizes it (without a hyphen) in terms of violence, and associates it with Erving Goffman's (1967) "cult of masculinity."
20  The band's popularity was evident in the large crowds it attracted wherever it performed (Morrison, 2006). Canadian and US women's military bands, formed in the 1940s and 1950s, also enjoyed extra attention compared with men's military bands of the time, a phenomenon suggested as a possible contributing factor to their dissolution (Cape & Nichols, forthcoming).

## References

Abeles, H. F., & Porter, S. Y. (1978). The gender-stereotyping of musical instruments. *Journal of Research in Music Education, 26*(2), 65–75.

Birge, E. B. (1928). *History of public school music in the United States*. Boston: Oliver Ditson Company.

Block, A. F. (1988). The status of women in college music, 1986–1987; A statistical report. In N. B. Reich (Ed.), *Women's studies/Women's status* (pp. 79–158). Boulder, CO: College Music Society.

Brett, P. (2006). Musicality, essentialism, and the closet. In P. Brett, E. Wood, & G. C. Thomas (Eds.), *Queering the pitch: The new gay and lesbian musicology* (2nd ed.) (pp. 9–26). New York and London: Routledge.

Britton, A. P. (1961/1985). Music education: An American specialty. In P. H. Lang (Ed.), *One hundred years of music in America* (pp. 211–229). Reprint. New York: Da Capo Press.

Butler, J. (1993). *Bodies that matter: On the discursive limits of "sex."* New York and London: Routledge.

Camus, R. F. (1976). *Military music of the American Revolution*. Chapel Hill: University of North Carolina Press.

Canadian Community Band & Orchestra Resources. (2011). Retrieved from http://www.grahamnasby.com/misc/music_local-resources.shtml.

Cape, J. (2009). Athene's pipers: The Canadian Women's Army Corps Pipe Band. *Piping Today, 38*, 30–34.

Cape, J., & Nichols, J. (Forthcoming). Engaging stories: Co-constructing narratives of women's military bands. In M. Barrett and S. Stauffer (Eds.), *Narrative soundings and resonant lifework*. Dordrecht, The Netherlands: Springer.

Coffman, D. D., & Sehmann, K. H. (1989). Musical instrument preference: Implications for music educators. *Update: Applications of Research in Music Education, 7*(2), 32–34.

College Music Society. (2008). *Directory of music faculties in colleges and universities, United States and Canada, 2008–2009 ed.* Missoula, MT: College Music Society.

Connell, R. W. (1995). *Masculinities: Knowledge, power, and social change*. Berkeley, CA: University of California Press.

Cramer, K. M., Million, E., & Perreault, L. A. (2002). Perception of musicians: Gender stereotypes and social role theory. *Psychology of Music, 30,* 164–74.

Deleuze, G. (1990). *The logic of sense.* M. Lester (Trans.). New York: Columbia University Press.

Deleuze, G. (1994). *Difference and repetition.* P. Patton (Trans.). New York: Columbia University Press.

Deleuze, G., & Guattari, F. (1983). *Anti-Oedipus: Capitalism and schizophrenia.* R. Hurley, M. Seem, & H. R. Lane (Trans.). Minneapolis: University of Minnesota Press.

Delzell, J. K., and Leppla, D. A. (1992). Gender association of musical instruments and preferences of fourth-grade students for selected instruments. *Journal of Research in Music Education, 40*(2), 93–103.

Eaklor, V. L. (1994). The gendered origins of the American musician. *Quarterly Journal of Music Teaching and Learning, 4/5*(4-1), 40–46.

Edwards, J. M. (1997). Helen May Butler and her ladies' military band: Gender and image. Paper presented at the conference Feminist Theory and Music 4, University of Virginia, Charlottesville.

Fennell, F. (1961). Hardy perennial: Bands in the open. *Musical America, 81,* 14–17.

Fortney, P. M., Boyle, J. D., & DeCarbo, N. J. (1993). A study of middle school band students' instrumental choices. *Journal of Research in Music Education, 41*(1), 28–39.

Foucault, M. (1978). *The history of sexuality, Vol. 1: An introduction.* R. Hurley (Trans.). New York: Vintage Books.

Goffman, E. (1967). *Interaction ritual.* New York: Anchor.

Goldman, R. F. (1946). *The concert band.* New York: Rinehart and Company.

Goldman, R. F. (1961). *The wind band.* Boston: Allyn and Bacon.

Gordon, L. D. (1990). *Gender and higher education in the Progressive Era.* New Haven: Yale University Press.

Gould, E. (2003). Cultural contexts of exclusion: Women college band directors. *Research and Issues in Music Education, 1*(1). Retrieved from http://www.stthomas.edu/rimeonline/vol1/gould1.htm.

Gould, E. (2007). Thinking (as) difference: Lesbian imagination and music. *Women and Music: A Journal of Gender and Culture, 11,* 17–28.

Graham, A. P. (1951). *Great bands of America.* New York and Toronto: Thomas Nelson and Sons.

Graves, K. (1998). *Girls' schooling during the Progressive Era: From female scholar to domesticated citizen.* New York and London: Garland Publishing.

Green, J. P., & Vogan, N. F. (1991). *Music education in Canada: A historical account.* Toronto: University of Toronto Press.

Griswold, P. A., & Chroback, D. A. (1981). Gender role associations of music instruments and occupations by gender and major. *Journal of Research in Music Education, 29*(1), 57–62.

Hallam, S., Rogers, L., & Creech, A. (2008). Gender differences in musical instrument choice. *International Journal of Music Education, 26*(1), 7–19.

Handy, D. A. (1981). *Black women in American bands and orchestras.* Metuchen, NJ: Scarecrow Press.

Haraway, D. J. (1991). *Simians, cyborgs, and women: The reinvention of nature.* New York: Routledge.

Hartley, L. (1995). A preliminary study of gender imbalance among college band directors: An investigation of low female population. Paper presented at the Women's Music Symposium, Boulder, CO.

Hazen, M. H., & Hazen, R. M. (1987). *The music men: An illustrated history of brass bands in America, 1800–1920.* Washington, DC: Smithsonian Institution Press.

Holland, J., Ramazanoglu, C., & Thomson, R. (1996). In the same boat? The gendered (in)experience of first heterosex. In D. Richardson (Ed.), *Theorising heterosexuality: Telling it straight* (pp. 143–160). Buckingham, UK: Open University Press.

Keene, J. A. (1982). *A history of music education in the United States.* Hanover, NH: University Press of New England.

Keillor, E. (2006). *Music in Canada: Capturing landscape and diversity.* Montreal and Kingston: McGill-Queen's University Press.

Kerbey, T. (2008). 14th Army Band WAC, 1942–1976. Arizona State University. Retrieved from http://www.public.asu.edu/~tmontgom/.

Kessler, S. Ashenden, D. J., Connel, R. W., & Dowsett, G. W. (1985). Gender relations in secondary schooling. *Sociology of Education, 58*(1), 34–48.

Kopstein, J., & Pearson, I. (2002). *The heritage of Canadian military music.* St. Catharines, ON: Vanwell Publishing.

Koza, J. E. (1993). The "missing males" and other gender issues in music education: Evidence from the *Music Supervisors' Journal,* 1914–1924. *Journal of Research in Music Education, 41*(2), 212–232.

Lamb, K. (1975). Kitchener Ladies' Band. *Waterloo Historical Society Annual Volume, 63,* 4–10.

La Rue, H. (1994). Music, literature and etiquette: Musical instruments and social identity from Castiglione to Austen. In M. Stokes (Ed.), *Ethnicity, identity, and music: The musical construction of place* (pp. 189–206). Oxford, England: Berg Publishers.

Lesko, N. (2001). *Act your age! A cultural construction of adolescence.* New York and London: Routledge Falmer.

Maloney, S. T. (1986). *Canadian wind ensemble literature* (Unpublished doctoral dissertation). Eastman School of Music, Rochester, NY.

marching on . . . (2009). The history of the kilties. Retrieved from http://sps.k12 .mo.us/CHS/Kilties.html.

Mark, M., & Patten, A. (1976). California bicentennial festival of marching bands. *The Instrumentalist, 30*(11), 36–37.

McCarrell, L. K. (1971). A historical review of the college band movement from 1875 to 1969 (Unpublished doctoral dissertation). Florida State University, Tallahassee.

McClary, S. (1994). Same as it ever was: Youth culture and music. In A. Ross & T. Rose (Eds.), *Microphone fiends: Youth music and youth culture* (pp. 29–40). New York: Routledge.

McElroy, C. (1996). The status of women orchestra and band conductors in North American colleges and universities: 1984–1996 (Unpublished doctoral dissertation). University of Missouri–Kansas City, Kansas City.

McLain, B. P. (2000). Teaching music in the American university: A gender analysis. Paper presented at the biennial meeting of MENC: National Association for Music Education, Washington, DC.

Mellor, J. (1988). *Music in the park: C. F. Thiele, father of Canadian band music.* Waterloo, ON: Melco.

Milburn, D. (1982). The development of the wind ensemble in the United States (1952–1981) (Unpublished doctoral dissertation). Catholic University of America, Washington, DC.

Morrison, M. (2006). Playing their part: The role of the Kitchener Musical Society 1925–1950. *Waterloo Historical Society Annual Volume, 94,* 117–159.

msn Encarta Dictionary. 2009. Hyper. Retrieved from http://encarta.msn.com/encnet/refpages/search.aspx?q=hyper.

Nandy, A. (1983). *The intimate enemy: Loss and recovery of self under colonialism.* New Delhi: Oxford University Press.

Nichols, J. (2008). The United States Air Force Women's Band (WAF), 1951–1961. Arizona State University. Retrieved from http://www.public.asu.edu/%7Ejmsulli/WAF_NICHOLS.htm.

Rich, A. (1986). Notes toward a politics of location. In *Blood, bread, and poetry: Selected prose 1979–1985* (pp. 210–231). New York and London: W. W. Norton.

Richardson, D. (1996). Heterosexuality and social theory. In D. Richardson (Ed.), *Theorising heterosexuality: Telling it straight* (pp. 1–20). Buckingham, UK: Open University Press.

Rosenberg, R.. (1982). *Beyond separate spheres: Intellectual roots of modern feminism.* New Haven: Yale University Press.

Scheff, T. J. (1996). Hypermasculinity and violence as a social system. *Universitas, 2*(2). Retrieved from http://www.uni.edu/universitas/fall06/tocforum03.htm.

Sedgwick, E. K. (1990). *Epistemology of the closet.* Berkeley and Los Angeles: University of California Press.

Sheldon, D. A., & Price, H. E. (2005). Gender and instrumentation distribution in an international cross-section of wind and percussion ensembles. *Bulletin of the Council for Research in Music Education, 163,* 43–51.

Silverman, E. L. (1998). *The last best west: Women on the Alberta frontier, 1880–1930.* Calgary, AB: Fifth House Publishers.

Smith, R. T. (2005). Characteristics of hypermasculinity: A relational perspective (Unpublished doctoral dissertation). Fielding Graduate University, Santa Barbara, CA.

Sperry, G. L. (1954). Women are here to stay. *The Instrumentalist, 8*(7), 30–31.

Sullivan, J. (2006). Women's military bands in a segregated army: The 400th and 404th WAC Bands. *Journal of Band Research, 41*(2), 1–35.

Sullivan, J. (2007). Music for the injured soldier: A contribution of American women's military bands during World War II. *Journal of Music Therapy, 44*(2), 1–43.

Sullivan, J. (2008). A century of women's bands in America. *Music Educators Journal, 95*(1), 33–40.

Sullivan, J. (2008a). Women's bands. Arizona State University. Retrieved from http://www.public.asu.edu/~jmsulli/Webpages/historical_main.html.

Tucker, S. (1999). The Prairie View Co-Eds: Black college women musicians in class and on the road during World War II. *Black Music Research Journal, 19*(1), 93–126.

University of Washington Libraries. (2008). Franklin High School girls band, Seattle, April 15, 1948, *Digital collections*. Retrieved from http://content.lib.washington.edu/cgi-bin/viewer.exec?CISOROOT=/imlsohai& CISOPTR=3987&CISOBOX=1&REC.

Uttley, W. V. (1937/1975). *A history of Kitchener, Ontario*. Waterloo, ON: Wilfrid Laurier University Press.

White, P., & Young, K. (1999). Is sport injury gendered? In P. White & K. Young (Eds.), *Sport and gender in Canada* (pp. 69–84). Don Mills, ON: Oxford University Press.

Whitehill, C. D. (1969). Sociological conditions which contributed to the growth of the school band movement in the United States. *Journal of Research in Music Education, 17*(1), 179–192.

Williams, F. (1989). *Social policy: A critical introduction: Issues of race, gender, class.* Cambridge: Polity Press.

Woody. T. (1929). *A history of women's education in the United States*. 2 volumes. New York: Science Press.

Zervoudakes, J., & Tanur, J. M. (1994). Gender and musical instruments: Winds of change? *Journal of Research in Music Education, 42*(1), 58–67.

# EIGHT

# Community Music Making:
## Challenging the Stereotypes of Conventional Music Education

*Kari Veblen*

Why is it important for music and arts educators to consider community as a frame of reference for music education in the public sphere? How does this expansion sit with older, narrower conceptions of music education? How might community music (CM) interact, intersect, or enhance what happens in schools, and vice versa. What are the implications of CM activity for the future of Canadian music education? Everything suggests that music education is undergoing a transformation as all forms and all interactions of formal, informal, intentional, and incidental music making become questioned, recognized, valued, or devalued. In fact, if music education does not undergo massive transformation to keep pace with new learnings, as found in the research and to reflect the multiple aspects of our pluralistic society, then the limited music education we currently have in public education could be at risk. From a postmodern vantage point, we need to acknowledge that music education in Canada is about music making and education in many contexts, including both formal and informal settings that may or may not exist side by side and which may or may not interact in a variety of ways. These experiences are not limited to public schooling, but extend more broadly into the community where music education is known as community music — often music education at its most diverse. This chapter offers a perspective on the broadening views of music education that CM engenders when we consider music education in Canada through discussions of the Canadian context for CM, an examination of who is involved in CM, structures of CM in Canada, and challenges facing music education in the community.

## Community Music in a Canadian Context

As in the United States and much of Europe, community music in Canada accommodates many networks, organizations, and individual enterprises.[1] Although CM persists heedless of outside or central organizing forces, music educators seem to take an interest in this area only periodically. Peter Dykema, an early advocate, defined CM in 1916:

> Community music is a term that has obtained great vogue the past three years and yet so far as I know it has never been defined. It may be worthwhile, however, for the sake of definiteness in this paper and the discussion, which may ensue, to indicate one conception of a proper definition. First of all, it may be said that community music is not the name of a new type of music ... It is not so much the designation of a new thing as a new point of view ... Stated positively and concretely, community music is socialized music. (p. 218)

Dykema went on to talk about the efforts in his day to give all people opportunities to hear and make music. He described some programs as being profit-motivated and some as initiatives of public-spirited citizens. Dykema felt that all of these new programs were important because they were "giving the opportunity to every man and woman for free and frequent participation in music" (p. 223).

Although CM has expanded and grown in complexity, almost one hundred years later Dykema's comments remain central to an understanding of CM and its place in our postmodern society. Music making and music teaching/learning are certainly a major part of the CM dynamic. However, social factors — "socialized music" as Dykema puts it — are also essential. These include aspects of community building, self-expression, identity, awareness of national heritage, recreation of myth, group solidarity, networking, bonding, consciousness raising, healing, and others. Clearly, CM as a force in Canada is developing rapidly. Factors such as expanded life expectancy, increased leisure time, prosperity, access to technology, and rapid movement of people play their part. I also think that there may be unique aspects — particularly "Canadian" aspects — in this development. Some parameters of the Canadian scene will be explored in the next section.

### Those Who Take Part: From Infants to Raging Grannies, Klezcampers to Young Offenders

CM programs in Canada, including intergenerational events, accommodate a wide range of people from the prenatal to the elderly, serving the privileged and the hard-to-serve populations. Participants include people from diverse cultures, ability levels, socio-economic circumstances, political, and religious traditions. While some programs are geared to marginalized and disadvantaged populations, taking place in site such as hospitals and prisons, others are intended to celebrate and entertain, with community centres and parks as their settings. A variety of alternative structures, formal and informal, and planned and unplanned, exist to teach, experience, and perform music. In contrast to conventional music education, a trained professional or a volunteer, either a specialist or generalist, may facilitate such activities. For example, many community music programs are geared toward early learning that include specific activities for pregnant mothers, infants, toddlers, and pre-school children. One such example is Nova Scotia's Kids First, which features parent and child interactive music and movement programs as well as many other services (Kids First, n.d.). Some programs for infants and young children are formalized, traditional, and affiliated with conservatories, university outreach programs, libraries, or community programming, while others occur in informal settings as parents of young children come together within their own communities for their children's well-being as well as their own. In both cases, however, the emphasis is on parental interaction with their children through traditional nursery repertoire, finger and toe plays, bouncing rhymes, and lullabies, such as espoused by the Parent-Child Mother Goose Program, a free program with chapters throughout Canada (The Parent-Child Mother Goose Program, n.d.). There are also a variety of CM programs that target school-aged children in the form of summer camps, community groups, religious-based groups, university outreach programs, and private or group music instruction.[2]

Music education, however, is no longer only the domain of the young. Adult learners are valuable contributors to CM activities and frequently form voluntary groups who perform in secular or religious areas. One such is the London Jazz Orchestra from Ontario, composed of community musicians from high school students to seniors, who meet together every week to play. Once in a while they may perform, but public performance is not a significant part of their mandate. Other groups come together for a purpose beyond music making. For example, the Raging Grannies — a singing group for social justice that formed in Victoria, BC, in 1987 to protest US warships containing nuclear weapons docking at Canadian ports — now have forty chapters worldwide (Roy, n.d).

Music education also plays a role in the rehabilitation and healing of hard-to-serve populations through therapy programs in institutions and the community (Knox, 2004; Knox et al., 2005; Curtis & Mercado, 2004). Numerous small-scale opportunities exist for prisoners to learn and play music. One such example, called "New Music in New Places," occurred in Dorchester, New Brunswick, and is sponsored by the Canadian Music Centre. There, twelve inmates took part in "Humming and Drumming," an experimental, meditative, and improvisatory musical project (Canadian Music Centre, 2005). Another resource of note that provides rehabilitation and healing is the Canadian Music Therapy Trust Fund, which provides powerful opportunities to experience and participate in the many roles that music plays in hospitals and other healing facilities.[3]

**Context and Structures in Canadian Community Music**
CM in Canada takes place through various structures, some highly organized, others informal. The following discussion represents both formal organizations and contexts, and is expanded from an earlier typology.[4]

*Community Music Schools*
Community music schools offer private or group lessons and workshops in music. While generally of excellent quality, often these schools are only accessible to the privileged, who are able to pay fees for private instruction. However, most would agree that private instruction provides the foundation for Canada's professional performers in the classical genre.

*CM Performance Organizations*
Community music performance organizations promote performance ensembles ranging from choirs to jazz quartets, punk bands, orchestras, and drum and bugle corps. For example, most large cities that have a professional symphony orchestra also have one or more youth symphonies for aspiring young professional musicians.

*Ethnic/Preservation Groups*
These groups exist to preserve traditions for both immigrant groups and indigenous First Peoples or Native North American groups. Such groups not only preserve traditions, but they may adopt, improvise, recreate, or invent traditions. Cherished customs and gatherings preserve old ways,

celebrate passages, mark uniqueness, and recreate idealized versions of a former context. As one First Nations participant describes the significance of a powwow:

> [The powwow] gives you a sense of identity... it makes you realize that you're a First Nation's person and dancing is just a way to celebrate that... I guess it's a universal thing where all tribes can come together and celebrate... And then as well we have our own different cultural rites and rituals as Ojibwe, Cree... the different nations. (Broad, Boyer, & Chataway, 2006, p. 44)

### Space and Place Sponsorship

Some community music groups exist to provide space or room for music making. Coffeehouses, community drop-in jams, open-mike night at bookstores, clubs, and pubs all serve to nurture local musicians and local genres.

### Festival Gatherings

Festivals are another structure created to allow people to come together for an exciting occasion, often with chances to hear and learn a variety of musics, to dance, to eat, to make art, and to connect. A great deal of recent research has been done on festival gatherings, including Fernandez (2006), who documented the Desh Pardesh Arts Festival, a diasporic arts and culture festival rooted in the South Asian gay and lesbian communities of Toronto, and Snell (2005), who explored the growth and empowerment of an alternative arts and music community through the Om Festival in Ontario. A multitude of music festivals bring people together for blues, country, jazz, pop, folk, classical, and various traditional musics. There are significant annual choral festivals in Laval, Quebec, and Newfoundland. Other festivals celebrating history, dairy or farm products, seasonal themes, and so forth have musical events as a major theme.

### Religious-Based Community Music

Church musicians and choirs representing traditional and modern musics are often the mainstay of smaller, rural communities in Canada. However, as Canadian society becomes more secular and more diverse, the Praise Band — with new facilities that support a huge stage, band pit, electronic keyboard, drums, and electric guitars — is replacing the traditional music of Christian-based churches that usually centred on an organ and choir loft. Gospel and "Jubilation" choirs are common. Not to be forgotten in this discussion is the growth of religious institutions in many communities that support religions from all over the world.

## Associative Community Music

Many non-profit and professional organizations, such as orchestras and opera companies, maintain associative relationships with schools. The fabric of association may take place through collaborations limited in a relatively short time frame; however the influence of such events may have far-reaching results. Band Aid is one such initiative that provides band instruments to deserving schools and seeks to provide "musical instrument grants to schools whose music programs have great potential yet are in need of funding to ensure their sustained growth" (Canadian Academy of Recording Arts and Sciences, n.d).

## Outreach Initiatives Associated with Universities and Schools

A number of universities and colleges sponsor outreach programs, which may include initiatives in schools, hospitals, senior centres, and early childhood centres. Other kinds of outreach may include sponsorship of local arts and music events, collaborations with community music groups, or formation of choirs, bands, orchestras, and other ensembles.[5] Documentation of successful programs includes Lamb's (2006) description of university/symphony/school partnership in Kingston, Ontario, and Babineau's (2000) research with outreach initiates such as the Music in Medicine through Dalhousie University in Halifax, Nova Scotia. In addition, Carruthers (2005) described partnerships in Manitoba and (2006) suggested changes in university structures to meet needs of lifelong music learners.

## Informal Affinity Groups

This category takes its name from Slobin (1993), who deemed such groups to be "charmed circles of like-minded music-makers drawn magnetically to a certain genre that creates strong expressive bonding" (p. 98). This category allows for very informal gatherings, cyber groups, new ways of music making, and new reasons for making music.

## A Penny for the Piper: Funding in Canadian Community Music

Funding for CM and community arts projects is limited, and most structures operate as non-profit organizations. Some initiatives may be aided with government grants; however, a critical point is that the federal Canadian and provincial governments make minimal provisional support for arts programs through grants and awards. Most CM groups are self-funding, non-profit groups supported by participant fees and the tireless work of volunteers. As Sealey (2005) pointed out:

Democratization of the arts is not making art available to every-one, it's making art meaningful to everyone. Citizen musicians will also become very important…We are seeing the return of micro-artistic production. In classical music, house concerts are making a comeback. This is just like in the age of Schubert. And it's usu-ally practicing amateur musicians who are hosting these events in their homes…In the Communist régime of Russia, samizdat were the primary way of communicating new and, as it was at the time, illegal writings. Today, under ground and over ground music mak-ers are putting their music on the net in a sort of samizdat way. It's just electronic instead of dog-eared photocopies. In the old days of the USSR it was raging against state controlled culture; today it is raging against the cultural hegemony of international corporate giants — like Sony…We must be more encompassing in thinking about arts and the community. New economic models have to be put into practice. We must also be aware of new ways of participating in and creating the arts, staying in tune with new movements and trends. Above all, we must listen to our kids. (n.p.)

With government, foundation, and non-profit funding structures lacking, the entire territory of CM seems to be populated by enterprising individu-als. CM workers/independent musician-teachers use their entrepreneurial skills to make music education possible, often renting or borrowing space in public venues. Volunteers are the heavy lifters for much CM, and not only do volunteers make up the ensembles and audiences, they also initi-ate, shape, lead, and often finance them. The scene for funding in CM in Canada is fluid and rapidly changing, with much potential.

## Challenges to Community Music and to Music Education

Community music in Canada is lively, follows multitudinous courses, and changes frequently in response to particular contexts and specific needs. It happens energetically and takes place in a variety of ways on its own terms as a result of individual and collective energies. The diversity of music making in the community sometimes interacts, intersects, or enhances what happens in schools. And, at the same time, this vital area certainly complements and augments deficiencies in music education as offered through school systems. Although responsive to school systems, especially the limitations of opportunities for students to make and create music, in my opinion, CM is not in competition with schools. By acknowledging the significance of CM, music educators can open their minds to enlarge per-spectives and see music education's mission in Canada as beyond schools

or school-aged students. Nevertheless, while CM can support music education in schools, it cannot, will not, and should not save or replace music
education. CM is another form of music education and, although it offers
a varied spectrum of musical activities to a wide range of participants, it
lacks basic mandates, such as access.

Music education is about *access*, and every Canadian has the right to a
comprehensive, sequenced, and excellent education in and through music.
However, the reality is that both public music education and CM programs
fall short of this ideal. Like school music courses, some CM programs are
available for all, while some admit only those who can afford them; some
are available in one place and not another; some support broad views of
the world in which we live, while others profess a dogma and proselytize
to its adherents. As a result, a major challenge is to somehow yoke together
structured and unstructured programs to serve the common good — if one
could determine what that is. The bigger question, however, is how can
we make connections and structures so that all Canadians of all ages and
circumstance can learn and make music in ways that are meaningful and
fulfilling for them.

Community music faces numerous challenges, some of which are shared
with public education. Some critics of CM challenge the quality or worth,
in the artistic domain, of some forms of music making, and equate CM
with not-so-good music. This is clearly a misconception of what CM may
be about. This particular notion arises without consideration of at least
four factors: (1) that genres of music may be understood and heard differently (i.e., one expects crystalline voices from a children's choir and smoky
vocalizing from a jazz chanteuse); (2) that creative processes and emergence
of new forms of expression may take a variety of forms; (3) that music has
many purposes in lives; and (4) that each possible CM function (thera-
peutic, social, political, advocacy, bonding, heritage, identity-asserting)
may sound distinct from each other and from, say, a concertgoer's musical
experience. However, there is a challenge here — not just that music making happens, but how to make links, support, and work for excellence in
expression in whatever way a particular group defines excellence. Another
challenge faced by the music education community concerns funding and,
indirectly, recognition and professionalization. What things are important to Canadians? Should music making be accessible to marginalized
populations and to those who can't afford to pay? What about accredita-
tion, adequate wages, and benefits for community musicians? Community
musicians are fellow music educators who do valuable work, often without
pay or recognition, and sometimes find themselves working in subversive
ways to bring about social change or, at the very least, recognition. As we

expand the definition of music educator beyond the customary to take in wider-ranging ideas and ideals, this discussion may help music education grow closer to what it could be.

## Notes

1  While music making in communities is certainly not new, the notion of CM as a research field, a unifying ideal, or an emerging professional practice is still a new idea in some places. For a discussion of community music as it is defined variously and internationally, please see Veblen and Olsson (2002) and *Proceedings of the 2000 ISME Commission on Community Music Activity* over the past decade, as well as recent research in the *International Journal for Community Music*.

2  For example, the University of Saskatchewan sponsors both summer band camps (http://www.saskband.org) and music camps (http://cede.usask.ca/community-music) for children. Canada's National Arts Centre Orchestra sponsors the Music Alive Program to bring school music programs to rural areas in Alberta, Saskatchewan, and Nunavut (see www.nac-cna.ca/pdf/education/education_newsletter_spring2010.pdf).

3  See Canadian Music Therapy Trust Fund for an exhaustive listing of their many programs (http://www.musictherapytrust.ca/). In Regina, Saskatchewan, Cool Moves combines research and practice for severely disabled individuals. This project enables users to play instrumental sounds by their physical movements linked through electronic devices. Montreal-based Auberge Transition is a shelter for abused women and families that uses vocal and instrumental improvisation combined with relaxation and empowerment strategies. Doctor Peter Centre in Vancouver, BC, is a day centre and hospice for adults living with HIV/AIDS. In addition to other things, this centre makes contemporary instruments and amplifiers available for jamming, forming bands, and musical creating.

4  I've expanded an early North American CM typology here (Veblen & Olsson, 2002). The initial configuration was drawn from Leglar and Smith (1996), who surveyed community music groups in the United States and found what they describe as "compatible pockets of diversity" (p. 95). They classified CM groups as belonging to: (1) community music schools; (2) community performance organizations; or (3) ethnic/preservation groups. In 2002, Bengt Olsson and I augmented Leglar and Smith's model with four other classifications: (4) religious; (5) associative organizations with schools; (6) outreach initiatives of universities and colleges; and (7) informal affinity groups. After some study and reflection, it occurred to me that there were two other distinct categories: (8) spaces for music making sponsored by volunteer groups, such as coffeehouses and pubs for Irish session musicians; and (9) festivals of all kinds. Research seems to indicate that similar configurations are found throughout Canada and the United States; thus this typology is meant to include all of North America at this time.

5  McGill's Conservatory is a hybrid of this category and community music schools.

## References

Babineau, N. (1998). Partners in the arts — the orchestra as community resource. In B. Roberts (Ed.), *Connect, combine, communicate: Revitalizing the arts in Canadian schools* (pp. 223–236). Pictou, NS: University College of Cape Breton Press.

Babineau, N. (2000). Enriching the curriculum — enriching the community: Canadian partnerships for arts education. In M. Taylor & B. Gregory (Eds.), *Music of the spheres ISME conference proceedings* (pp. 12–28). Regina: Impact Printers.

Broad, G., Boyer, S., & Chataway, C. (2006). We are still the Aniishanaabe Nation: Embracing culture and identity in Batchewana First Nation. *Canadian Journal of Communication, 31*, 35–58.

Canadian Academy of Recording Arts and Sciences. (n.d.). Band Aide grants. *Musicounts*. Retrieved from http://www.musicounts.ca/?page_id=10.

Canadian Music Centre. (2005). *Newsletters: Notes Atlantic #74 from the CMC Atlantic region*. Retrieved from http://www.musiccentre.ca/atl.cfm?subsection=new&pgname=n74.

Carruthers, G. (2005). Community music and the "musical community": Beyond conventional synergies. *The International Journal of Community Music, 3*. Retrieved from www.intijcm.com/articles/carruthers.html.

Carruthers, G. (2006). Universities and the music-learning continuum. *International Journal of Community Music, 4*. Retrieved from http://www.intijcm.com/article/volumepercentage204/Carruthers4/.

Curtis, S. L., & Mercado, C. S. (2004). Community music therapy for citizens with developmental disabilities. *Voices: A World Forum for Music Therapy 4*(3). Retrieved from https://normt.uib.no/index.php/voices/article/view/185.

Diamond, B. (2000). What's the difference? Reflections on discourses of morality, modernism, and mosaics in the study of music in Canada. *Canadian University Music Review/Revue de Musique des Universités Canadiennes, 12*(1), 54–75.

Dykema, P. W. (1916). The spread of the community music idea. *Annals of the American Academy of Political and Social Science, 67*, 218–228.

Elliott, R. (1997). *Counterpoint to a city: A history of the Women's Music Club of Toronto*. Toronto: ECW Press.

Elliott, R. (2005). Community music schools in Toronto. *ICM Institute for Canadian Music Newsletter, 3*(2), 1.

Fernandez, S. (2006). More than just an arts festival: Communities, resistances, and the story of Desh Pardesh. *Canadian Journal of Communication, 31*, 17–34.

Gallo, A. (1998). A lone sacred space, an old musical tradition: The dynamics of the Ethiopian Orthodox Church in Toronto through its music (Unpublished doctoral dissertation). Université de Montréal, Montréal.

Kennedy, M. (1999). The music *is* the message: The "how" and "what" of communication. In B. Hanley (Ed.), *Leadership, advocacy, communication: A vision for arts education in Canada* (pp. 265–278). Victoria: University of Victoria/ CMEA.

Kids First. (n.d.). About us. Retrieved from http://kids1st.ca/about-us/.

Knox, R. (2004). Adapted music as community music. *The International Journal of Community Music, 1*(1). Retrieved from www.intijcm.com/articles/knox.html.

Knox, R., Lamont, A., Chau, T., Hamdani, Y., Schwellnus, H., Eaton, C., Tam, C., & Johnson, P. (2005). Movement-to-Music: Designing and implementing a virtual music instrument for young people with disabilities. *International Journal of Community Music, B*(1). Retrieved from http://www.intljcm.com/archive.html.

Lamb, R. (2006). Symphony education: The story of a successful community arts partnership. In K. K. Veblen & S. A. Johnson (Eds.), *Proceedings of the 2000 ISME Commission on Community Music Activity.* Toronto.

Larkin, I. (2006). Foundations. In J. H. Marsh, L. N. Bonikowsky, et al. (Eds.), *Encyclopedia of music in Canada.* Toronto: Historica Foundation of Canada. Retrieved from http://www.thecanadianencyclopedia.com/.

Leglar, M.A., & Smith, D.S. (1996). Community music in the United States: An overview of origins and evolution. In M.A. Leglar (Ed)., *The role of community music* (pp. 95–108). Athens: University of Georgia Press.

Lyon, G. W. (1999). *Community music in Alberta: Some good schoolhouse stuff!* Calgary: University of Calgary Press.

Messenger, S. J. (in press). Digital community: Sharing, teaching, exploring. In K. K. Veblen, S. J. Messenger, M. Silverman, & D. J. Elliott (Eds.), *Community Music Today.* Lanham, MD: Rowman & Littlefield.

Neel, B. (1955–56). Music in Canada. *Tempo, 38,* 7–8.

Parent-Child Mother Goose Program, The. (n.d.). About us. Retrieved from http://www.nald.ca/mothergooseprogram/about.htm.

Roy, C. (n.d.) The original Raging Grannies: Using creative and humorous protests for political education. *Raging Grannies International: Herstory.* Retrieved from http://raginggrannies.org/herstory/.

Sealey, R. (2005). Keynote speech 2: The contributions of the citizen musician to the social economy. *The International Journal of Community Music, B*(1). Retrieved from http://www.intljcm.com/articles/sealey.html.

Slobin, M. (1993). *Subcultural sounds: Micromusics of the west.* Hanover: Wesleyan University Press.

Snell, K. (2005). Music education through popular music festivals: A study of the *OM Music Festival* in Ontario, Canada. *Action, Criticism & Theory for Music Education, 4*(2), pp. 2–35. Retrieved from www.mas.siue.edu/ACT/v4/SNELL4_2.pdf.

Veblen, K. (2003). Compelling connections: Community and music making in Canada. *Canadian Music Educator, 45*(2), 25–28.

Veblen, K. (2008). Many ways of Community Music. *International Journal of Community Music, 1*(1), 5–21.

Veblen, K., & Olsson, B. (2002). Community music: Toward an international overview. In R. Colwell and C. Richardson (Eds.), *The new handbook of research in music teaching and learning* (pp. 730–753). New York: Oxford University Press.

# NINE

# Still Wary after All These Years: Popular Music and the School Music Curriculum

*June Countryman*

The use of popular music in the school music curriculum was given its first enthusiastic endorsement in 1967 at the influential Tanglewood Symposium when leaders from the American education, music education, and professional music worlds met to discuss the role of music education in a changing world. One of Tanglewood's resulting eight goals was for the National Association for Music Education (MENC) to "advance the teaching of music from all periods, style, forms and cultures" (Mark, 2000, p. 2). Yet, after all these years, Canadian music educators are still uneasy about how much popular music to include in their programs and how best to incorporate it. Why are music educators still wary? What are the factors that continue to make popular music's place in Canadian music education programs such a difficult issue? In this chapter, I ponder three interrelated themes that help account for our ongoing insecurities with bringing popular music into our secondary music classrooms: (1) our own musical preparation, (2) our large-group performance emphasis, and (3) our professional isolation and role socialization.

## Music Teacher Preparation

Music teachers typically begin specialized musical training in their child-hood or early teen years. This training almost always includes private lessons outside of the public education system. Admission to postsecondary music programs includes a solo audition requiring an advanced level of performance skill. This is virtually the only route to becoming a school music educator. While a few teachers with other majors do teach music, most secondary school music teachers are products of Bachelor of Music programs. In university music study

> the music education paradigm is strongly aligned with classical music, which today includes jazz as concert music, and musical theatre. However there is still an implicit hierarchy of "taste" and, consequently program definition that favours real (serious) classical music. Along with this there is a general intolerance of popular music. (Bartel, 2004, p. xiv)

Music performance is prized, of course, and this creates a product — as opposed to a process — orientation, which, if unexamined, functions as tacit confirmation of how music education should be. Naturally, many music graduates who choose to teach in the school system want to recreate the kinds of musical experiences that were so profoundly meaningful for them in their own high school and university lives. The cycle continues: many new music educators envision school music programs as revolving around students performing in large ensembles, learning their music by reading traditional music notation, and being led by a teacher/conductor. Elevating students' musical tastes with "serious" repertoire is an overarching goal.

In addition to the primarily classically oriented university music students, there is a second group of music majors who combine their classical music studies with a rich "outside" life performing various popular music styles. They lead bands, write songs, develop arrangements, find gigs, play bass in one group and guitar in another, and many of these musicians become music educators too. They would appear to have the skill set to enable them to more readily introduce popular music performance and small-group improvising and arranging into the secondary school music program, and some of them do. Others, in my experience, continue to lead the double musical lives they began in university, keeping their popular music performing as a personal, after-hours passion, and running traditional band and choral programs in their schools.

Senyshyn (2004) believes that many music teachers feel there is something unethical about popular music. It merely entertains, whereas "good" music uplifts and ennobles. He notes that "this false and misleading elit-ism...distorts the power of music. We do this at the expense of students' identities and values which are passionately based on the very music that is, at times, suppressed" (p. 119). This attitude may be true for some music educators. Others, I think, embrace various popular musics, and recognize their students' investments in these styles, but do not see how popular music can have any role in their school music program beyond program-ming the occasional pop arrangement for their ensembles.

Musician Robert Fripp (in Green, 2001) distinguishes between popular culture, where "the musician calls on the highest part in all of us," and mass culture, where "the musician addresses the lowest parts of what we are. In mass culture our singers shout what we want to hear. In popular culture, our musicians sing to us in our own voice" (p. x). This distinction is profound and it hints at a discourse that may be alive and well in cul-tural studies programs but that has been largely absent from undergradu-ate university music study. The academic study of popular music has been dominated by cultural critics and sociologists who address different schol-arly issues than do musicians — "a distinction between text and context" as Covach (1999, p. 455) explains it. If scholarly investigation of popular musics is not part of future music educators' professional preparation, its absence may function as another of those tacit messages about how school music should be. The sociological understanding of musicking as a human practice (e.g. Martin, 1995; Stokes, 1997; Small, 1998; DeNora, 2000; Clay-ton, Herbert, & Middleton, 2003; Keil & Feld, 2005; Turino, 2008) offers the profession a richly expanded sense of its work. Gracyk's (2007) expla-nation of the importance of aesthetic value in our experiences of popular musics provides an important counterbalance to the social relevance the-ory of popular music's significance. Bayles (2003) observes that "there is no 'great divide' between the ideas, practices, and values of the traditional arts and those of popular culture: Popular culture is a living tradition which, like all traditions, throws off a ton of junk, a lot of diversion, some bits that are vile, and some bits that are lovely" (pp. 15–16).

Charles Leonhard (in Bartel, 2004) believed that music educators turn students away by focusing on musical grammar, technique, and analysis at the expense of the essence of music — its expressiveness: "Music educa-tion operates in the realm of feeling and can educate for humanness in an increasingly mechanistic and depersonalized society" (p. xi). Leonhard urged teachers to include the best contemporary popular music and to develop students' abilities to sing and play by ear, as well as to make inde-pendent musical judgments. These recommendations, made over thirty years ago by one of the profession's most influential academics, remain elusive in practice. I believe that the heavily classical orientation of university music programs, when not contextualized within a broader framework that situates the Western composed tradition as one among many ways of musicking, is a key factor in status-quo practice.

## Music Education's Large-Ensemble Performance Emphasis

Large ensembles have always been the major performance vehicles in secondary school music programs. This is because of such factors as tradition, expedience, the physical design of facilities, and the immutability of school scheduling.

Most instrumental and choral ensembles perform classical (or classically derived) repertoire, Broadway tunes, movie themes, and pop songs arranged for large performing groups. These pieces are "sanitized" (Bartel, 2004, p. xiv) to accommodate large numbers of musicians using instruments and making sounds that are classically based. The students in these performance classes and ensembles usually have developed sufficient skill on their instruments to enable them to derive personal enjoyment from performing. Many are motivated to practise. They tend to have strong academic skills that enable them to develop fluency with musical notation and/or great ears that enable them to fake the reading. They also value the experience of being part of a musical community. These music students are clearly a select group. They and their teachers share a vision of developing musical excellence and of celebrating an ongoing communal experience. When they perform popular music, they accept the compromises involved in translating the music to a large-group setting. Some of these young musicians have the combination of skill and passion to form small combos where they can play contemporary music in more authentic contexts, either within the school's extracurricular music program or independently.

But what about the much larger group of students who stop taking school music as soon as they have a choice because of insufficient performing skill (on a school-approved instrument), frustration with the emphasis on traditional notation, disenchantment with the large-ensemble setting and pedagogy, or a combination of these? Many students might be drawn to, and enriched by, a program that did not require years of prior experience and that featured the kinds of music they love, performed in small combos where the participants' musical agency is central. The professional literature offers ideas and models for such courses, which are based on rock group performance, on close listening to contemporary music, and on technologically enabled composing in contemporary styles (Rodriquez, 2004; Green, 2008; Mantie, 2008).

Popular music's inclusion in school music programs is, I think, more a pedagogical issue than a repertoire issue. When music educators do bring popular music into the classroom, Green (2001) contends, they strip it of its informal learning practices so that "it bear[s] little resemblance to any music that exists in the world outside" (p. 7). Green's study of informal music practices shows that pop and rock musicians work radically differently than do classical musicians, making intensive use of imitation/listening/improvisation and, of course, largely ignoring traditional notation. The Musical Futures initiative in England, begun in 2003, is based in part on Green's research on informal learning practices. Musical Futures is a well-documented, longitudinal, research-based series of models and approaches to music education for eleven- to eighteen-year-olds, focusing on student performance through informal learning, beginning with popular music, highlighting student choice, and branching in many directions (e.g., composition, world music fusions, classical music ensembles) depending on local interests, expertise, and resources. One of Musical Futures' distinguishing features, regardless of musical style, is the emphasis on student-driven musicking, with the teacher as a guide and a knowledgeable resource.

In the Canadian context, we have guitar, steel pans, drumming, and keyboard courses offered as additions to or replacement for the traditional instrumental and choral programs. Typically, the pedagogy still centres on full-group instruction (or, with keyboards, in plugged-in isolation). Reading standard notation may receive less emphasis and the repertoire may include much more popular music, but formal pedagogy continues to dominate, presumably because of a lack of models for teaching music differently.

Adopting the informal pedagogy that Green (2008) describes will not, by itself, develop students' musicality and musical independence. Lindgren and Ericsson (2010) provide a cautionary tale in their research into Swedish music education practices, where small-group learning in rock-band formations has long been the norm. They documented the antagonism between the supposed freedom of musical creation in a rock-combo setting and the school requirements of self-regulation, efficiency, and standardization. They note that musically skilled students thrived in these settings, but those with insufficient performing skills did not: for these students, little or no musical learning took place.

When the pupils in our study were given a free hand to run their own learning and to choose by themselves what type of music and lyrics they wished to create and perform, they became incapable of doing their musical tasks. The freedom the pupils are offered is transformed to a kind of self-discipline in order to learn how to manage and give an account of their time. Ideas of open, collective, authentic, and creative music practices outside school have been put together with today's somewhat contradictory discourses around self-reflection, control, and rules. (p. 49)

Broadening the repertoire to include popular music and adopting pedagogical approaches that best suit that repertoire is no simple thing. Music educators must still develop students' performing skills and musicianship.

Within any performance-based music program is an expectation that we listen to lots of music. If our programs are teaching open-mindedness to various musical styles and a deepening ability to listen creatively and critically, then popular music's inclusion here, as listening material, is a necessity. Musical concepts can be clarified or expanded through listening across styles[1] and rich questions about the reasons for various approaches to making music can be explored. Once we start acknowledging that the music our students are passionate about holds interest and value for us, an exciting shift can happen. We become learners, too, and can then authentically model that which we desire in our students: excitement, curiosity, and respect for honest musical expression in any style. If we create a genuinely shared conversation about music in our classrooms, our students will start finding and sharing unexpected and wonderful music connections as part of that ongoing conversation.[2] And yet, in many high school music programs students never have opportunities to listen to and discuss music beyond their own ensemble repertoire.

### Professional Isolation and Role Socialization
Having experienced an intense and highly focused musical preparation, it is hardly surprising that many music educators see themselves as custodians of the Western European classical heritage. In the past thirty years jazz has gradually won respect as a musical style worthy of being taught, and musics from some non-Western traditions continue to be an important repertoire area, albeit one with its own set of challenges. These three broad areas, then — Western classical, jazz, and musics of some non-Western traditions — comprise the performing and listening repertoire of most Canadian music programs. If we are "rocking out" in our own classrooms (and, at least in our guitar programs, some of us are), we certainly don't advertise the fact. We worry about being judged by our peers as having low standards or questionable tastes. We know the arguments about just giving students more of what they already know, and of messing with a youth cultural practice that students perhaps don't want us messing with. And

yet, if music education is to connect with students' lived realities, popular musics need to be part of any music education program.

We have in music education an increasingly sophisticated theoretical literature that supports a broad, inclusive, inspiring notion of music as a human practice, a social action (e.g., Small, 1998; Regelski & Gates, 2009). Yet, in the context of school music education, our professional preparation and our experience as musicians lead most music educators to continue to treat *musical literacy* in the narrow sense of reading and manipulating the complex notation system of the Western European musical tradition. This emphasis on notated music is another reason for the exclusion of much popular and participatory music. The oral/aural nature of these musics is mistakenly construed as making them less rigorous, and therefore less worthy of educational time. Further, our pedagogical traditions have prepared us to teach music reading, but we are much less equipped to effectively and authentically teach oral and improvisational musical traditions. As a result, when we have attempted to broaden the school music repertoire, we have acted "as if these musics could be simply added and stirred — as though we needed to challenge or change nothing but our assumptions about the relative worth of these various traditions" (Bowman, 2007, p. 116).

I contend that our professional isolation keeps us either as prisoners of status-quo teaching or as clandestine change agents within the privacy of our own classrooms. Missing in the professional lives of most music educators are ongoing opportunities for professional dialogue, for honest articulation of doubts and fears, for genuine sharing of fleeting successes, crushing defeats, and moments of clarity. The life-world of a secondary music educator is intense. The political reality of maintaining a thriving music program and making that program fit within a school's many competing interests requires constant energy. In the Canadian context, music teachers teach a full load of courses and then perform their second role as extracurricular coach and director. The job can be both exhilarating and all-consuming. It leaves little or no time for the kind of continuous professional dialogue necessary to encourage reflective practice and collaborative pedagogical experimentation. Indeed, opportunities for this kind of dialogue do not exist for most music teachers, and it is not part of the professional culture to wonder why they do not.

Paul Woodford, in *Democracy and Music Education* (2005), argues that music educators have isolated themselves from the political arena since the 1950s and 1960s, when they were publicly advocating for strong music education programs. They have "reverted to traditional performance-based models, repertoires, and pedagogies divorced from the real musical world and its social problems" (p. 58). Woodford writes bluntly:

A growing body of research suggests that many [music education majors and even experienced music teachers] are intellectually passive in the sense that they are too accepting of received knowledge, including highly prescriptive methods and the latest fads. Perhaps worse, there seems to be impatience among them and perhaps among teachers in general with things intellectual. Many music education majors and performance teachers — as practitioners charged with acquiring and replicating traditional performance and teaching methods — are not intellectuals in the sense of being politically aware and disposed to question and challenge the professional status quo. Nor are they disposed to engage in public criticism of wider educational, social, and political values. (p. 23)

Bowman (2002) warns music teachers that "failure to 'theorize practice,' to reflect critically on the ends to which our musical and instructional practices may lead leaves open the very real possibility that our musical engagements miseducate rather than educate" (p. 64). Woodford and Bowman both suggest that music educators have made their marginal curricular status even more precarious by failing to keep up with societal changes and the intellectual foment that these changes create.

I agree with this assessment, but as a long-time high school music teacher, I protest too. Music teachers are professionally isolated. They work in a culture that is (ironically) anti-intellectual. Public displays of their work (at concerts and festivals and in the community) help to substantiate the contours of professional identity. The infrequent professional development opportunities that exist are usually workshop-style events that model transmissive pedagogy. At the local level, professional development for music educators is often the responsibility of the teachers themselves, and music educators do not feel empowered to create for their peers professional development initiatives that are theoretical and exploratory in nature. Discussion sessions intended to share individual pedagogical moves turn out to be superficial: participants have little confidence in sharing ideas from their practice and no trust in admitting pedagogical or philosophical confusions. This is because there is no tradition of genuine collegial learning as part of the profession. The "nature of teaching as a cultural activity that follows scripts deeply inscribed by tradition" and the "traditional norms of individualism" (Sykes, Bird, & Kennedy, 2010, p. 465) together define "occupational competence" in teaching.

The culture of (music) teaching is the opposite of what Greene (1995) envisions as "a kind of collaborative search" (p. 23). Greene believes that education should be focused on making our world a more humane place, which means actively resisting practices that routinize and standardize and that accept the status quo. "Made aware of ourselves as questioners, as meaning makers, as persons engaged in constructing and reconstructing realities with those around us, we may communicate to students the notion that reality is multiple perspectives and that the construction of it is never complete, that there is always more" (p. 131). Teachers are not socialized to see themselves as questioners and meaning makers.[3]

Occasionally, serendipity may prevail and we find a colleague with whom to discuss and share ideas. Most of the time, though, we work alone, without the benefit of regular, thought-provoking, revitalizing professional conversation. I believe that two kinds of ongoing professional development experiences are vital for music teachers' professional growth: (1) opportunities to actively observe and critique actual classroom practice where new pedagogical approaches are being tried, and (2) opportunities to experiment in their own classrooms, buttressed by regular sharing sessions in a community of peers where honest, open dialogue about practice is the norm.

**Conclusion**
Woodford (2005) decries the lack of "musical conversation, of mutual curiosity, respect, and criticism" when music teachers try to deal with popular music (p. 25). He insists that music teachers must treat popular music and world musics with the same kind of intellectual rigour they apply to classical music. He cautions against teaching popular music for the wrong reasons, such as mere entertainment or as a stepping stone to the "real" (i.e., classical) repertoire. Finally, he reminds educators that meeting a democratic standard in teaching also necessitates taking up political and ethical issues, going "beyond the music to consider issues of class, power, and control" (p. 101). While some individual music educators are incorporating popular music in compelling and authentic ways, the majority, Woodford suggests, do not. Here, I respectfully submit, is an illustration of the disconnect between the academy and what Turner-Bisset (2001) calls *the chalkface*. Woodford's arguments are strong. The next paragraph, though, is missing; he provided no specifics. We need tangible recommendations for how to teach popular music — as a performance repertoire, as a springboard to creativity, and as social critique. We need help translating elegant theory into possible practice. We do not lack the inquiring spirit or the intellectual capacity for this work. We lack a workplace culture that frames teachers as public intellectuals, and we lack a professional culture among music educators that cultivates honest dialogue and meaningful collaboration, and that welcomes challenges to status-quo practice.

Examining the question of music education's connection to real life, Allsup (2003) considers the difficulty music educators have with popular musics. He advocates "real dialogue" or "intercultural exchange" (p. 7) with students in order to "reconnect formal education to everyday culture" (p. 10):

> When children examine popular music, and learn to ask critical questions, they are beginning the Arnoldian search for perfection. For these explorations to work, the questions educators ask must be age-appropriate, yet praxial: what songs do you consider a master-piece? How do they inspire you? What do these works say about who we are? Are we allowed to perform them differently? How does your contribution reflect who you are? Here we have located a Freire-ian understanding of praxis: a view of learning that appropriates the revolutionary tradition of Marx, while using bourgeois culture and its ideological tools for self-transformation. (p. 11)

Allsup emphasizes that "the study of perfection is a subversive operation in today's consumer society. To think critically, in spite of culture, is a revolutionary act, and one that may lead to self-transformation" (p. 12). Theorizing about aspects of practice, such as Allsup does here, provides teachers with a virtual dialogue that enriches and dignifies their own teaching. Yet music teachers, unless they are involved in graduate study, do not have access to the rich theoretical literature of which Allsup's article is one example.

What we are wary of, I believe, is not popular music itself, but the changes in pedagogy and in performable product that authentically embracing popular musics require. Hargreaves and Marshall (2003) suggest that the level of autonomy and control students experience in their music making might be even more important than the genre or style involved, and my own research (Countryman, 2008) bears this out. Some of my young adult participants had been involved in music programs where opportunities to develop their musical independence were featured. Their comments about the value they place on experiences of *musical creativity* (improvising, arranging, small-group composing, and performing with one's individual-ity honoured) and *musical independence* (running small combos, coaching younger students, and providing musical leadership) were strong endorse-ments for sharing power through a broadening of pedagogical approach.

Popular musics, authentically performed, demand independent musi-cianship enacted in small-combo settings without a conductor. Our pro-grams, K–12, should be developing students' performing and listening skills so that they are equipped to engage in both teacher-led and peer-led musicking. The matter of popular music in music education draws attention to broader philosophical and pedagogical issues. We must find the space to push against status-quo music teaching through dialogue and experimentation. That space should exist between the academy and the chalkface.

## Notes

1 An exploration of the appropriateness of applying the analytic constructs from art music to popular music is beyond the scope of this paper. I do not wish to imply a *musical elements* approach here.

2 It would have been as unlikely for me to have encountered, for example, the asymmetrical metres in the music of Nine Inch Nails or the polyrhythms in Tool (including the Fibonacci sequence in *Lateralus*) as it would have been for most of my students to have discovered the static harmonic power of Gorecki's *Amen* or the hauntingly spiritual experience of Tuvan overtone singing.

3 For example, see Dolloff's (2007) exploration of the complexities of role socialization and music teacher identities.

## References

Allsup, R. E. (2003). Transformational education and critical music pedagogy: Examining the link between culture and learning. *Music Education Research* 5(1), 5–12.

Bartel, L. (2004). Introduction. In L. Bartel (Ed.), *Questioning the music education paradigm* (pp. 7–11). Toronto: Canadian Music Educators' Association.

Bayles, M. (2003). The (proper) place of popular culture in liberal education. *Arts Education Policy Review, 104*(4), 13–16.

Bowman, W. (2002). Educating musically. In R. Colwell & C. Richardson (Eds.), *The new handbook of research on music teaching and learning* (pp. 63–84). New York: Oxford University Press.

Bowman, W. (2007). Who is the "We"? Rethinking professionalism in music education. *Action, Criticism and Theory for Music Education, 6*(4), 109–131.

Clayton, M., Herbert, T., & Middleton, R. (Eds.) (2003). *The cultural study of music: A critical introduction.* London: Routledge.

Countryman, J. (2008). *Missing voices in music education: Music students and music teachers explore the nature of the high school music experience.* Unpublished doctoral dissertation, University of Toronto, Toronto.

Covach, J. (1999). Popular music, unpopular musicology. In N. Cook & M. Everist (Eds.), *Rethinking music* (pp. 452–470). London: Oxford University Press.

DeNora, T. (2000). *Music in everyday life.* Cambridge, England: Cambridge University Press

Dolloff, L. (2007) "All the Things We Are": Balancing our Multiple Identities in Music Teaching. *Action, Criticism, and Theory for Music Education, 6*(2), 2–21.

Gracyk, T. (2007). *Listening to popular music, or, how I learned to stop worrying and love Led Zeppelin.* Ann Arbor, MI: University of Michigan Press.

Green, L. (2001). *How popular musicians learn.* Aldershot, Hants, England: Ashgate.

Green, L. (2008). *Music, informal learning and the school: A new classroom pedagogy.* Aldershot, Hants, England: Ashgate.

Greene, M. (1995). *Releasing the imagination: Essays on education, the arts and social change.* San Francisco: Jossey-Bass.

Hargreaves, D., & Marshall, N. (2003). Developing identities in music education. *Music Education Research, 5*(3), 263–274.

Keil, C., & Feld, S. (2005). *Music grooves* (2nd ed.). Tuscan, AZ: Fenestra Books.

Leonhard, C. (1981). The great masquerade: Means become ends. In L. Bartel (Ed.), *Questioning the music education paradigm* (pp. 7–11). Toronto: Canadian Music Educators' Association.

Lindgren, M., & Ericsson, C. (2010). The rock band context as discursive governance in music education in Swedish schools. *Action, Criticism, and Theory for Music Education, 9*(3): 35–54.

Mantie, R. (2008). Getting unstuck: The "One World Youth Arts Project, the music education paradigm, and youth without advantage." *Music Education Research, 10(4),* 473–483.

Mark, M. (2000). From Tanglewood to Tallahassee in 32 years. *Music Educators Journal 86*(5), 25–28.

Martin, P. (1995). *Sounds and society: Themes in the sociology of music.* Manchester: Manchester University Press, 1995.

Musical Futures. Retrieved from http://www.musicalfutures.org.uk/.

Regelski, T., & Gates, J. T. (Eds.). (2009). *Music education for changing times: Guiding visions for practice.* New York: Springer.

Rodriquez, C. X. (Ed.). (2004). *Bridging the gap: Popular music and music education.* Reston, VA: National Association for Music Education.

Senyshyn, Y. (2004). Popular music and the intolerant classroom. In L. R. Bartel (Ed.), *Questioning the music education paradigm* (pp. 110–120). Toronto: Canadian Music Educators' Association.

Small, C. (1998). *Musicking.* Middletown, CT: Wesleyan University Press.

Stokes, M. (1997). *Ethnicity, identity and music: The musical construction of place.* Oxford: Berg.

Sykes, G., Bird, T., & Kennedy, M. (2010). Teacher education: Its problems and some prospects. *Journal of Teacher Education 6*(5), 464–476.

Turino, T. (2008). *Music as social life: The politics of participation.* Chicago: University of Chicago Press.

Turner-Bisset, R. (2001). *Expert teaching.* London: David Fulton Publishers.

Woodford, P. G. (2005). *Democracy and music education.* Bloomingdale, IN: Indiana University Press.

# TEN

# E-Teaching and Learning in Music Education: A Case Study of Newfoundland and Labrador

*Andrea Rose, Alex Hickey, and Andrew Mercer*

## Introduction

Distance education in Newfoundland and Labrador grew from a need to create equal access to high school courses, university programs, and other learning opportunities. Small, geographically isolated rural schools in the province have challenged the province's ability to provide students with sufficient teacher and resource allocations. Out-migration, educational reform, the collapse of the cod fishery, and the resulting economic restraint have yielded a dramatic change in the demographics of coastal communities and their schools. The inevitable reality is that school enrolments and teacher availability are both declining at rates beyond the capacity of traditional face-to-face teaching and learning models. The purpose of this chapter is to provide a descriptive overview of new and emerging technologies in music education currently being used in e-teaching and learning contexts in Newfoundland and Labrador.[1] Because the application of e-teaching and learning in music is still in its nascent stages and remains relatively unstudied in the literature, the purpose of the following discussion is to provide a foundational description of current developments. Topics include: historical contexts for the current initiatives in web-based teaching and learning music, ongoing developments in e-teaching and learning, emerging questions for research, and potential roles of community partnerships and collaborations.

## Historical Context: Music Education and Technology

The relatively recent development and application of virtual learning technologies to education in Newfoundland and Labrador is part of a century's worth of innovations intended to address the necessity of distance education in the province. In 1936, the Department of Education introduced the "School Car" initiative, which provided children living along the railway with access to a mobile school and teacher, who taught according to the available correspondence studies curriculum, learning materials, and equipment. The rail car also housed books from the Travelling Library headquartered in St. John's and was in service until 1942 (Noseworthy, 1997). In 1939 the Department of Education organized a Correspondence Division to educate children living in small, isolated communities without schools. Lessons were sent to the children, who returned them by mail for evaluation (Noseworthy, 1997).

These initial attempts at distance education were augmented by the introduction of the Canadian Broadcasting Corporation (CBC) Radio School Broadcast Series, which ran from the 1950s until the 1980s. Content for this series was dovetailed to fit the prescribed provincial curriculum, and schools were encouraged to tune in for the "Schools Broadcast." These broadcasts included large amounts of music and cultural content, which ranged from plays commissioned for this series, to interviews with artists and authors, to recordings of musical performances — all of which were accompanied by information on their relationship to the curriculum. Newfoundland joined the CBC network in 1949 and began contributing to the Maritimes School Broadcasts in 1952. In 1967, a music series ("Music in the Classroom") for Grades 1 to 4 was created and remained part of the Atlantic school broadcasts from 1968 to 1973. Although Atlantic school broadcasts terminated in June 1975, local programs including "Let's Sing a Song" (1974–75), "Something to Sing About" (1976–77), and "Old Times and New" (1978–79), continued to be heard in Newfoundland (Historical Foundation of Canada, 2008).

At the postsecondary level, Memorial University of Newfoundland (MUN) Extension Services offered some of the earliest postsecondary distance learning opportunities beginning in the late 1960s. Through a combination of teaching manuals, on-site teaching assistants, videotaped lectures, and hands-on support materials, these courses paralleled courses that were taught on campus. These courses were strictly aimed at teachers enrolled in undergraduate degree programs (Mugridge, 1986). In 1977, the Tele-health and Educational Resource Agency (TETRA, formerly known as Tele-medicine) was also established (House & Keough, 1989). The Department of Education used TETRA's network to provide distance education to the province's K–12 schools, and continued to do so until the establishment of the Centre for Distance Learning and Innovation (CDLI) in 2000 (Boone, 2008). The Virtual Teacher Centre (VTC), a division of the Newfoundland and Labrador Teachers' Association (NLTA), was established in 2001 with in-kind support from key education partners in the province and finan-cial support from Industry Canada. The ongoing mandate of the VTC is to develop, facilitate, and deliver online professional development and class-room content support to practising and pre-service teachers throughout the province (Virtual Teacher Centre, 2004). Working collaboratively with CDLI, the Department of Education, and MUN, the VTC currently offers a variety of online professional development opportunities to teachers.

The actual introduction of online, web-based learning as the primary mode of delivery for distance education is quite recent. The Centre for Distance Learning and Innovation emerged from a recommendation to government in the Sparkes-Williams's Ministerial Panel on Education Delivery in Newfoundland and Labrador Report (Government of New-foundland and Labrador 2000). In 2000, the province developed a new distance education program that included e-teaching/learning and related teacher professional development. CDLI now offers numerous high school courses in a variety of subject areas, including visual art and music. CDLI, a division of the Department of Education, Government of Newfoundland and Labrador, operates in partnership with Memorial University of New-foundland and the Newfoundland and Labrador Teachers' Association. The CDLI vision is that all learners will have *equitable access* to educational opportunities in a manner that *renders distance transparent*. To achieve this vision, the Centre works with its partners as a leader in the develop-ment and delivery of educational programs and services using information and communications technologies and the World Wide Web. To that end, CDLI's primary objectives are to develop web-based courses and services to learners of all ages, facilitate school districts in web-based delivery, and develop online professional development for teachers in the K–12 system (Government of Newfoundland and Labrador, 2007). Currently, 103 of 140 high schools are online via CDLI. Of the 21,768 high school students in the province, approximately 1,000, or 5.5 percent, are online. In 2008, 38 sec-ondary courses were offered through online, web-based formats. Presently, CDLI employs 45 staff, which includes e-teachers (one e-music teacher), administrators, technicians, and one guidance counsellor.

**Table 10.1** *Students and communities served by online arts courses (2005–2008)*

|  | 2005–6 | | 2006–7 | | 2007–8 | |
|---|---|---|---|---|---|---|
|  | Students | Communities | Students | Communities | Students | Communities |
| Art Technologies | 91 | 25 | 85 | 30 | 60 | 20 |
| Art & Design | 26 | 11 | 44 | 18 | 41 | 24 |
| Experiencing Music | 39 | 10 | 44 | 19 | 52 | 19 |
| Applied Music (pilot) | n/a | n/a | n/a | n/a | 19 | 7 |
| **TOTAL** | **156** | **46** | **173** | **67** | **172** | **70** |

### Current E-Teaching and Learning Contexts in Music Education

The history of delivering high school art/music courses via distance education formats is a relatively recent one. In 1998 (pre-CDLI), STEM~Net, in collaboration with School District Five in central Newfoundland and the Art Consultant at the Department of Education at the time, secured financing from Industry Canada to develop the newly implemented Art Technologies 1201 as Newfoundland and Labrador's first completely web-based distance course for high school students. CDLI currently offers two visual art courses and two music courses supported by three full-time arts specialist teaching positions. Plans are currently under way to develop Theatre Music 2200 for online delivery as well. The four arts courses, now redesigned for web-based delivery are: Art Technologies 1201, Art and Design 3200, Experiencing Music 2200, and Applied Music 2206 (in pilot). Experiencing Music 2200 is a two-credit high school general music course designed for students to explore music through a three-faceted approach: listening, performing, and creating. The focus of this course is on the experiential nature of music and music making in its many and varied forms (Government of Newfoundland and Labrador, 1994). Applied Music 2206 (guitar) was introduced as a pilot for the 2007–8 school year. It is a two-credit course in which students develop musical skills, literacy, and aural skills through the medium of guitar. CDLI plans to develop the course further by offering additional applied areas such as violin, piano, and accordion (Government of Newfoundland and Labrador, 1996). In addition, CDLI has offered an online fiddle ensemble, Online Fiddle Group (co-curricular music ensemble), since 2005. CDLI provides instruments to twelve students throughout the province, and, through use of the Polycom video conferencing system, students are taught fiddling and ensemble techniques.

These web-based courses continue to serve a wide range and large number of students in the province. Table 10.1 illustrates the breakdown of the number of students and communities served by these online arts courses for the three most recent school years.

**Pedagogical Uses of Technologies in E-Music Education: A Sampling**
The current distance delivery model in Newfoundland and Labrador is web-based, using computers, networks, and the Internet to deliver course content. Courses strike a balance between synchronous (online, real-time environments) and asynchronous (offline, independent environments) interactions based upon the nature of the course and the degree of interaction required. That balance is usually determined by the instructional designer and the e-teachers. In current music courses, the proportion is approximately 60 percent synchronous and 40 percent asynchronous. During synchronous periods, the teacher works with students to explore concepts, teach skills, engage in dialogue, interact via group work, and evaluate/assess students' progress. During asynchronous periods, students work independently on assigned tasks and projects. The e-teacher is available for individual consultations with students.

While CDLI courses are managed within a learning management system, teachers have latitude to employ technological applications beyond those provided by the current management system Desire 2 Learn (D2L). For example, Elluminate Live, a platform-independent web-conferencing tool that utilizes voice, chat, whiteboard, and a variety of other features, is frequently used in day-to-day interactions with students. The degree to which a teacher uses varied technological supports is driven by the instructional needs of the teacher and students as well as the demands of the discipline area.[2]

E-music teachers frequently collaborate to create short video clips of particular techniques, such as care for instruments, to support student learning. Clips developed as part of a course are embedded in web content and are viewable online, whereas teacher-developed clips are frequently stored on external sites such as YouTube. Live video transmission is also employed as a standard teaching/learning method. Using video tools, music teachers can provide interactive demonstrations and tutorials for students on how to perform specific artistic tasks as well as how to use music-based software.

Students in Experiencing Music 2200 have access to the basic CDLI equipment (e.g., computers, printers, fax machines, Polycom video system) in addition to equipment provided to address specific needs unique to music education. For example, students use tin whistles to learn basic literacy and applied music skills, complete compositional exercises, and demonstrate their understanding of applied musical concepts. Webcams are used to facilitate video conferencing, which allows for real-time instruction and performances during synchronous classes.

Both Experiencing Music 2200 and Applied Music 2206 are currently facilitated by three main pieces of software: Audacity, Music Ace, and Sonar-Home Studio. Audacity, an audio recorder and editor, is installed on each student computer. Using Audacity, students are able to record music and projects that can be shared with peers and teachers. Music Ace is a theory and ear-training software package designed to develop understandings and skills pertaining to music literacy. Sonar-Home Studio is a compositional tool. Using intuitive applications, students are able to create compositions in a variety of genres and styles. This tool uses a sample-based compositional approach by providing a bank of sample musical examples which students can select and manipulate in unique and creative ways.

Recent developments in internet technology have facilitated online student expression. Students in both Experiencing Music 2200 and Applied Music 2206 are provided with online areas in which they can freely express themselves, create and share content, and interact with their peers. Through tools such as wikis and blogs, students are able to take on the role of publisher/editor. Media such as podcasting, electronic journals, and digital portfolios all extend options for both teacher and student. For example, through the use of podcasts — digital media files distributed over the Internet for playback on portable media players and personal computers — instructors are able to supplement course content, add assignments, and so forth. Students are able to access course content according to personal learning preferences. Providing such alternative opportunities for students is important in creating a learner-centred teaching and learning environment (Hargis & Wilson, 2005). Similarly, electronic journals and blogs allow e-teachers to gather varied types of information for assessment from students (Greher, 2006). These include, for example, student compositions and videos in progress.

Digital portfolios, and portfolios in general, are excellent tools for formative evaluation (Davis, Sumara, & Luce-Kapler, 2000). Bauer and Dunn (2003) described two types of electronic portfolios: (1) working and (2) presentation. The working portfolio signifies a compilation in progress in which students continuously add representative exercises and resources. The final product may be shown along with documentation of work in various stages. A presentation portfolio is more focused on a particular topic area. Barrett (1998) stressed the importance of using standards to organize a portfolio. Bauer and Dunn (2003) encouraged the use of a portfolio template to aid in the creation and maintenance of student portfolios and stated that a portfolio is an excellent tool for authentic assessment. Several other new technologies hold promise for e-learning in the music and are currently being examined by e-music teachers in the province. These include: interactive whiteboards, portable audio/video devices, and online desktop applications.

## Challenges in Distance Learning

Challenges to the e-learning environment include: the need for privacy and security of student personal information; exposure to unwanted content; copyright and intellectual property rights and the determination of ownership; and constant technological development requiring upgraded hardware and software and access to greater bandwidth. The unique requirements for the effective delivery of a music education curriculum, however, have created problems that are unique to the field. Significant issues include:

### 1. Leadership Capacity

There is need for (1) increased instructional expertise and (2) greater awareness of current research in technologies and arts/music education. The significance of the e-learning environment in current educational practices requires greater awareness and training at the pre-service teacher education level as well.

### 2. Curriculum Design and Development

CDLI's role is to take the already developed and authorized provincial music curriculum and overlay that with an instructional design for the online environment. This work is usually contracted out to a recognized expert in the particular discipline. The music teacher then mediates that instructional design to the particular needs of the students in each class. One of the challenges with this approach is maintaining the integrity of the original curriculum philosophy and design. Some critical questions include the following: Are students in the online courses being exposed to the same content to the same degree as their face-to-face counterparts in music, or, conversely, is the online experience deeper than that in the regular classroom? Are learning outcomes that were conceived and constructed around the assumption of face-to-face learning now appropriate in the online environment? To what extent is innovation in the use of web technologies applied to the courses — how far removed are online courses from a strict linear model as opposed to capitalizing on the non-linear capacity of the Internet?

## 3. Creativity
The Newfoundland and Labrador Music Education Curriculum Foundations document states that "creativity does not occur in a vacuum. Art making is a process built on creativity and skill and is cultivated through setting the conditions that encourage and promote its development" (Government of Newfoundland and Labrador, n.d. b, p. 42). Are those conditions for creativity present in the current e-music courses? How much emphasis is placed on nurturing and developing creativity in the instructional design phase? How are teachers meeting the challenges and demands of "doing" and "creating," both individually and socially, in online contexts?

## 4. Receptivity to Innovation and Change
Online delivery of music education seeks to combine traditional and new technologies. As online initiatives increase, the challenge will be to find ways to live out the social and collaborative process of music learning and making in this digital environment and, at the same time, enable processes that lead to personal expression. There is a need to explore and understand the relationships between online delivery and face-to-face music education models, an issue that is particularly important given current levels of skepticism, and even fear, that exist among music teachers — skepticism relating to the value of online teaching and learning generally, and fear that face-to-face traditional contexts will be replaced by online formats. Ongoing communication and professional development are needed to confront these concerns.

## 5. Program Evaluation
Program evaluation/assessment incorporates both student performance data and critical analysis of content and instructional design as a means of determining whether a program is achieving its intended outcomes. Web-based music education courses need periodic external assessment to ensure agreement with appropriate instructional design, current pedagogical practices, and relevance of content. Part of this assessment should consider compliance and alignment with the provincially prescribed course as evidenced in the published curriculum guides. These courses and their curriculum guides are developed by teams of music education professionals who represent a cross-section of discipline knowledge. Online versions of the same courses are currently developed by a single e-music educator. This process has the potential to skew a course and its instructional plan

according to individual preferences and biases. With limited expertise in this area globally, there exists the need to develop a means for objective and consistent program review and evaluation relating to online course development and delivery in the province.

## 6. Teacher Education and Professional Development

A key area to be examined in e-teaching and learning in music education is the attention currently being given to the education (pre-service, in-service, and professional development) of e-music teachers and on-site management teams. There exist great opportunities and potential now to develop both face-to-face and online training and professional development in areas that are specific to K–12 music education. There are opportunities also to examine existing teacher education models in light of including the study of e-teaching and e-learning components (e.g., content, strategies, technologies), and to develop and document new pedagogies surrounding e-music teaching and learning. The need to include this new component in our teacher preparation programs means that e-teaching and e-learning components must also be aligned with ongoing professional development opportunities and contexts (e.g., institutes, seminars).

## 7. E-Teaching, Learning, and Cultural Production

In view of its effect on a culture's artistic content, the Internet can be regarded as having a double-edged sword. There was a time when the only way for a person to be exposed to a piece of art/music was to experience it first-hand, and, historically, many people were rarely exposed to artistic material outside of their local culture. As a result, the art of that culture was isolated and protected. With the advent of TV, radio, and the Internet, individuals can experience artistic content from virtually any culture, which can have the effect of diluting people's perception and valuing of their own culture's artistic content. On the other side of the sword, the Internet makes a culture's artistic content accessible to anyone worldwide wishing to experience it. This global audience can create opportunities for artists and musicians and help to strengthen their culture's identity by raising the appreciation level for its artistry and content. Through the music courses currently offered by CDLI, teachers are attempting to instill and nurture an appreciation for Newfoundland and Labrador culture in students. If students appreciate their culture's own artistic content and understand the positive and negative effects the Internet and globalization can have, they may be able to individually and collectively use the Internet to engage in and ultimately make and grow (i.e., produce) their own cultures. Access to global cultures is now a key factor in broadening our students' exposure to and experiences with a varied repertoire of musics, cultural traditions, and practices. Synchronous technologies allow for musical and dialogical interactions with musicians and culture bearers throughout the world. The ongoing production of music and culture by our students and emerging musicians will certainly be influenced by this opportunity.

## 8. Community Access

Music-based content is currently restricted to the high school students who access CDLI courses. The success of a variety of lifelong learning initiatives (e.g., New Horizon's Band programs) suggests the existence of a demographic population outside of the schools that is interested in music and music education yet currently excluded from the province's online learning initiatives. Extending access to a wider community of youth and adult learners provides a potential area for future growth. Current school-based initiatives in the province include the provision of professional development experiences in online and web-based teaching and learning resources for all music teachers. These teachers can now avail themselves of, and adapt as appropriate, the new and ever-emerging online technologies and resources as they teach in traditional spaces and contexts.

## 9. Research Funding and Support

Financial support for instructional and technological research and innovation is necessary in order to facilitate the growth of and protect current investments in K–12 music-based e-teaching and learning. While there exists some research pertaining to postsecondary online contexts, there is an urgent need and demand for new research to focus around bridging theory and practice in online K–12 music classrooms, investigations of classroom technological applications, transitions from teaching in the traditional classroom to the digital classroom, the changing role of instructional design in curriculum development, and the changing nature or music and music education as it now "lives" in the virtual world.

## Research Initiatives and Future Directions

Though e-learning and teaching in secondary music education contexts is a new pedagogical approach in Newfoundland and Labrador, and indeed the world, a number of recent research initiatives are emerging to provide a foundation for the future development of virtual classrooms. In 2003, CDLI supported the development of a foundational document on web-based music education courses (Rose, 2003). In 2005, the Departments of Education and Tourism, Culture, and Recreation commissioned a one-year study (*State of the Art: Music and Cultural Education in Newfoundland*

*and Labrador* [Rose, 2006]) that resulted in a report with implications for the ongoing development of e-teaching and learning in music education, as well as for the creation of potential collaborations between government, MUN, CDLI, and the VTC. In March 2006, the Community-University Research Alliance (CURA) Program, funded by the Social Sciences and Humanities Research Council of Canada, was created to foster innovative research and training, and to generate new knowledge about e-learning, particularly as it relates to opportunities in isolated rural areas. In addition to these specific initiatives, a number of related master's theses and projects have recently been completed at MUN on this topic. Relevant projects include: (1) a study of learner-centredness and the development of learning objects for web-based music education (Mercer, 2007); (2) a critical case study of issues and challenges in developing Experiencing Music 2200 for web-based delivery (Nakashima, 2009); and (3) a critical-constructivist study of the perceptions of students, teachers, administrators, and policy makers of distance learning in Newfoundland and Labrador (Bennett, 2010).

**Emerging Questions**
These initial research initiatives provide the basis for future developments in virtual teaching environments, but also suggest a broad range of questions for future investigation. Some of these emerging questions include:

*1. Equality of Access*
Do all students in CDLI-qualifying schools have unfettered, discretionary access to online music education? Will increased accessibility to online materials/resources be made available to all teachers and students in the province? Might this lead to an improvement in the delivery of classroom music programming throughout the province? Are online opportunities providing increased access to specialist/expert teachers in the music?

*2. Communication, Collaboration, and Social Interaction*
Are there sufficient levels of teacher-student, student-student, teacher/student-artist interactions built into the instructional plans for online courses? Are there effective opportunities to make music and art socially and to engage with practising artists/musicians? Will growth in online music programming lead to increased opportunities for building on community/local resources, expertise, and tradition/culture bearers?

*3. Social Interaction and Human Relationships*
How do teachers and students deal with emotional and physical needs as well as cognitive ones in regard to learning, individually and collectively?

What are the effects of the changing relationships between student-student and teacher-student as they occur in virtual contexts?

### 4. Online Learning in Traditional Contexts

What is/might be the potential social and cultural impacts of the introduction of networks/technologies into "traditional" small, rural, and isolated communities and its school(s)? How will/might these technologies affect the educational, social, and cultural contexts of these communities? Might there be opportunities for these schools that are now outfitted with state-of-the-art technologies to play a significant role in rural and economic development for the province?

### 5. Pedagogy

Does/will e-music education, as an alternative mode of program delivery, improve the quality of and increase accessibility to music education provided to rural students? Are teachers' and students' needs and interests met/enhanced in online formats? Is music teaching effective in these new contexts? Are e-music students meeting intended outcomes of curriculum? Is there indeed enhancement of individualized attention and learning through this medium? What is the impact of small classes, much one-to-one teacher/student interaction, and flexible scheduling on motivation, retention, and achievement in music education? Amid ever-changing technologies, is there an appropriate balance between the learning and the management of these technologies?

### 6. Diversity

Might web-based music programming lead to increased possibilities and opportunities for addressing student diversity, engagement, and choice (e.g., pacing, timing, and depth and breadth of experiences for both gifted and special needs students)?

### 7. Nature of Music Education

How might the nature and status of music education be transformed in web-based delivery formats? As new contexts and technologies emerge, how will thinking and practice in music (as an art from) and music education be shaped?

### 8. Role of Music in Culture and Society

How might the nature and role of music be transformed in culture and society? As new ways of making and learning music are created and practised in online formats, what new artistic/cultural traditions are being/

might be created? Is there a new musical identity emerging in Newfoundland and Labrador as well as in culture and society at large? What *is* this new identity and musical culture?

### 9. Professional Development for Teachers
Might greater awareness of and experiences with e-teaching and learning in secondary music education in Newfoundland and Labrador lead to an increased emphasis on the need for professional development for all music teachers, especially in regard to mastery of technology?

### 10. Change and Innovation
Might web-based music programming lead to increased possibilities for "new" experiential and hands-on learning modes (e.g., new sounds, symbols, forms) in music education generally? How might these innovations have an impact on developing effective and meaningful creative contexts in music education?

### 11. Leadership and Globalization
Might web-based music programming lead to increased possibilities for the nurturing and development of an expanded world/global view and experiences, perspectives, and interactions? What is this province's role, and indeed Canada's role, in developing leadership capacity in the area of e-music teaching and learning? Is this of general interest and importance to us?

## Opportunities
In Newfoundland and Labrador, e-teaching and learning contexts have been created out of a very real need to provide education in general, and music education in particular, to students living in a province that is small in population and vast in geography. Virtual environments now provide unique opportunities for students to interact with music specialist teachers as well as with community music makers, professionals, and each other, regardless of their respective locations. For example, students in remote communities in Labrador are able to be taught and mentored by students and faculty at Memorial University through online, synchronous workshops and master classes. Similarly, teachers and students in St. John's can investigate Inuit musical and cultural traditions through the use of e-learning technologies. In the current application of e-learning, the focus is principally on the delivery of high school courses. There is, however, enormous potential for e-learning technologies to be integrated into traditional classrooms, allowing for the enrichment of current curriculum and the sharing of learning with the community beyond the schools. Things such

as podcasts, video clips, learning objects, lesson extensions, online professional development, artistic production demonstrations tutorials, access to
performances and exhibitions — or contact with musicians from disparate
locations — can enrich traditional music programs. Virtual learning environments make integrating these experiences into classrooms across the
province — regardless of location and community resources — an achiev-
able possibility.

   While there is general agreement that online settings have created exciting and new opportunities for music teaching and learning, there is also
acknowledgement that there exist real challenges. Many of these challenges
are reflected in the questions posed earlier in this chapter. One of the greatest challenges facing educators in general is how to deal with "physicality"
in a virtual environment. In music education, we are continuously exploring ways to "do" and "perform" music in authentic and meaningful ways.
How does the social and collaborative nature of music get lived out when
students may be separated from each other, and from the music teacher,
by hundreds of miles? Through constant research and experimentation,
new technologies are utilized and adapted to attempt to meet these challenges (some have been described earlier in this chapter). There rests a huge
responsibility for the e-music teacher to play many roles (e.g., researcher,
instructional designer, technician, musician, educator) and dance deli-
cately between the needs and interests of individual students, available
technologies and resources, and the integrity of the music curriculum.
The goal now is to develop a solid strategy for ongoing development and
growth, one that includes research and knowledge acquisition, human
capacity building, teacher education, and professional development.

## Conclusions

Through this case study, we have examined how e-teaching and learning provide new possibilities for music and cultural education in Newfoundland and Labrador. The provincial Department of Education, CDLI,
NLTA, and MUN are currently leading the development of this field
through innovative application of evolving technologies to the creation of
new instructional designs and course offerings. School, community, and
musician/artist collaborations are currently under way and recent research
initiatives are in place to help explore the many questions, problems, and
challenges that have been noted throughout this chapter. One of the most
important questions yet to be answered is how the application of e-teaching and learning to music education will influence the development of
Newfoundland and Labrador society and culture. Previous research has
established that there is a significant relationship between K–12 music

education and cultural reproduction and production in general (Rose, 1990). Hence, we are reminded of the importance to continuously take time to reflect on, examine, and analyze the potential connections between e-teaching and learning in music education and traditional forms of music curriculum delivery. We need also to be conscious of how school-based e-teaching and learning in music contexts and practices may ultimately serve the ever-transforming nature and role of the music and artists in culture and society. Might we see new forms of music emerge from our students, music classrooms, and communities? Might we see new brands of musical identities emerging in those students and teachers immersed in virtual contexts? Might music education be assisted, through these new and ever-emerging technological applications and pedagogies, in becoming even more relevant to local and global contexts? Might music and the arts in general be created in ways beyond even the currently imagined?

It is our hope that this description of current e-music education contexts in Newfoundland and Labrador, and our many questions posed throughout the chapter, will both set the stage for and encourage needed local/global research and critical analysis pertaining to the new practice of delivering K–12 curricular-based music education in online (synchronous and asynchronous) contexts.

## Notes

1 This chapter is based on a paper presented at Symposium 2008: Post-Confederation Education Reform — From Rhetoric to Reality (May 7–9, 2008), Memorial University, St. John's, NL.

2 Elluminate Live functions as a classroom in which primary learning interactions between teacher and students occur. In the words of an e-art teacher, Elluminate Live is important "to convey such course materials as slide shows, to conduct demonstrations and web tours of galleries, to demonstrate concepts stored in video clips, on YouTube, and to use the web camera to illustrate a technique such as gesture or contour drawing" (J. Deeley, personal communication, April 7, 2008).

## References

Barrett, H. C. (1998). *Electronic portfolios*. Retrieved from http://www.electronic portfolios.com/ portfolios/encyclopediaentry.htm.

Bauer, W., & Dunn, R. E. (2003). Digital reflection: The electronic portfolio in music teacher education. *Journal of Music Teacher Education, 13*(1), 7–20.

Bennett, K. W. (2010). *A case study of perceptions of students, teachers, and administrators on distance learning and music education in Newfoundland and Labrador: A constructivist perspective.* Unpublished master's thesis, Memorial University of Newfoundland, St. John's.

Boone, W. (2008). *The evolution of e-learning in small rural schools in Newfoundland and Labrador.* Unpublished manuscript.

Davis B., Sumara, D., & Luce-Kapler, R. (2000). *Engaging minds: Learning and teaching in a complex world.* Mahwah, NJ: Lawrence Erlbaum Associates.

Government of Newfoundland and Labrador. (1976). *Art 1201.* Retrieved from http://www.ed.gov.nl.ca/edu/sp/shart.htm.

Government of Newfoundland and Labrador. (1994). *Experiencing music 2200 curriculum guide.* Retrieved from http://www.ed.gov.nl.ca/edu/sp/music2200.htm.

Government of Newfoundland and Labrador. (1996). *Applied music 2206 curriculum guide.* Retrieved from http://www.ed.gov.nl.ca/edu/sp/music_2206_3206 .htm.

Government of Newfoundland and Labrador. (2000). *Supporting learning: report of the ministerial panel on educational delivery in the classroom.* Retrieved from http://www.edu.gov.nf.ca/panel/panel.pdf.

Government of Newfoundland and Labrador. (2007). *The centre—mandate.* Retrieved from http://www.cdli.ca/index.php?PID=AnnounceFull& NewsID=6612.

Government of Newfoundland and Labrador. (n.d. a). Art and design 2200-3200 draft. Retrieved http://www.ed.gov.nl.ca/edu/sp/sh/Art/art_design 2200-3200/ a_d.htm.

Government of Newfoundland and Labrador. (n.d. b). *Foundation for the province of Newfoundland and Labrador music education curriculum.* Retrieved from http://www.ed.gov.nl.ca/edu/sp/foundations/art/music_found.pdf.

Greher, G. R. (2006). Transforming music teacher preparation through the lens of video technology. *Journal of Music Teacher Education, 15*(2), 40–60.

Hargis, J., & Wilson, D. (2005). *Fishing for learning with podcast net.* Retrieved from http://www.unf.edu/dept/cirt/tech/podcast/HargisPodcastArticle.pdf.

Historical Foundation of Canada. (2008). *Provincial school broadcasts.* Retrieved from http://www.thecanadianencyclopedia.com/index.cfm?PgNm=TCE& Params= U1SEC840949.

House, M., & Keough, E. (1989). *Telemedicine and distance education: The Memorial University of Newfoundland experience.* World Prosperity through Communications, IEEE International Conference, Boston, MA.

Mercer, A. (2007). *Web-based music education: An exploration of learning objects as examined through the lens of the American Psychological Association's Learner-Centered Psychological Principles.* Unpublished master's thesis, Memorial University of Newfoundland, St. John's.

Mugridge, I., & Kaufman, D. (Eds.). (1986). *Distance education in Canada.* London: Croomhelm.

Nakashima, J. (2009). *Experiencing music 2200 online: A critical case study of the curriculum transfer process.* Unpublished master's thesis, Memorial University of Newfoundland, St. John's.

Noseworthy, R. P. (1997). *The school car: Bringing the three r's to Newfoundland's railway settlements (1936–1942).* Whitbourne, NL: R. P. N. Publishing.

Rose, A. (1990). *Music education in culture: A critical analysis of reproduction, production and hegemony.* Unpublished doctoral dissertation, University of Wisconsin, Madison.

Rose, A. (2003). *The role of distance learning in music education — Theory to prac-tice*. St. John's. NL: Centre for Distance Learning and Innovation, Government of Newfoundland and Labrador and Memorial University.

Rose, A. (2006). *State of the art: Music and cultural education in Newfoundland and Labrador*. St. John's, NL: Dept. of Education and Dept. of Tourism, Culture and Recreation, Government of Newfoundland and Labrador.

Virtual Teacher Centre. (2004). *External report*. Retrieved from http://www.virtualteachercentre.ca/pd/uploads/External_Report.pdf.

# ELEVEN

# Focusing on Critical Practice and Insights in the Music Teacher Education Curriculum

*Betty Anne Younker*

## Introduction

The profession of music education encompasses multiple aspects, including educating students (1) in school-based settings, (2) in undergraduate programs for those who will go on to teach in school-based settings, and (3) in graduate programs for those who currently teach in school-based settings. In each, it is essential that students be thoughtfully engaged as they think in and about music. For those who work with prospective music teachers in university settings, it is imperative that questions be asked about the diverse student population that they may teach, the content that will be covered, and the way in which their students will be engaged with music, thus positing questions about the who, what, and how of teaching. Such an examination should include thinking that is critical and that contributes to one's reflective practice. To think critically about the various aspects of music education and reflect on one's practice can contribute to growth and evolution at the individual and professional levels.

This chapter, then, is about critical thinking and reflective practice, the definitions and characteristics of each, the relationships between the two, and the applications to students' development as thinking musicians throughout their undergraduate experience, all of which can inform the profession about structure and process of curriculum. With an aim to transform curriculum through the lens of critical thinking and reflective practice, the chapter closes with suggestions for curricular renewal, in terms of structures and process, for undergraduate curricula in North American schools of music.

With the inception of Schools of Music in the United States, circa 1900 (Mark, 1996), came criteria for core curriculum and requirements for specific degree programs in music, which continue to be "felt" in schools of music across North America. Present curricula are grounded in the Western European conservatory model that consists of a required set of core courses in music theory, music history, aural skills, studio, ensemble, and piano. While there has been minimal change in the content of the core curriculum since the inception of Schools of Music, there has been an increasing dialogue about pedagogical issues with a focus on critical thinking, reflective practice, and engaged learning with students serving as change agents within the profession (e.g., Bowman, 2002; Woodford, 2005).

Based on various philosophical writings about education, early writers within the growing field of psychology, such as John Dewey, began to examine issues of teaching and learning. From these early writings, there grew a divide between those who supported a traditional method based on behaviourism (e.g., Thorndike) and those who supported a progressive notion of education (e.g., Dewey). This divide still remains; however, some believe that both exist in various forms across a continuum that is more context-based.

Typically speaking, a traditional method of education is one in which textbooks and faculty serve as the "owners" of knowledge, with the transmission or transaction of knowledge flowing from the faculty member to students. Students are assessed through paper-and-pencil testing, some of which includes standardized tests, and behaviours of teaching and learning are studied empirically. The belief is that behaviours can be modified and changed according to expectations outlined by those of authority.

A progressive model of education, espoused since Dewey and still embraced today by leading educators and business people (e.g., Goodlad, 2004; Friedman, 2005), involves students being transformed through active engagement with content that requires flexibility, adaptability, curiosity, and imagination (e.g., Dewey, 1938; Eisner, 1998; Bransford, Brown, & Cocking, 2000; Goodlad, 2004). Performances of understanding might involve pencil-and-paper tests, but also projects, performances, debates, interviews, speeches, and papers, to name a few.

Integral to critical thinking is the acceptance that (1) learners come to the classroom with much to offer and construct new understandings with minds that are curious and evaluative; (2) the focus is not just on the content, method, or theory, but on the student; and (3) both teacher and learner shift on a continuum between teaching and learning as reflective practitioners. This acceptance serves as an underlying premise for this chapter, which examines critical thinking and reflective practice as the theoretical framework for considering implications for the undergraduate music experience.

### Theoretical Framework[1]

A variety of writers who have offered definitions for critical thinking and described how such thinking is experienced have done so in the context of learning (e.g., Ennis, 1980, 1987; McPeck, 1981, 1984, 1990; Paul, 1987, 1993; Noddings, 2004; Bransford et al., 2000; Woodford, 2005). One underlying influence on these authors' thinking is the work of Dewey (1933/1991), who identified critical thinking as the ability to respond to an experienced dissonance by examining and re-examining held assumptions before adopting an action or belief as conclusions are reached (see also Bowman, 2002, 2005; Jorgensen, 2003). These actions include identifying, framing, and solving problems; generating and evaluating possible solutions; converging on a solution; and further evaluating that solution in a context (Dewey, 1933/1991). Recent writers have echoed that this process of critical thinking is an integral part of learning. For example, Noddings (2004) reminds us that "critical thinkers raise questions about claims and about the motives of those who make them, they identify logical flaws in arguments, they evaluate the premises from which arguments are launched, they search for evidence to support claims, and they explore the likely consequences of proposed actions" (p. 489). Examining and re-examining held assumptions stifles dogmatic and anti-intellectual thinking, and assumes critical inquiry as the norm, and thus as the habit of an inquiring mind (Bowman, 2002). More recent writers (e.g., McPeck, 1981, 1984, 1990; Ennis, 1980, 1987; and Paul, 1987, 1993) expand upon Dewey's initial definitions and offer specific dispositions and abilities (see Younker, 2002, for expansions of these definitions and applications to research in music education).

At the centre of Dewey's thinking on learning is the notion of "experienced-based education," a theme that became prominent in a variety of Dewey's writings within the contexts of progressive education (1938) and experiences with art (1934), and later in the writings of those who espoused constructivism (e.g., Bruner, 1960, 1996). These writings reflect teaching and learning as "a continuous reconstruction of experience," in which students are involved in educative experiences, that is, in experiences that generate, as opposed to impede, growth. Educative experiences produce sensitivity and responsiveness; connect with the past and future; provide challenges that are accessible and yet evoke reflection; involve active and persistent inquiry that is mindful; and are organic as experiences are constructed and re-constructed (Vygotsky, 1978; Bruner, 1996; Bransford et al., 2000; Noddings, 2004).

Integral to these experiences is the kind of thinking that makes interpretative judgments about complex issues (King & Kitchener, 1994) within the students' discipline. With this action comes responsibility for interpretations and decisions that involve judgment making. The process of critical inquiry, which contributes to reflective judgment, goes beyond simple logic or formulas (both of which involve types of critical thinking) in that it involves identifying relevant facts, formulas, and theories, and also generating solutions to bring closure to situations that are uncertain or controversial (Dewey, 1933/1991, 1938). The opposite side of this involves accepting formulaic, logical solutions that do not involve controversy or doubt, that provide answers for the present, and that dominate absolute and preconceived assumptions. This notion of absolutism allows for the generation of "truths" and the pervasion of dogmatic thinking. With this notion, there is no room for the "messiness" of reflective judgment, which requires continuous examination of beliefs and assumptions, and experiences the limitations of data and the investigator. In the continuous, messy, constructive world of critical inquiry, there are only beliefs that are always questioned and only meaningful when viewed as situated in socially and culturally contextual settings (Vygotsky, 1978; Lave & Wenger, 1991; Bruner, 1996; Wiggins, 2001; Jorgensen, 2003; Bowman, 2005).

In addition to writings relevant to progressive education, Dewey (1934) wrote extensively about the artistic (aesthetic) experience within the framework of critical (reflective) thinking. He believed that "educative" interaction with the arts could transform and promote growth affectively and otherwise. Essential to the transformation and growth through artistic experiences is the role of critical thinking. One is reflective as the art works on the artist and the artist works on the art during creation and re-creation. Integral during the process is mindful involvement as problems are identified, solutions are generated, choices are made, and evaluation occurs. This is what artists do as they create and re-create. The process can be messy, constructive, and uncertain (Jorgensen, 2008). If the desire is to nurture such thinking in our students, then we need to engage students in what artists (musicians) do — that is, thinking about and within music during the process while reflecting on the product. Enabling these engagements fosters musical experiences that are educative and transformative, and involves students as mindful human beings who learn to negotiate the uncertainty of life. Bowman (2005) reminds us that education, including arts education, must prepare us for the unknown through critical inquiry and curiosity, which leads to growth. Being knowledgeable when creating art, then, requires one to be thoughtful and engaged; creating the art requires the intertwining of process and product (Bowman, 2005), all of which contributes to growth as an artist and as a connoisseur of art.

### The Role of Critical Thinking in Reflective Practice

Instead of training teachers to be technicians — that is, to realize specific practices and theories in a "recipe" fashion — we need to ensure that they are reflective practitioners (Schon, 1987) who are required to reason through options before choosing and to justify choices as decisions are made. A necessary activity of being an educator is diagnosing specific situations, designing appropriate activities, improvising instructional strategies, and evaluating changes for future situations (Jorgenson, 2001) while interacting with colleagues, peers, and mentors (Bruner, 1996; Schon, 1987). Reflective practice is engaging in one's practice through critical thinking and includes improvising throughout the process of active translation (Schon, 1987). Throughout, ideas are experienced, examined, and clarified as dialogue within each of them occurs, resulting in new possibilities (Merleau-Ponty, 1964). Thus openings are found and choices made — a critical aspect of teaching and learning (Greene, 1995) — and ambiguity, doubt, and dissonances are experienced. In such dialectical or paradoxical worlds (Jorgensen, 2001) options are less clear-cut, and thus critical thinking is necessary as teachers embrace ambivalence, vulnerability, surprise, and joy as found in the classroom; and all while learning occurs.

A critical, but often neglected aim, when preparing future teachers for these paradoxical worlds is to "inculcate habits of mind" to think (Bowman, 2002, 2005). Requiring students to question and inquire and to value curiosity should constitute foundational aspects of education. This concern has been raised in educational circles, including music education (e.g., Allsup, 2003; Jorgensen, 2003; Woodford, 2005) and visual art education (see Galbraith, 2002, for a summary of research in visual art education that focuses on questioning strategies and conversations in classrooms). Questioning, inquiring, and being curious in communities of learning involve all participants, who are recognized as stakeholders and knowledge bearers, and who construct understanding and meaning through active participation. Bruner (1996) often queries about who "owns" the knowledge and who is expected to be the knowledge bearer, with the understanding that all participants bring valuable understanding and knowledge to the communities of learning. Oftentimes, it is assumed that only the teachers are knowledge bearers and that it is their job to *give it* to students. In classes where students are required to question and construct understanding in collaboration with others, a realization occurs at the individual level that the teacher is not the sole "owner" of knowledge, but that the students also have knowledge. This recognizes the wealth of knowledge that is to be shared, constructed, and understood as a community. Hence, a community of learners is recognized and valued, the focus becomes learning and not teaching, and the examination of pedagogic practices focuses on intra- and inter-engagement and activity that is organic.

If we adopt the same frame of mind that school-based music programs should be communities of music activity, then the pedagogical approach becomes clear. "Creating and opening spaces" (Allsup, 2003) includes actions of discovery as decisions are made. This process reflects "a material process of democracy" — i.e., "democratic action" (p. 35) — which allows for experiences of individual and collaborative musical worlds that emerge from the music-making processes. During this process, constraints and freedoms are formed at individual and collective levels (Burnard & Younker, 2004) as students are engaged in musical problems not unlike those encountered by performers, composers, musicologists, and music theorists. Involving students in musical problems as encountered in daily musical lives requires thoughtful, reflective, and contributing minds, and resembles project-based learning, which in turn resembles working and learning as a musician. This differs from the traditionalist approach in which textbooks and teachers serve as the transmitters of content and assessment depends on the packaging, distribution, and standardizing of teaching and learning (Goodlad, 2004). With the flattening of the world in terms of technology-based information, the focus becomes less on teacher-directed learning, in which students are given information, and more on student-centred learning, in which students are required to utilize information when solving problems (Friedman, 2005); we have moved from an information to a conceptual age. Such constructive learning (e.g., Bruner, 1960) and project-based learning in music exemplifies a contextual, experience-based learning; the structure, and thus experience, is non-linear, and the process and product are equally noted and valued.

One example of the kind of learning as described above is the work by Jaffurs (2004), who described not only her discovery about the community of learners that existed among a group of her students, but how her observation of that group of students in their learning environment became a transformative experience and a catalyst for reflecting on her own practice. Using the thinking of those who have written extensively about practices in formal and informal music education (e.g., Green, 2002; Small, 1998), Jaffurs conducted an ethnographic study to "describe a developing 'rock group'" (p. 189). She experienced a rich reflection on her own practice, all of which led her to understanding the many lessons she learned from the group's collaborative practice of music making. This study clearly identified the knowledge bearers and how social construction can occur in collaborative practices (Wiggins, 2001) as well as the power of transformative experiences (Jorgensen, 2003).

### The Practice: Thinking Musically and Critically about Music

How do experiences of self-reflectiveness in life, with all of its pluralities, contribute to creating habits of mind such as curiosity, imagination, and inquiry (Greene, 1995)? How can there be consistent thoughtfulness on and in one's practice that demands asking questions and challenging ideas for clarity and authenticity? Those who write about educative environments that are relevant, meaningful, and student-directed suggest that the classroom must reflect life and consist of a constant stopping and thinking, attending to all that is encountered (e.g., Adams, 2000; Goodlad, 2004). This is in contrast to submissively accepting that which is given (Woodford, 2005) and promoting the growth of passive receptacles in which knowledge remains inert (North Whitehead, 1929). There needs to be an explicit acceptance that students will be required to think musically and critically about music throughout their courses.

The questions, therefore, that need to be asked when constructing coursework for undergraduate music students include, but are not limited to, these initial queries:

1. How do musicians think and act?
2. How do musicologists think and act?
3. How do music theorists think and act?
4. How do music educators think and act?
5. How do composers think and act?

If we accept that students are to be involved in the problems of the profession — that is, as active agents in the process of learning — and that content is to be relevant and known, then initial questions must uncover how musicians address uncertain or unique situations by "devising new methods of reasoning ... and constructing and testing new categories of understanding, strategies of action, and ways of framing problems" (Schon, 1987, p. 39). By understanding the rules, operations, and techniques within a context, the necessary knowledge base is provided to generate and assess new possibilities, and to continue to generate new forms of understanding and action. The following section examines how undergraduate curricula, typically found in Schools of Music, are constructed, and presents suggestions for possible curriculum renewal.

## Curriculum Renewal
### Redefining the Structures
For the most part, Schools of Music undergraduate curricula consist of sets of courses that are required for specific degree programs. The structures often are the same as those found in course syllabi and may contain, but may not be limited to, answers given to the following questions: Why is this course offered? What are the rationale and objectives of the course? How will students be assessed? What content will be covered? To whom is the course directed? When will the class meet? Where will the class meet?

The focus, then, is the content, materials, and subject — as opposed to the student, the student's fund of understanding, musical problems, and the processes of inquiry. While individual professors may incorporate problem-based approaches and content known to the student, the professor with reference to the textbook often determines the content.

To transform a curriculum based on the above questions into one that is flexible and fluid, one that makes critical inquiry explicit, and one that involves students in the profession of music making and thinking about music, we need to examine the supportive infrastructure for systemic changes that directly affect the system as a whole in response to such questions as why, how, to whom, where, and what. This inquiry can occur only if all stakeholders within the school of music are consulted. As a collective whole, the questions that begin with "why," "how," "to whom," where," and "what" would be investigated to determine the effectiveness of and relationships within and among the various departments. How efficiently and effectively are both faculty time and school resources being used? What are the goals of the department? What are the assumptions about the why, how, and what? And why are such assumptions influencing curriculum decisions? What is being conserved and why? Are we preparing students for day-to-day musical problems or just possible future jobs? Should all students complete the same broad array of courses as found in present-day core curriculum, or can the core be constructed around the ways in which musicians engage with musical problems? Would this restructuring allow for multiple offerings, thereby allowing individual students to become more enriched in specific areas after a core is experienced? Would such a restructuring allow for greater depth and less breadth, and an understanding of the vast availability of knowledge and the increasingly critical need for knowing what to do with the knowledge as constructive contributors to the profession (Friedman, 2005)? Would such restructuring make better use of faculty members' areas of research and provide a connectedness between the student and the faculty member's research and performance specialties? Responses to and implementation of the many possibilities generated throughout the process of answering these questions would require a culture renewal, a process that extends far beyond infusions of reform and requires more substantial changes than do infusions of reform. Many reforms are short-lived in that they allow for temporary changes as opposed to long-term renewal (Goodlad, 2004, p. 224).

*Redefining the Process*
Using the theoretical framework outlined earlier, we can view the process of education as combining what is done in the practice, and how it is done, with the inclusion of critical-thinking abilities and dispositions (Donovan, Bransford, & Pellegrino, 1999; Ferguson, 2004). In such experiences, students would construct (make things), be involved in inquiry (as they find out), express themselves artistically (show their musical understanding), and communicate what they understand (Dewey, 1938). Traditionally, students attend classes, memorize, recall, pass exams, complete papers, and pass proficiency tests all within what Dewey (1938) refers to as "watertight compartments" (p. 48). Within a progressive approach to education, Dewey suggested that students are active agents in the learning experience, and thus are required to access their fund of experience to bring understanding to the present context. So what could this look like in an undergraduate music education curriculum that spans the freshman and sophomore years?

A starting point would be to examine present content and students' involvement with that content across courses within the core curriculum and music education programs, and, in turn, compare those findings with how those in the field think and act (Schon, 1987). From the comparative analysis, one could begin to organize content and expectations so that students' involvement would represent the actions and thinking processes of those in the field — i.e., musicologists, music theorists, music educators, composers, and performers. The next step would be to identify characteristics of the students' musical worlds and compare those with the developed disciplines that are typically interpreted in traditional coursework. This would reveal the relevancy of musical problems and content encountered in their present world and how it differs from or is similar to content and actions required in typical courses within core curriculum and music education programs. This would allow for structures to be developed that enable meaningful relationships between what is known and what is newly acquired (i.e., associational learning), thus enhancing understanding of newly constructed knowledge and skills. During this process, students could explore the present musical world within music history, music theory, and music education courses; investigate new knowledge; and make comparisons between what they discover and what is known, gradually expanding knowledge about musical cultures, styles, and genres through inquiry and performance. Throughout, students would be required to problem solve, reason, communicate, conjecture, and represent their understanding through multiple means, including performances, critiques, interviews, journals, presentations, abstracts, analysis, teaching, conducting, and reporting. These processes of engagement require understanding of previously encountered content and allow for (1) the application of intelligence to new contexts, (2) an understanding of how present knowledge and skills are related to new knowledge and skills, and (3) the development of insights about the organizational structures of each discipline and possible interrelationships among the disciplines (e.g., music history, music theory, music education, composition, studio, ensemble, piano class). Throughout, transfer would be made not only possible, but explicit (Donovan et al., 1999; Bransford et al., 2000).

*A Possible Model*
What is offered below is a skeleton of a model that could serve as a beginning structure for a redefined core curriculum. The model is based on the theoretical framework as provided earlier in this chapter and reflective of the suggestions for curriculum renewal. To adopt such a beginning, the following is necessary: (1) acknowledging the importance of students' fund of experience (Dewey, 1933/1991; 1938); (2) embracing a constructivist's approach (Bruner, 1996), which has roots in Dewey's notion of educative experiences; and (3) accepting that critically thinking about music and thinking musically are at the core of all experiences (see Dewey, 1938, 1933/1991; Schon, 1987; Bransford et al., 2000; Noddings, 2004). For students to think critically about something they must have ownership of related facts and skills. For an arena of understanding new facts and skills to exist, activities must begin with what the students know and under-

**Figure 11.1**  *A Suggested Model for a Redefined Core Curriculum*

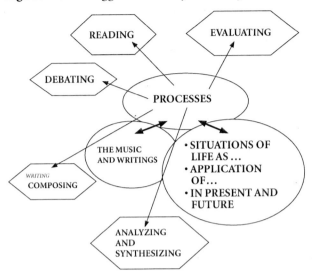

stand, and how they can act on what they know and understand. Students can think critically as new understandings are acquired, and not just serve as receptacles of knowledge for periods of time before they can interact with the knowledge.

### The Nuts and Bolts: Reflective Practice

How might we construct a course in core music curriculum that involves understanding content; cultivating artistry; thinking like musicologists, theorists, performers, composers, and educators; and inculcates habits of mind for lifelong learning and involved citizenship? Using the above model as a guide, this section provides possible processes and content within the areas of musicology, music theory, performance, composition, and music education. The examples are not meant to be comprehensive, but rather to serve as a guide for generating further involvement. Content of the courses would include music and readings about the lives of musicologists, theorists, composers, music educators, and performers.

*Musicology, Music Theory, and Composition*

A musicologist could teach the following in two class periods per week, and a music theorist in two class periods per week, with the fifth class being reserved for tutorials about applying the materials in music composition.

Guiding questions:
1. How do musicologists think, apply understanding, and utilize methods of inquiry?
2. How do music theorists think, apply understanding, and utilize methods of inquiry?
3. How do composers think, apply understanding, and utilize methods of inquiry?

Readings:
1. historical narratives and representations;
2. archives to identify the past and present situations, to infer relationships between them, and to determine relevancy to present investigations; and
3. lives of composers and descriptions of their processes.

Debating:
1. reasons for studying the disciplines;
2. the study of music within and extracted from its context;
3. the functions of music across genres and styles; and
4. the representations of people in opera and musical theatre productions.

Writing:
1. descriptions of music;
2. critiques of music performed;
3. descriptions of musical performances;
4. critiques of musical performances;
5. summaries of musical reviews;
6. critiques of musical reviews; and
7. music within parameters determined by style and genre, with guidelines for each exercise determined by the instructor and student.

Analyzing and synthesizing:
1. reading about, debating, and listening to music and musical materials;
2. identifying issues (problems) and generating solutions; and
3. identifying perceptions and understandings of the authors who wrote the materials encountered throughout the semester.

Evaluating:
1. own performances and creations;
2. own reviews and critiques;
3. peers' performances; and
4. peers' reviews and critiques.

*Performance*

Guiding questions:

1. How do performers think, apply understanding, and utilize methods of inquiry?
2. How do I as a performer think, apply understanding, and utilize methods of inquiry?

Debating:

1. knowledge gained in music history and music theory courses as musical problems are encountered and solutions offered throughout rehearsals and performances;
2. my own and others' performance practices; and
3. musical solutions.

Analyzing and synthesizing:

1. investigating, analyzing, and reflecting on the related performance practices encountered in music history, theory, and studio classes; and
2. practising, refining, and performing music created by others and by myself.

Evaluating:

1. own performances; and
2. peers' performances.

*Music Education*

Guiding question:

1. How do music educators think, apply understanding, and utilize methods of inquiry?

Reading and writing:

1. philosophies of music teaching and learning;
2. research methodologies of music teaching and learning;
3. curricula of music teaching and learning;
4. psychologies of music teaching and learning;
5. sociological aspects of music teaching and learning; and
6. multiple theories, approaches, and methods of music teaching and learning.

Debating:

1. the various viewpoints within the subjects as identified above; and
2. the relevancy of context.

Analyzing and synthesizing:
1. the various related issues that result from reading, writing, and debating;
2. identifying relevant music-making experiences and implementing them in school-based music classes; and
3. one's own growth as a reflective performer and teacher.

Evaluating:
1. appropriate music-making activities as implemented in school-based music classes; and
2. one's own growth as a reflective practitioner and musician.

## Conclusions

As we move into the twenty-first century, those of us who work with prospective and current music educators in the profession must examine how we involve students throughout their undergraduate and graduate experiences and ask questions that begin with "why," "how," "to whom," "where," and "what." It is only through careful, thorough scrutiny that we can examine and challenge beliefs and assumptions, and make informed decisions about the structures, content, and processes that define music programs in university settings. From such inquiry, we can ask questions about the characteristics of students' involvement as they make music, think musically, and think critically about music — that is, as they interact with music in ways that resemble the involvement of musicologists, music theorists, composers, music educators, and performers. Then, and only then, will our future educators and, hopefully, their students think and act as musicians do, as they construct and understand musical experiences in meaningful ways.

## Note

1 For a more condensed discussion about critical thinking, see Younker (2006).

## References

Adams, J. E., Jr. (2000). *Taking charge of curriculum*. New York: Teachers College Press.

Allsup, R. (2003). Mutual learning and democratic action in instrumental music education. *Journal of Research in Music Education, 51*(1), 24–37.

Bowman, W. (2002). Educating musically. In R. Colwell & C. P. Richardson (Eds.), *The new handbook of research for music teaching and learning* (pp. 63–84). New York: Oxford University Press.

Bowman, W. (2005). *More cogent questions, more provisional answers: The need to theorize music education*. Keynote address given at the Fourth International

Research in Music Education Conference, University of Exeter, School of Education and Life Long Learning, Exeter, England, April.

Bransford, J. D., Brown, A. L., & Cocking, R. R. (Eds.). (2000). *How people learn: brain mind, experience, and school.* Committee on Developments in the Science of Learning and Committee on Learning Research and Educational Practice, National Research Council. Washington, DC: National Academy Press.

Bruner, J. (1960). *The process of education.* Cambridge, MA: Harvard University Press.

Bruner, J. (1996). *The culture of education.* Cambridge, MA: Harvard University Press.

Burnard, P., & Younker, B. A. (2004). Problem-solving and creativity: Insights from students' individual composing pathways. *International Journal of Music Education, 22*(1), 59–76.

Dewey, J. (1933/1991). *How we think.* Buffalo, NY: Prometheus Books.

Dewey, J. (1934). *Art as experience.* New York: Perigee Books.

Dewey, J. (1938). *Experience and education.* New York: Collier Books.

Donovan, M. S., Bransford, J. D., & Pellegrino, J. W. (Eds.). (1999). *How people learn: Bridging research and practice.* Washington, DC: National Academy Press.

Eisner, E. (1998). *The kind of schools we need.* Portsmouth, NH: Heinemann.

Ennis, R. H. (1980). A conception of rational thinking. In J. R. Coombs (Ed.), *Philosophy of education 1979* (pp. 3–30). Normal, IL: Philosophy of Education Society.

Ennis, R. H. (1987). A taxonomy of critical thinking dispositions and abilities. In J. B. Baron & R. J. Sternberg (Eds.), *Teaching thinking skills: Theory and practice* (pp. 9–26). New York: Freeman.

Ferguson, L. (2004). *Mus201: Development of western music.* Course outline given as a handout at Teaching Music History Day. School of Music, University of Michigan, Ann Arbor, MI (October).

Friedman, T. L. (2005). *The world is flat.* New York: Farrar, Straus, and Giroux.

Galbraith, L. (2002). Research in visual art education: Implications for music. In R. Colwell & C. P. Richardson (Eds.), *The new handbook of research for music teaching and learning* (pp. 962–976). New York: Oxford University Press.

Goodlad, J. I. (2004). *Romances with schools.* New York: McGraw-Hill

Green, L. (2002). *How popular musicians learn: A way ahead for music education.* London, England: Ashgate.

Greene, M. (1995). *Releasing the imagination.* San Francisco, CA: Jossey-Bass.

Jaffurs, S. (2004). The impact of informal music learning practices in the classroom or how I learned how to teach from a garage band. *International Journal of Music Education: Practice, 22*(3), 201–218.

Jorgensen, E. R. (2001). A dialectical view of theory and practice. *Journal of Research in Music Education, 49*(4), 343–359.

Jorgensen, E. R. (2003). *Transforming music education.* Bloomington, IN: Indiana University Press.

Jorgensen, E. R. (2008). *The art of teaching music*. Bloomington, IN: Indiana University Press.

King, P. M., & Kitchener, K. S. (1994). *Developing reflective judgment*. San Francisco, CA: Jossey-Bass.

Lave, J., & Wenger, E. (1991). *Situated learning: Legitimate peripheral participation*. Cambridge, England: Cambridge University Press.

Mark, M. (1996). *Contemporary music education* (3rd ed.). New York: Schirmer Books.

McPeck J. E. (1981). *Critical thinking and education*. New York: St. Martin's Press.

McPeck J. E. (1984). Stalking beasts but swatting flies: The teaching of critical thinking. *Canadian Journal of Education, 9*(1), 28–44.

McPeck J. E. (1990). *Teaching critical thinking*. New York: Routledge & Kegan Paul.

Merleau-Ponty, M. (1964). *The primacy of perception*. Evanston, IL: Northwestern University Press.

Noddings, N. (2004). War, critical thinking, and self-understanding. *Phi Delta Kappan, 85*(7), 489–495.

North Whitehead, A. (1929). *The aims of education*. New York: Free Press.

Paul, R. W. (1987). Dialogical thinking: Critical thought essential to the acquisition of rational knowledge and passions. In J. B. Baron and R. J. Sternberg (Eds.), *Teaching thinking skills: Theory and practice* (pp. 127–148). New York: Freeman.

Paul, R. W. (1993). Accelerating change, and the complexity of problems, and the quality of our thinking. In J. Willsen & A. J. A. Binker (Eds.), *Critical thinking: What every person needs to survive in a rapidly changing world* (pp. 1–16). Santa Rosa, CA: Foundations for Critical Thinking.

Schon, D. (1987). *Educating the reflective practitioner*. San Fransico: Jossey-Bass.

Small, C. (1998). *Musicking*. Middletown, CT: Wesleyan University Press.

Vygotsky, L. (1978). *Mind in society: The development of higher psychological processes*. M. Cole, V. John-Steiner, S. Scribner & E. Souberman (Eds. and Trans.). Cambridge, MA: Harvard University Press.

Wiggins, J. H. (2001). *Teaching for musical understanding*. Boston: McGraw-Hill.

Woodford, P. G. (2005). *Democracy and music education: Liberalism, ethics and the politics of practice*. Bloomington: Indiana University Press.

Younker, B. A. (2002). Critical thinking. In R. Colwell & C. P. Richardson (Eds.), *The new handbook of research for music teaching and learning* (pp. 162–170). New York: Oxford University Press.

Younker, B. A. (2006). Reflective practice through the lens of a fifth grade composition-based music class. In P. Burnard & S. Hennessy (Eds.), *Reflective practice in arts education* (pp. 159–168). Norwell, MA: Kluwer Academic Publishers.

# TWELVE

# Marching to the World Beats: Globalization in the Context of Canadian Music Education

*Carol Beynon, Kari Veblen, and David J. Elliott*

### Defining Globalization

Globalization was originally coined as an economic term that described how business practices in local nations around the world developed, comingled, and unified into global economic communities. It is not a new phenomenon; globalization has been occurring since the dawn of civilization as peoples moved from place to place, crossing borders and creating new boundaries in peace and war — imposing, sharing, and trading expertise, customs, cultural traditions, ideologies, business, and even family members. Since then, concepts of globalization have expanded slowly and surely. However, recent technological advancements have propelled globalization into a central role as one of the concrete pillars of global society as the various components of our world accelerate, expand, and reinvent themselves every hour. All areas and forms of civilization and education are trying to keep pace, and like every other facet of society, globalization has been blamed or commended for the uneven challenges and impacts that have occurred with and without warning. At its most extreme, our world could be identified as one society in one community functioning as one entity. Metaphors abound to describe the impact of globalization — the global village, global marketplace, virtual world, or the world economy.

No longer is globalization simply related to economics; it is associated with political, sociological, psychological, cultural, educational, and technological influences and practices. Countries, once totally isolated by oceans, communicate, renegotiate, and integrate their values, ideologies, and cultures instantly with each other. It is the impact of globalization on Canadian music education that forms the topic of this chapter. At the outset, we note that in comparison to the histories of music education in other nations, Canadian and North American music education has been impacted by globalization far more and for far longer than in other countries due to the mass immigration of outsiders to these countries during the last four hundred years. Consider Canadian music education in these scenarios:

- Until the 1980s, school music education programs in Canada looked a lot like music education programs in Britain. But almost twenty-five years ago, a high-profile secondary school in one of Canada's largest cities began offering courses in steel drums for music credit, and now steel drums are the foundation of all music courses offered in the school's flourishing music program (Doyle-Marshall, 2000).
- In many schools where no keyboard accompanists are available, choral conductors regularly use accompaniment tracks created and played on synthetic, digitized instruments. Some students have never sung with an acoustic piano.
- Young people's concerts are a well-known formula for concert outreach. But one alternate and uniquely Canadian approach is Litaehkanao'pi — The Meeting Place Project. Initiated by Wasiak (2005), this Alberta pilot project brought students, symphony, university, and others into an artistic collaboration that bridged traditional Blackfoot and contemporary art music (plus dance, new media, and mythology).
- Music students all across Canada use computers to interact on a daily basis with students in other school boards, provinces, and countries around the world in order to listen to and perform musics of the "other" (Polin, 2006, pp. 73–74).[1]
- A gifted twelve-year-old Métis violinist in the Northwest Territories is taking private lessons from Pinchas Zukerman, world-renowned violinist and conductor of the National Arts Centre Orchestra in Ottawa, without either leaving his school or community. Zukerman has online private violin students in countries around the world and never needs to leave his studio.

Such scenarios tend to jolt music educators who may have become complacent with the traditional instrumental or choral class/rehearsal educational experience yet who seek ways to develop better strategies for bringing music to their students. As globalization, with its increasing and inequitable flows of information, people, and culture, steadily disrupts modernist notions of educational monoculture (Taylor, Bernahard, Garg, & Cummins, 2008, p. 271), we need to reframe music education as an expressive artistic trajectory rather than a static curriculum. The following questions are the foundation of this chapter:

1. What does the term globalization mean in relation to Canadian music education?
2. What will the future hold for music education in Canada in the context of the global village?

In this chapter, we use two theoretical concepts to begin a discussion and frame the impact of globalization on Canadian music education in the twenty-first century — one based in economic theory and the other in sociological cultural theory. Pulitzer Prize–winner Friedman's provocative and controversial book *The World Is Flat: A History of the Twenty-First Century* (2006), is one of the leading academic and professional interpretations of the impact of globalization on our twenty-first-century world and frames globalization in economic contexts. Because music is a critical component of culture, the second framework we use is Rochon's seminal work on cultural theory as outlined in his book *Culture Moves: Ideas, Activism and Changing Values* (1998).

## Friedman's View of Globalization and Potential Impacts on Canadian Music Education

Friedman's main thesis about globalization is that the world is no longer round; it has become flattened, not simply economically, but in every aspect including the cultural. He noted that, ironically, Christopher Columbus began the flattening process in 1492 when he discovered that the world was indeed round, and that this single discovery reunited civilizations that had been separated for millennia. Friedman cites ten examples of flatteners that have relevance for music education. The first is the *collapse of the Berlin Wall* in 1989, an event that not only ended the Cold War but symbolically and figuratively flattened the world, giving free access to the "other." Artistic barriers also crumbled and free exchanges and sharing of music have become the norm, especially with the *rise of the Internet and the World Wide Web* as the primary communication medium; the *new technology of workflow where machines, rather than people, talk to each other*; the development of *wikis, blogs, Flickr, Twitter, social networks, and integrators,* which has allowed people across generations, counties, and countries to communicate openly and share everything, including musics in real time; the rise of *Internet search engines such as Google*; and *personalized digital communications devices* such as cellphones, iPads, personal digital assistants, instant messaging, and Voice-Over Internet Protocol (VOIP), which have taken over people's lives in both helpful and unhealthy, addictive ways in the search for immediate answers. Friedman wrote: "Never before in the history of the planet have so many people — on their own — had the ability to find so much information about so many things and about so many other people" (p. 152). He called search engines *in-formers*, where information is instant and people have no privacy. Interestingly, Friedman believed these technologies disrupt communities more than they unite them — an interesting thought as we ponder the topic of this chapter.

Friedman also refers to new patterns of doing business in every industry, from manufacturing to the arts, as world flatteners: *outsourcing,* a common process in which companies lay off or overlook their own employees or local citizens to have materials manufactured or services rendered elsewhere to save money; *offshoring,* where companies in foreign lands take advantage of cheap labour practices. Countries such as India are competing for foreign investment, making it cheaper to manufacture and then ship the products than to use domestic labour. Fresh or canned peaches sold in Canadian stores all year round, for example, likely are not grown in the local orchards but have been shipped more cheaply from China to North American markets while Canadian fruit growers' produce rots on the trees in August; *supply chaining in the retail industry* by huge retail box stores, such as Walmart and Costco, that sell everything from groceries to furniture, much of which is imported cheaply. The bottom line for these retailers is reasonable goods for the consumer, and increased profits for shareholders, all at the expense of the workers who toil for minimum wage with no benefits. It matters not whether the consumer is in Mississauga or Mexico, there is a Walmart somewhere nearby in the McWorld with the same products for sale. The final flattener is *insourcing,* in which the employees of one company actually perform the services of another company. As an example, Friedman notes that UPS repairs Toshiba's computers.

Friedman adds a number of cautions to his flat-world theories, of which two are relevant here. First, while most of the world has been flattened, there are pockets of the world that are still rounded and are suffering terribly because of it. Africa and other Third World countries are languishing in poverty and disease and have not been able to access global markets. The wealthy countries are not willing to share their surpluses to support growth and development in these areas, and, in fact, drain even further resources from them, making them weaker and poorer. Second, while globalization has impacted the entire global population economically, culturally, and financially, it has also opened the world to global crime. As Friedman stated in a 2005 interview,

> The flat world is a friend of Infosys and of Al-Qaeda. It's a friend of IBM and of Islamic Jihad. Because these networks go both ways. And one thing we know about the bad guys: They're early adopters. Criminals, terrorists — very early adopters. The person who understands supply chains almost as well as Sam Walton [founder of Walmart], is Osama Bin Laden. We have an issue there with the most frustrated and dangerous elements of the world using this flat planet in order to advance their goals. Our job is to try to soak up those tools, so that we can use these collaborative tools in a more constructive way. (YaleGlobal, April 18, 2005)

While this concept of global flattening has obvious implications for educational structures and music education in particular, Friedman's flatteners have created what he refers to as a triple-convergence model. As of the year 2000, when work flow and software converged, so too did the flatteners enhance each other to level the global playing field. This convergence made producers realize that vertical, isolated, smoke-stack dealings were no longer possible or effective; a form of horizontalization has emerged where partners collaborate and work together to increase their influence. Friedman (2006) emphasizes that a vast amount of brain power has been invested in global developments that have come from former and current communist and socialist countries as they have redrawn borders and communications with and around the world. There is no doubt that globalization has affected the world industrially, financially, economically, politically, legally, culturally, ecologically, socially, and technologically and that it continues to have a major impact on information, language and literacy, and competition. As an example, consider the financial and economic impact on global markets and the creation of world governmental structures such as the World Bank and the International Monetary Fund or the predictions that if China continues to grow in all ways at current rates, it will emerge within twenty years as a world leader, reallocating the base of power, wealth, industry, and technology away from the West. All of these factors affect education in general; financial and economic forces naturally affect education along with other corresponding changes in technological, ecological, social, and cultural practices. To examine globalization and music education in an appropriate context, one needs to start with the big picture of arts and, even more broadly, culture.

## Rochon's Sociocultural View of Globalization and Its Potential Impact on Canadian Music Education

Culture is a large umbrella term that includes the arts and, specifically, music. The concept of flatteners within globalization has certainly had an impact on culture in general, and music in particular, in obvious ways that are not always positive. New forms of culture have emerged that reflect both simple and complex forms of diffusion, as well as harmonious and contentious blendings of cultures. In some cases, one sees new forms of socially conscious culture, environmentally and ecologically conscious culture, assumed acculturation, and the development not just of cross-cultural or multicultural innovations, but of world cultures. Rochon's (1998) three theories of cultural change can continue to play a major role in conceptualizing the development of new cultural forms and are useful in this discussion. He described the first theory as "value conversion," in which values play a significant role in creating new cultural norms to replace current but unacceptable practices. The current debate about torture in the prisoner-of-war camp at Guantanamo Bay is an example of a value conversion under debate. The second theory is "value creation" in which new cultural artifacts are created to adapt to new local or world situations. The final theory is "value connection": "the development of a conceptual link between phenomena previously thought either to be unconnected with each other or be connected in another way" (p. 54).

## So What Does This Have to Do with Music Education?

Friedman's and Rochon's works are useful as we look at music education on a national level and in the context of Canadian music education's place in the larger conception of culture. Music education is but one small aspect of culture buffeted on all sides by the global flatteners and the concomitant influences and impacts of the twenty-first-century world. In fact, Friedman and Rochon would have us realize that it is naive to think there really is such a distinct entity as Canadian music education.

Thirty years ago, educators were becoming cognizant of the issues of non-dominant and non-traditional cultures as students from non-Eurocentric countries began to move into larger Canadian communities and schools in larger numbers. The social and cultural exchanges that developed because of this increased mingling of peoples resulted in three phenomena: (1) multicultural mixed communities where difference was noticeable and often awkward, and where the dominant, traditional Western cultures maintained their superiority; (2) distinct and separate ethnically based communities with little mixing of cultures even in the public institutions of schools and churches; and (3) diffuse communities with blurred boundaries and marked blending as circulation among community members increased. Technological advances — or the flatteners as Freidman called them — continue to obscure these contexts even further, especially in educational institutions. Canadian communities, schools, and school districts in both urban and rural areas now have access to technology that links them in real time with communities around the world, and cultural artifacts are now being acculturated, diffused, and blended. What we formerly knew as the *other* or the exotic, is now a known part of lived experience for many people in the flattened parts of the world. The relationship between globalization and music education has not been unique. Professionals in all fields have faced and continue to face a complex set of related challenges as they attempt to carry out their central and ancillary missions. But pertinent to music and the arts is the fact that today's extraordinary connectivity has resulted in the collapse of geographical and cultural borders; an enormous increase in new migratory populations; unprecedented collaborative teaching, learning, and research; and a massive back-and-forth transfer of media — including all sorts of music media. Thus, public education and its music education can no longer be conceived as having inevitable ties to its meaning in one nation, or one location, or even in the traditional locus of the school or the students. All cultures, meanings, and institutions are morphing into a hybrid mix as people migrate geographically and electronically.

Learning in music not only occurs in an organized, top-down fashion in schools or community groups; it happens spontaneously, planned, and serendipitously in public and private spaces, both individually and in groups who intersect through technology around the entire globe. Accordingly, globalization has opened vast opportunities for the creation of new hybrid forms of cultural products, musics, and productivity as it relates to music education. Bresler and Stake (2006) confirmed the changes in curriculum:

> On the cultural level, globalization seems to blur distinctions between national, regional and local music communities. At the same time, globalization discloses musical diversity and heterogeneity through increased hybridization, highlighting historical, social and cultural

contexts. The prevalence of popular music, combined with the post-modernist erosion of the traditional distinction between high and low art, accelerated the research on various types of folk, popular and rock music. (p. 286)

In the 1960s and '70s, the exotic multicultural music of choice for performance might have been a negro spiritual. In the 1980s, songs from other countries would have primarily included western European countries such as Germany, France, Italy, or perhaps Mexico, Spain, or even the Caribbean. School children might have felt they were stretching their boundaries and awareness if they learned and performed one Japanese song — "Cherry Blossoms" ("Sakura"). Fast-forward to 2010 to an interesting juxtaposition in which the format of music education remains much the same as it did fifty years ago with bands, orchestras, choirs, and guitar programs as the predominant mode of delivery,[2] but the repertoire in the music curriculum looks much different with combinations and diffusions of rock, popular, jazz, and ethnic hybrids of music being studied and performed.[3]

In a pan-Canadian study of elementary schools,[4] Mundy and Manion (2008) explored curricular strands that integrate successfully with globalization themes and the current state of implementation. While their study looks at the school system as a whole, music makes an appearance. They cite a principal from Alberta who reports: "We certainly find global education in the social studies curriculum. Our music department fits global education in the program" (p. 953).

Suarez (2009), in her discussion of the impact of globalization on music education, promoted a concept not of diversity, but of universality. She suggested that the classroom should no longer be confined to the classroom walls and that the learning environment needs to be both transparent and porous, creating an environment of musical osmosis with students and teachers nourished by living in the context of equally rich cultures:

Each generation brings unique perspectives to a dynamic society. The Internet has resulted in a globalization and transformation of our teaching environment. As part of this, world music is immediately accessible through a variety of media and can be embraced as an aid to music educators in the classroom. In response to these changing needs and opportunities, the classroom has become a glorious mosaic, one in which the emphasis begins to shift from "diversity" to "universality." (p. 39)

More than ever before, music holds an important place in school-aged children's lives, especially teenagers. In a study about media use and the importance of media in the lives of youth, Livingstone and Bovill (1999)) found that music was especially significant to the lives of the participants, coming second only to television in terms of importance. Not surprisingly, young people use music to distance themselves from parents and teachers but also to help them make the transition from childhood to adolescence. And they use music to communicate with peers in two ways: to belong, yet also to show individuality. But if music is so important to youth, why do so few choose to study music in school? Simply put, their music is not the music of most schools.[5]

## Summary
To summarize this chapter, we return to the original two questions around which this paper was written:

### 1. What does the term globalization mean in relation to Canadian music education?
Globalization has not resulted in fairness, here or abroad. This is partly because the main motivations of economic globalization — more efficiency for more profit — have penetrated and compromised socially oriented governments to the extent that job security, pension plans, health coverage, and public education have been diminished. More specifically, the extreme economic competitiveness of the global marketplace and the attendant need for corporate efficiency have caused many educational institutions to take a right turn toward capitalist values and business models of curriculum, instruction, and evaluation. Conservative politicians, business leaders, policy makers, and taxpayers now see education as a commodity to be bought, sold, controlled, standardized, and evaluated by corporate standards and bottom-line results. The turn toward conservatism and a business-based foundation of education seems to relate to the current call for back-to-the-basics learning, standardized testing, and the further marginalization of music and arts education as a frill in the curriculum.

Nevertheless, the news can be hopeful if we as music educators learn to be adaptable. Because globalization depends on horizontal networks and interactions, we are being given a teachable moment as students network musically at home, in schools, and even on street corners to learn to create new knowledge, new culture, new media, and personal meaning in their own interactive world context. The benefits of globalization will come about only if music educational opportunities become more accessible for everyone. Music education that is well conceived and carried out, raises people's dignity, wellness, and economic productivity. Education fuels innovation through creative, interconnected local, regional, and global technologies. Globalization is also pressuring higher education to address community needs and social ills, not just academic needs. This is causing universities to reinvent their missions in relation to local economic, social, and racial problems.

Clearly, globalization is dramatically altering the ways in which all people live, learn, love, interact, work, and create self-identity and self-respect. Marcelo Suárez-Orozco (2005), a renowned scholar of globalization, explained what this means for education in general (and his words apply equally well to music education):

> An education for globalization should aim for nothing more — and nothing less — than to educate "the whole child for the whole world"... An education for the global era must engender life-long habits of body, mind, and heart. It must tend to the social and emotional sensibilities needed for cross-cultural work: empathy and learning with and from others who happen to differ in race; religion; national; linguistic, or social origin; values; and worldviews. (p. 212)

*2. What will the future hold for music education in Canada in the context of the global village?*
There are those who believe, naively or not, that music "is the very essence of globalization. The real potential for cross-cultural communication and understanding lies in many small moments of interaction rather than in anything large, state run, or commercial" (Paul, 2008). Canadian music education in this global context requires media-rich, humanistic learning-learning situations

- by having teachers continue to see themselves and their students as learners, with both students and teachers learning openly from each other;
- by engaging more diverse teacher and student populations in collaborative artistic projects;
- by combining teacher and student musical understandings with new sources;
- by developing multiple musical/cultural/artistic perspectives;
- by learning how to value, while moving across, culture preferences;
- by tearing down classroom walls and opening up opportunities where they exist;
- and, perhaps most importantly, by scrutinizing and dissecting the very foundational term of this book, "music education," and being brave enough to consider supplanting it with something more educationally sound.

Canadian music education cannot afford to exist in isolation; in fact, this chapter has questioned whether there really is such a phenomenon as "Canadian music education" given the nature of how public education has developed. The solutions offered above will be difficult and perhaps even impossible to implement in their entirety, but further scrutiny and discussion are necessary if music education is to survive and have any sort of relevance in the present century.

## Notes

1  In Polin (2006), Andrea Rose describes programs in Canada, including the Centre for Distance Learning and Innovation, which is developing online music education courses geared especially toward rural populations so that they can gain better access to music learning opportunities. Learn Canada, a music grid project, connects music education courses with those in several other countries. Rose notes, "As a result of launching these new delivery methods, Canadians find themselves in the process of deconstructing all definitions of what is music, and what is music education" (p. 75).

2  See chapter 1 for a general overview of music education across Canada.

3  See Bradley (2006) for a timely and critical ethnography of one choir's globally oriented repertoire and subsequent viewpoints.

4  Field research included interviews at provincial, district, and school levels in British Columbia, Yukon, Alberta, Manitoba, Ontario, Quebec, and Nova Scotia as well as an analysis of curriculum guidelines.

5  The question of whether it should or could be needs to be a subject of further research.

## References

Bradley, D. (2006). *Global song, global citizens? Multicultural choral music education and the community youth choir: Constituting the multicultural human subject.* Unpublished doctoral dissertation, University of Toronto, Toronto.

Bresler, L., & Stake, R. (2006). Qualitative research methodologies in music education. In R. Colwell (Ed.), *MENC handbook of research methodologies* (pp. 270–311). New York: Oxford University Press.

Doyle-Marshall, W. (2000). Steelbands move from lobby to concert hall. *Performing Arts and Entertainment in Canada 33*(1), 26–30.

Friedman, T. L. (2006). *The world is flat: A history of the twenty-first century.* (2nd ed.). New York: Farrar, Straus and Giroux.

Livingstone, S., & Bovill, M. (1999). *Young people, new media.* Retrieved from http://www.mediaculture-online.de/fileadmin/bibliothek/livingstone_young_people/ livingstone_young_people.pdf.

Mundy, K., & Manion, C. (2008). Global education in Canadian elementary schools: An exploratory study. *Canadian Journal of Education, 31*(4), 941–974.

Paul, A. (October 21, 2008). Music: True agent of globalization. *Wall Street Journal.*

Polin, J. L. (2006). International music education policy symposium. *Journal of Arts Management, Law and Society, 36*(1), 66–80.

Rochon, T. R. (1998). *Culture moves: Ideas, activism and changing values.* Princeton, NJ: Princeton University Press.

Suárez, E. R. (2009). Globalization and transformation in the local music classroom. *Global Studies Journal, 1*(2), 39–44.

Suárez-Orozco, M. (2005). Rethinking education in the global era. *Phi Delta Kappan: A Professional Journal for Education, 87*(3), 209–212.

Taylor, L.K., Bernahard, J.K., Garg, S., & Cummins, J. (2008). Affirming plural belonging: Building on students' family-based cultural and linguistic capital through multiliteracies pedagogy. *Journal of Early Childhood Literacy,* 8(3), 269–294.

Wasiak, E. (2005). Iitaohkanao'pi — The Meeting Place Project: An alternative approach to young people's concerts. *International Journal of Music Education, 23*(1), 73–88.

YaleGlobal. (April 18, 2005). "Wake up and face the flat earth": In an interview, columnist and author Thomas L. Friedman says globalization has outpaced its critics. Retrieved from http://yaleglobal.yale.edu/content/wake-and-face-flat-earth.

# THIRTEEN

# Epistemological Spinning:
## What Do We Really Know about Music Education in Canada?

*Carol Beynon, Kari Veblen, and Elizabeth Anne Kinsella*

## Introduction

The chapters in this book have comprehensively considered Canadian music education over the first decade of the twenty-first century from several perspectives. In this concluding chapter, we explore the ways in which the chapters, in total, are more than the sum of their parts and how they may contribute to a holistic study of music education in Canada and elsewhere. We reflect on one philosopher/artist's depiction of epistemology in order to (1) illustrate the personal nature of epistemological beliefs about music education and (2) provoke readers' personal examination of their own beliefs. And finally in this chapter, we layer a methodological framework of critical ethnography over the preceding chapters to analyze and synthesize the rich data and to allow an epistemological model to grow out of the analysis. The chapters of this book provide the foundation to generate a meta-study of the various authors' contributions, not by beginning with extant theories about epistemology and music education, but by trying to perceive what theories or truths emerge from what is written here.

## What Is Knowledge in Canadian Music Education?

The task undertaken in compiling this book, vitally important to the understanding of music education as a discipline, implies a certain level of knowledge. In the Foreword, R. Murray Schafer stated that "Plato taught that there was an answer to every question. Socrates taught that there was a question to every answer, but that was something my teachers didn't seem to want to deal with" (p. vii). A clear aim of this book is to question, to answer, and then to question those answers. If Plato's assertion that knowledge is embedded in the intersection of truth and beliefs is worth considering, then the critical questions become "What is knowledge in music education?" and "What is *belief*?" Those questions propel us to the philosophical concept of epistemology — an important starting point in this discussion because epistemology makes us engage deliberately in the study of knowledge, truth, and beliefs and in a consideration of how these three elements intersect and relate to music education. *The Oxford Dictionary of Philosophy* defines epistemology as follows:

> (Greek, epistēmē, knowledge) The theory of knowledge. Its central questions include the origin of knowledge; the place of experience in generating knowledge, and the place of reason in doing so; the relationship between knowledge and certainty, and between knowledge and the impossibility of error; the possibility of universal scepticism; and the changing forms of knowledge that arise from new conceptualizations of the world. All of these issues link with other central concerns of philosophy, such as the nature of truth and the nature of experience and meaning. (Blackburn, 2008)

The discipline of epistemology has evolved from a Platonian notion of knowledge as fixed and universally true to contemporary understandings of knowledge as postmodern, culturally bound, contextually situated, and conditional. We might like to believe that the locus of study in this and all other chapters represents the knowledge of timeless forms rather than uncertain interpretation; however, any studies such as these are legitimately limited by boundaries that include the individual lenses, expertise, and experiences of the researchers, as well as by the changing foundations of knowledge as a central component of the changing times in which we live. The epistemologies of music education in Canada, as represented both in this chapter specifically and in the book as a whole, are based on the knowledge that emanates from varied interpretive truths in combination with the beliefs and values of the authors. English (2003) reminds us that truth changes and modifies over time; therefore, as our knowledge

**Figure 13.1**  *Epistemological Spinning*

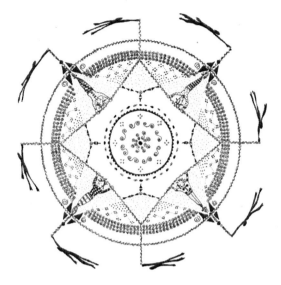

Source: Kinsella (2005).

increases, so too are our beliefs and values challenged and altered — indeed, the truth must change.

One of the authors of this chapter, Kinsella, an artist, educational philosopher, and health professions researcher who has studied the phenomenon of epistemology in education, has created an intricate drawing that helps illuminate this discussion. Entitled "Epistemological Spinning," the drawing conveys far more meaning through artistic representation than can be described in mere words. To understand the artwork comprehensively one might begin by looking at the drawing as a whole, taking in its intricate detail. In considering (1) what we have just written about epistemology and (2) what epistemology can mean in examining Canadian music education, we recommend looking at the drawing from the outside in, and then from the inside out, and then its parts, imagining each symbol and line as a part of each individual's knowledge of music education.

When creating this artwork, Kinsella had the concept of epistemology in mind, and the title — "Epistemological Spinning" — implies the fluidity and the constant and requisite change that educators' experience. In this artistic piece, various symbols are used to reflect on the epistemological question of what it means to know. As Kinsella looks at phenomena through different frames, a whole new meaning, conceptualization, or world view can emerge depending on the norms of the particular community within which she shares the gaze. As she moves into various fields of thought ranging from philosophical to social to psychological to spiritual, she has a sense of moving into different discursive communities, and of needing to learn a new language and set of assumptions before being able to discern the meanings and subtleties of the arguments and texts. At times, a theoretical perspective that is minuscule in one discipline is paramount in another. This causes her to reflect on the situated particularity of knowledge, as well as the historicity of disciplinary knowledge — in the sense that those who have gone before have influenced what is currently considered and accepted within particular domains. As she traverses various realms of thought, she has the sense of the carpet being pulled out from beneath her feet. Notions of an "objective" world "out there" crumble in the face of constructed worlds. She is confronted with the ambiguity of "official" knowledge and with a growing awareness of the self as a location of conversation within a cacophony of voices and intellectual communities. The centre suggests the possibility of transcending chaos to discover an implicit order where insight, connection, and unity emerge.

Kinsella's piece of art and her descriptive words illuminate a relationship, not only to music education as a specific, concrete discipline, but to the way in which music education shifts and engages in spiritual, aesthetic, social, psychological, and, of course, political communities. If nothing else, this drawing reminds us that the purpose of a book such as this is to find some forms of connection, some order or unity, some general insights out of the diverse perspectives about music education in Canada. In other words, we seek to discern meaning out of what those before us have done, and out of what we have each constructed, recognizing that this is a complex, confusing, and chaotic task: that it involves epistemological spinning.

## An Epistemology of Canadian Music Education: Our Study within a Study

With Kinsella's artwork as a conceptual underpinning, our goal is to use a critically reflexive approach to examine the contributions to this book. Critical reflexivity is defined by social philosopher Barry Sandywell (1996) as the "act of interrogating interpretive systems" (p. xiv). In this process, we begin at the outside and move inward to discern central understandings about the state of music education that permeate the contributions to this book, while acknowledging that our own beliefs and values inform the process. Our aim is to examine music education through various frames and to seek new or renewed conceptualizations, while acknowledging and accepting new and divergent assumptions, recognizing ambiguities, and searching for subtle interpretations that arise from the various discourses and texts. While each chapter of this book examines music education in unique contexts—from the contested tensions in trying to teach the traditional music of the Innu people to a group of high school Innu students in Nunavut, to recognizing and addressing the gendered patterns in music—it is important to reflect on the situated particularity of knowledge as well as the historicity of disciplinary knowledge in each instance. Music education in Canada is as vast and varied as Canada itself; it is unique in each iteration; nonetheless, there are also numerous similarities among the ways in which it manifests itself in distinct contexts. Each of the constituent pieces, as described in this volume, tells its own distinct, historicized, and socio-political story—each one certainly worth examining conceptually and in detail. But in order to understand how each of the parts contributes to the epistemological foundations of Canadian music education, we need to look further.

This meta-study draws upon Carspecken's (1996) model of critical ethnography to examine music education in Canada on a holistic basis. Carspecken stated that critical ethnography allows for an "emancipative" insider's point of view by allowing the researchers to study social action taking place in one or more social sites and to explain this action through examining locales and social systems intertwined with the sites of interest. The methodology is useful for accessing and assessing subjective experiences that are common to the various actors in the study, and focuses on identifying issues of power and inequality. Hence, we use this methodological protocol to provide an organizational device for this "study within a study," not in distinct phases, but as directional signposts to help us relate the various topics to and among each other.

Following the Carspecken model, the preliminary phase of this study was set up to promote social interaction and involved data collection through two distinct and significant components. First, a Pan-Canadian Symposium was held and sixty music education researchers, teachers, performers, and policy makers from across Canada—from north to south and east to west—were invited to come together for three days of intensive interaction, discussion, and recorded presentations. These scholars brought ideas in the form of approximately fifty delivered papers based on questions and considerations of various epistemological approaches specifically contextualized about Canadian music education. This was followed by a critical process of social integration which involved extensive and vigorous discussion. Over the past decades, music education departments in faculties of music and faculties of education throughout Canada have become smaller; prior to the meetings, many of the participant researchers worked alone and in isolation. However, despite the challenges, the individuals involved in this project — as well as others working independently — have sought to make change through music education networks and through schools. Throughout the initial, and then ongoing, dialogue, members of the group considered and reconsidered their values, beliefs, and ideologies in the context of the whole of Canadian music education, rather than remaining solely focused on the specifics of their own situations; the meetings provided a space for critical collective dialogue.[1]

In the second phase of this study, a phase which Carspecken calls *reconstructive analysis*, we examined the dialogue of the initial meetings and the revised papers. We considered the record of the discussions and read each paper carefully as we sought to make explicit the tacit, to underline the obvious, and to search for patterns that would allow a deeper and more analytical understanding of the data. Carspecken suggests that as participant-researchers we should look broadly and deeply to determine interactivity, meanings, power relations, roles, interactive sequences, evidence of embodied meanings, and inter-subjective structures. Our task was not to articulate the obvious but to reconstruct what is not always observable or articulated by action or word. Through this level of analysis and through the process of clarification, we considered coordination of action between the social sites and topics as they were separated in space and time. Further, we discussed impressions and examined boundaries, routines, and similar factors in an attempt to better understand how the system was integrated. Carspecken refers to this as *social integration*. This phase of analysis was the lengthiest and the most interesting, yet it was challenging because we, as the researchers, were as deeply immersed in the process as our colleagues. It was difficult to separate ourselves from the study in order to engage in impartial scrutiny; however once we acknowledged that it was impossible to look objectively, given our own personal lenses, biases, values, ideologies, and situatedness within music education, the process became more manageable and transparent. Not surprisingly, interactivity was the most demonstrable aspect of this phase. Bringing together sixty experts in Canadian music education — all passionately involved in various aspects of the same topic — provided fertile ground for lively, lengthy discussions that raised challenges, arguments, disputes, and sometimes concurrence.

Carspecken anchors the subsequent processes of a critical ethnographic study in dialogical data generation that leads to system analysis. As such, after three days of sharing of papers and discussions, the authors were invited to submit their work for a peer-reviewed publication — another form of dialogical data. Many attendees accepted this invitation, and the result was a series of revised papers that begged for comparative analysis. As a whole, the papers, while not always consistent, added to the understanding of the current context and offered significant snapshots of one point in time in Canadian music education history. And, most significantly, the discussion and ensuing papers no longer represented isolated Canadian voices. The anxieties, questions, affirmations, and issues shared by the authors had become issues for the group, and each paper contributed to creating a more complex, yet clearer, whole. While numerous issues were repeatedly raised by researchers in relation to their individual geographic areas, three primary issues of concern were: (1) limited music education teachers, resources, and programs in rural and remote areas across Canada; (2) the lack of specialist or trained generalist music teachers in the elementary schools across Canada; and (3) the immediate need for opportunities to collaborate with First Nations and diverse, non-mainstream populations in order to support authentic programs in music education in both specialized schools and the regular school system. These are issues that severely impair the growth of music education programs across Canada, and there was a demonstrable sense of shared commitment to collectively look for solutions. Rather than viewing these obstacles as insurmountable, the participants articulated and sought ways and means of collaborating together to seek solutions, rather than working in isolation in the face of current challenges. R. Murray Schafer underscored the centrality of creative expression essential to living music education; as he writes in his Foreword, "allowing children to become creative does not require genius: it requires humility" (p. viii). This discussion brings Kinsella's "Epistemological Spinning" back into clear focus as our shared common issues lead toward an openness to democratizing the process of working together in Canadian music education.

In sum, the chapters in this book powerfully emphasize the relationships among music educators brought about by the geographic, cultural, and hierarchical forms of music education in this country. The outcomes highlight the ambiguities, contradictions, and shifts of perception, not only in music education across Canada, but within this group of intelligent and esteemed individuals who work within the same discipline. In fact, in what might have been considered, at first glance, to be a homogeneous group, inside and outside views emerged that were often contentious, divergent, and the subject of scrutiny. The cultural power of music education intersects in complex ways with forces that reflect political, economic, and social power—all of which are external and none of which is artistically based. Yet each certainly affects the art and science of music education.

What are the conditions of the production of music education in Canada? Some, usually from outside education, see the inclusion of music or arts education as an expensive frill when what pupils truly need is a solid grounding in basic skills. Music education is often marginalized as an inferior subject and can be seen, by some, as providing useless information. Others give it credit for adding variety to a staid and stagnant curriculum. Still others support music education because it leads to the development of creative minds in pupils that, in turn, leads to a more productive future for the Canadian economy. Some believe that the existence of mandated accessible music education in many provinces has literally kept a higher level of music making alive in some communities. These varied beliefs and values held by outsiders contrast sharply and are often incongruous with those held by the insider participants in this manuscript, resulting in the question, "What is the reality of music education in the Canadian context?" This question poses further challenging questions, such as:

- What are the realistic conditions for the production of music education in Canada given that the findings in these chapters illuminate more concerns and problems than good news about the current context?
- Can music education continue to be autonomous[2] as a subject discipline in schools and communities? Should it be?
- How does one negotiate the varied intents and meanings of process and product in music education from the various societal perspectives of music: (1) Is it an expensive frill subject that adds variety to the curriculum through basically useless information or (2) does it support the development of the creative mind in pupils, which leads to a productive and creative future for the economy?
- How does the reality of Canadian music education compare with music education in other countries around the world that also have similar institutions of public education?
- What are the dominant values that permeate the education of Canadians, and what are the implications for music education in this country?

The realities reported in the pages of this book illuminate an entirely different, but critical, path for music education possibilities and research, while simultaneously altering and refining our current theories of behaviour, beliefs, and possibilities. It might be helpful to summarize this study by using the metaphor of "depth of field" as understood by professional photographers. When a photographer composes a picture, focus is a prime consideration. However, the human eye is subject to an optical phenomenon such that it perceives a finite number of things in focus. The depth of field — or the area that appears to be in focus — does not change dramatically but, rather, occurs in a gradual transition. Thus, objects in that zone will appear sharply focused to the eye, but the eye will actually bring into focus objects just in front of and just behind the centre or heart of the picture. As the lens's aperture becomes smaller, the depth of field and area that appears to be in focus increases, leading us to a *circle of confusion*:

> Since there is no critical point of transition, a more rigorous term called the "circle of confusion" is used to define how much a point needs to be blurred in order to be perceived as unsharp. When the circle of confusion becomes perceptible to our eyes, this region is said to be outside the depth of field and thus no longer "acceptable sharp." (Cambridge in Colour, n.d.)

Indeed, the purpose of this book has been an ambitious one: to try to bring the huge and varied expanse of the current state of Canadian music education, as presented in the preceding chapters by many of our country's leading scholars, into some kind of focus. We cannot look forward unless we know where we have been and where we are now. Like the optics in cameras, our minds can only perceive a finite number of objects in focus at one time, and while it might be easier to look only at a tiny portion of the whole picture at any one time, it is essential to do our best to take the big picture into account.

As we consider the epistemology of Canadian music education, we might recall Kinsella's artwork and the metaphor of epistemological spinning that she proposes. Through this ongoing dialogic process and in each chapter of this book, the authors contribute a unique perspective, a narrower depth of field that allows for greater detail and depth about the particularities of music education to come into view; these individual situated reports each contribute to the bigger picture. Contributions of music and related arts position the image. It is our intention and our hope that the insights offered here will afford readers an opportunity to view music education in Canada from a variety of perspectives — to focus in on specific areas and to broaden their gaze in order to take in a larger perspective. As in photography, the point is in the artfulness of seeing and in the juxtaposition of familiar things in order to see and to think about the epistemology of Canadian music education in new ways.

### Future Research and Future of Music Education in Canada
This project began as an attempt to understand and to challenge the status quo of music education in Canada between 2000 and 2010. We began by imagining a greater number of critical perspectives than we have actually addressed in this book. At this juncture, we are struck that the ideas we

previously espoused as daring and innovative now seem mundane and customary. Has the system changed? Have we changed? Or have the dialogues that were initiated herein simply shown us how conventional our thinking is? As we consider the future (with hopes and fears, predictions, plans and dreams), it is clear that slow-moving systems are at work in education. For example, while there are forces that are both progressive and conservative, the field has been slow to accept popular culture as a window to music understanding and music making. Furthermore, older notions of what types and genres of music are valuable are still being played out in the repertoire and in teacher education. Does music competency in schools entail knowledge of self[3] or the meticulous training of, for example, a principal violinist? We predict that the schisms that are now apparent will become wider with each passing year.

Our hope is that every student in every classroom and every citizen throughout Canada has access to learning about, through, with, and in music. We dream of a time when the multiplicity of musical expressions are not just tolerated, but supported, celebrated, and continued throughout life. Perhaps the means that will carry us to a more courageous and open place will be accomplished through the work of individuals. Each musician, educator, and community worker carries his or her own social construction of musical being in the world, as well as a world of creating, performing, and teaching.

We need the courage of our convictions. And we need many, many more Murray Schafers.

## Notes

1  Since the initial meeting in 2005, a small but resolute cohort who were determined to continue discussing Canadian music education has consistently networked, sought funding, and come together for various projects. There have been two other Pan-Canadian Symposia, one held at Memorial University in Newfoundland in 2007, and another at the University of Victoria in 2009, with another scheduled for 2012 in Quebec.

2  By *autonomous* we mean a separate discipline apart from integrative curriculum, such as instances where "the arts" are clumped together and taught by non-musician, non-specialist teachers. Currently, music education in many secondary schools and some primary schools is taught by music educators who *are* musicians as well as teachers.

3  Or selves, since we live in a pluralistic social order, even though the dominant culture powerfully controls all aspects of education.

## References

Blackburn, S. (2008). Epistemology. *The Oxford dictionary of philosophy*. Oxford: Oxford University Press. Retrieved from http://www.oxfordreference.com.

Cambridge in Colour. (n.d). Tutorials: Depth of field. Retrieved from http://www
.cambridgeincolour.com/tutorials/depth-of-field.htm.

Carspecken, P. F. (1996). *Critical ethnography in educational research: A theoretical and practical guide.* New York and London: Routledge.

English, F. (2003). *The postmodern challenge to the theory and practice of educational administration.* Springfield, IL: Charles C. Thomas Publishers.

Sandywell, B. (1996). *Reflexivity and the crisis of western reason: Logological investigations* (Vol. 1). London: Routledge.

# About the Authors

**Carol Beynon** is Associate Vice Provost of the School of Graduate and Post-doctoral Studies and former Acting Dean of Education at the University of Western Ontario. She is the founding co-artistic director of the renowned and award-winning Amabile Boys and Men's Choirs. Her research focuses on teacher development, teacher identity, and gender issues in music education; she is the first author of the book *Learning to Teach* (Pearson, 2001). She is currently a co-investigator on two federally funded SSHRC funded projects in music education and singing. Carol was named the Woman of Excellence in Arts, Culture and Heritage 2007.

**Benjamin Bolden**, music educator and composer, is an Assistant Professor of music education at Queen's University. His research interests include the teaching and learning of composing, community music, and Web 2.0 technologies in education. As a teacher, Ben has worked with preschool, elementary, secondary, and university students in Canada, England, and Taiwan. An associate composer of the Canadian Music Centre, Ben has seen his works performed by a variety of professional and amateur performing ensembles. He is editor of the *Canadian Music Educator*, official journal of the Canadian Music Educators' Association/L'Association canadienne des musiciens éducateurs.

**Wayne D. Bowman**'s work is extensively informed by pragmatism, critical theory, and conceptions of music and music education as social practices. He is particularly concerned with music's socio-political power and ethically informed understandings of musical practice. His publications include *Philosophical Perspectives on Music* (1998), the *Oxford Handbook of Philosophy in Music Education* (2012), numerous book chapters, and articles in prominent scholarly journals. The former editor of the journal *Action, Criticism, and Theory [ACT] for Music Education*, his university teaching experience includes positions at Brandon University (Manitoba), Mars Hill College (North Carolina), the University of Toronto, and New York University.

**June Countryman** teaches aural skills and music education courses in the Music Department at UPEI. She holds B.Mus., B.A., and B.Ed. degrees (Mount Allison), M.Mus. (UWO), and Ed.D (OISE/UT). She has lengthy experience as an elementary music teacher, a curriculum writer and program consultant, and a high school choral teacher. Her research interests include improvisation as a tool for musical growth, children's informal musicking on school playgrounds, sharing power in teaching contexts, and teacher professional development. Dr. Countryman was awarded UPEI's Hessian Award for Teaching Excellence in 2008.

**David J. Elliott** joined NYU in 2002 after twenty-eight years as Professor and Chair of Music Education at the University of Toronto. He has also served as a Visiting Professor of Music Education at Northwestern University, the University of North Texas, Indiana University, the University of Cape Town, and the University of Limerick. He is the author of *Music Matters: A New Philosophy of Music Education* (1995) and editor of *Praxial Music Education: Reflections and Dialogues* (2005/2009). He has published numerous journal articles and book chapters and presented more than 200 invited lectures and conference papers worldwide.

**Elizabeth Gould** serves as Associate Professor at the University of Toronto Faculty of Music. Her research in gender and sexuality in the context of feminisms and queer theory has been published widely, including *Philosophy of Music Education Review, Women and Music: A Journal of Gender and Culture, Educational Philosophy and Theory*, and the Brazilian journal *labrys: études féministes estudos feministas*. She served as lead editor for the book *Exploring Social Justice: How Music Education Might Matter* (2009) and organized the conference *musica ficta*: A Conference on Engagements and Exclusions in Music, Education, and the Arts (2008).

**Betty Hanley** is Professor Emeritus at the University of Victoria, BC, Canada. An outstanding contributor to arts and music education in Canada, Dr. Hanley has organized symposia and conferences, written and edited books, and conducted research in music pedagogy and arts policy. She has published articles in the *Canadian Music Educator, British Journal of Music Education, Arts Education Policy Review, Canadian Journal of Education, International Journal of Community Music, Journal of Music Teacher Education*, and *Journal of the Canadian Association for Curriculum Studies*. She is an honorary member of the Canadian Music Educators Association and has received its Jubilate Award.

**Alex Hickey** has a broad scope of experience in K–12 education and teaches part-time in the Faculty of Education at Memorial University. He has worked as a sole-charge teacher in a one-room school, as a high school art teacher, as an art and technology education coordinator at the school district level, and as a curriculum consultant at Department of Education. He is a former Director of Program Development (English and French) for the Department of Education in Newfoundland and Labrador and is currently Coordinator of the Virtual Teacher Centre, an online professional development entity for teachers. Alex is a practising visual artist with a fascination for digital technology, media education, and peering over the horizon of invisibility.

**Elizabeth Anne Kinsella** is Associate Professor in the Faculty of Health Sciences and the Faculty of Education at the University of Western Ontario, Canada. Her work draws on social science perspectives in the study of professional education and practice, with a particular focus on the health professions, epistemologies of practice, and reflexivity in professional life.

**Andrew Mercer** has taught music in Newfoundland and Labrador since 1994 and has been involved with Internet-based music education since 1995. In 2004 he joined the Centre for Distance Learning and Innovations, where he pioneered the practice of teaching of high school music via the Internet. His work on Internet-based music education has been featured in *Canadian Music Educator, Popular Science, The Wall Street Journal, CNN, Nippon TV*, and elsewhere. He has presented his work on web-based music education at numerous conferences, including the 2008 ISME Conference, the MTNA National Conference, and the MENC. Andrew's most recent work explores the educational uses of such new technologies as Second Life and Apple's iPhone.

**Mary Piercey** is a Ph.D candidate in Ethnomusicology at Memorial University of Newfoundland. Her research explores how the Inuit of Arviat, Nunavut, use their musical practices to negotiate social diversity within the community in response to the massive sociocultural changes caused by resettlement in the 1950s. Ms. Piercey lived and taught music at Qitiqliq High School in Arviat, Nunavut, founding and directing the Arviat Imngitingit Community Choir, a mixed-voiced group specializing in traditional and contemporary Inuit music originating from the Kivalliq region of Nunavut. Mary now lives in Iqaluit, Nunavut, where she directs the Inuksuk Drum Dancers and teaches music at Inuksuk High School.

**Andrea Rose** is Professor of Music Education at the Faculty of Education at Memorial University of Newfoundland, Canada. Artistic Director of Festival 500 International Choral Festival and Co-Director of The Phenomenon of Singing International Symposia, Dr. Rose is active as musician, educator, lecturer, and collaborator. Her primary research interests include the development of critical pedagogy, leadership, and citizenship in music/arts education, the nature and role of indigenous music/arts in school curricula, the development of web-based contexts for music/arts education and dialogue-based education.

**R. Murray Schafer** is a noted Canadian composer of interdisciplinary works performed worldwide. Author, iconoclast, and founder of soundscape ecology, R. Murray Schaefer has contributed to educational thought and practice. Murray's books *The Composer in the Classroom* (1965), *Ear Cleaning* (1967), *The New Soundscape* (1969), *The Tuning of the World* (1977), *A Sound Education*, and *The Thinking Ear: On Music Education* continue to catalyze educational thinking in Canada and elsewhere.

**Patricia Martin Shand** taught at the University of Toronto Faculty of Music from 1968 to 2011. She has published ten books and more than fifty articles on Canadian music in education, music curriculum, string pedagogy, and music performance. She has served on the boards of OMEA, CMEA, and ISME, and has chaired the ISME Music in Schools and Teacher Education Commission. She received the Jubilate Award of Merit for outstanding contribution to music education in Canada, and the Friends of Canadian Music Award for lifetime achievement in Canadian music scholarship.

**Kari Veblen**, Assistant Dean of Research, teaches cultural perspectives in music education, elementary methods, and graduate courses at the Don Wright Faculty of Music, University of Western Ontario. Musician and educator, Veblen studies international trends in Community Music. She also pursues a twenty-five-year fascination with transmission of traditional Irish/Celtic/diasporic musics. Lectures and learning have taken her worldwide.

**Betty Anne Younker** is Dean and Professor of Music Education of the Don Wright Faculty, University of Western Ontario. Previously, Betty Anne was Associate Dean for Academic Affairs and Associate Professor of Music Education at the University of Michigan. Her research interests include critical and creative thinking within the disciplines of music philosophy and psychology. Publications include articles in national/international journals and chapters in several books. Dr. Younker was teacher in band, choral, and general music settings in the public school system. Presently she serves on several editorial boards and committees for a variety of professional organizations.

# Index

**A**

Alberta: development of music education, 4; music curriculum, 22, 76, 183; music programs, 24–25, 131n2, 183; teacher training and qualifications, 26

Allsup, Randall Everett, 144

Association of Canadian Choral Communities, 39

**B**

bands: attitudes toward, 95–96, 102–3, 110–11; Band Aid, 128; Canadian Wind Band Repertoire Project, 40–41; community music and, 126, 127, 128, 131n3, 136; development of in Canada and United States, vii, 22, 91, 93–94, 96–97, 103–5, 188; exclusionary nature, 25, 102; gender and, 102–3, 108, 109–14; growth of, 96–97, 106–8, 110; in Manitoba's schools, 59–63; New Horizon's Band, 156; notable Canadian bands, 32–33, 103–7, 114, 116n10; role and influence, 101, 103, 104, 109–11, 113–14; women's bands, 105, 106, 107–8, 114, 116n10, 116n11, 116n14. *See also under* music education. *See also names of individual provinces and territories under* music programs

Beatty, Rodger, 40

Bowman, Wayne, 22–23, 28, 29–30, 32, 142, 169

Brandon University, 67n2, 73, 81

Britain, viii, 10, 14, 91–92, 139, 182

British Columbia: development of music education, 4; music curriculum, 22; music programs, 24–25; public education, 93; teacher training and qualifications, 24, 27–29, 31

British Columbia Choral Federation, 40

British Columbia Music Educators' Association, 32

## C

Canada: American influence, 94, 96; British colonization, 91–92, 94, 98, 110; defining "music education" in, 1–2, 186, 197; as democracy, 7–8, 109; development of music education programs, ix, 2, 8, 91–97, 101, 106, 107–8, 110, 123, 140–41; geographical considerations, 4, 92–93, 187; multiculturalism, 12, 46, 186–87; public and Catholic education, 4, 6, 91, 93, 95, 96, 110, 187; role of official languages, 4

Canada Council, 11

Canadian Broadcast Corporation, 92, 148

Canadian Conference of the Arts, 11

Canadian Music Centre, viii, 39, 126

*Canadian Music Educator,* 5

Canadian Music Educators' Association, xiv, 4, 10–11, 39

Canadian Teachers' Federation, 11

Canadian Wind Band Repertoire Project, 40–41

Carspecken, P. F., 197–99

Centre for Distance Learning and Innovation, 25, 149–61, 191n1

choral music: attitudes toward, 93–94, 95, 96, 98; Canadian, 39–40; community music and, 126, 127, 128, 131n3; early music education in Canada and, 4, 90–91; Festival 500: Sharing the Voices, 81; as mass entertainment 92; notable Canadian choirs, 32–33, 73, 81, 90; popularity in schools, 93, 95, 87, 188; teacher training and, 55, 93, 95, 97, 99n1. *See also under* music education. *See also names of individual provinces and territories under* music programs

citizenship, vii, 96, 109–11, 124, 129, 175, 202

Coalition for Music Education in Canada, 10, 11, 49, 63

community music: challenges facing, 130–31; definition, 124; e-learning and, 156, 157, 158, 187–88; frame for public music education, 123; funding, 128–29; globalization and, 187–88; organizational structures, 126–29; participants, 98, 125–26, 131n4; purposes, 7, 104, 113, 115n6, 124–28, 130, 131n1, 131n4, 138. *See also under* music education

composers, viii, 39–46, 75, 171, 173–74. *See also* John Adaskin Project

composition, 44, 138–39, 144, 170, 175–76

Conference Board of Canada, 97

Council of Ministers of Education Canada, 11

creativity, viii, 29, 44–45, 64, 139–40, 144, 154, 168–69, 200

Cringan, Alexander, 4, 5

critical ethnography. *See under* music education

critical thinking: curriculum reform and, 171–78; described, 144, 167–70, 173–74; in educational philosophy 166–67; music teacher training and, 165–66, 169–78. *See also under* music education

curriculum. *See under names of individual provinces and territories. See under* critical thinking, music education

## D

Dalhousie University, 28, 128

Davies, Peter Maxwell, viii

democracy, 7–9, 12–13, 109, 129, 143, 170,

Dewey, John, 7–8, 166–68, 173

# E

e-learning, 25, 147, 149–50, 182;
assessment, 152, 154–55; community
music and, 156, 158–59; further
research, 156–59; globalization
and, 155–56, 159, 183–84, 187–88;
pedagogy, 151–52, 158; teacher
training, 153, 155–56, 159;
technologies in music education,
151–53, 158, 160; vs. traditional,
153–54, 161. *See also under* music
education
elementary education. *See under* music
education
epistemology, 193–96; used to examine
Canadian music education, 196–99,
201
European influence on music
education, 2, 6, 9, 14, 41, 68n4, 109,
140, 141, 166, 188

# F

Fenwick, Roy, 5
First Nations Peoples, 2, 6, 32, 47, 72,
74–76, 77–78, 82, 84n1, 84n2, 84n3,
86n12, 126–27, 182, 199. *See also*
Inuit, Nunavut

# G

globalization, 12, 95–96, 129, 155–56,
170; descriptions of, 181–82, 183–
86; Friedman and, 183–86; theories
of cultural change and, 186. *See also
under* music education
Green, Lucy, 17n9, 139
Green, Paul, 1–2, 3, 4–5, 6, 14, 15, 17n2,
17n11, 95
guitar education, 25, 50, 62, 79, 127,
136, 139, 140–41, 150, 188

# H

Horsley, Stephanie, 10, 11, 17n2
Hutton, Charles, 5

# I

identity. *See under* music education
immigration: education and, 4, 91;
music education and, 2 6, 65, 91,
182. *See also* multiculturalism
improvisation, ix, 61, 131n3, 136, 139,
141, 144
International Association for Jazz
Education, 60
Inuit: curriculum, 75, 77–78; effects
of colonization, 74, 75–77, 79;
traditional musical practices,
6, 32–33, 71–72, 74–76, 79–82,
159; traditional vs. oral teaching
practices, 72–73, 74, 77–82. *See also*
First Nations Peoples, Nunavut

# J

Japan, xi
jazz, viii, 47, 125, 126, 127 136, 140,
188; in Manitoba schools, 60–62
Jessop, John, 4
John Adaskin Project, viii, 39–42
Johnson, Deral, 90, 95

# K

Kinley, Ethel, 5
knowledge bearers, 169–71

# L

Little, George, 5

# M

Manhattanville Music Project, viii
Manitoba: development of music
education, 4, 65; future of music
education, 63–65, 128; music
curriculum, 22–23, 51–54, 56–58,
59–60, 63; music programs, 26, 49–
54, 56–63; music teacher training
and qualifications, 28–29, 50–52,
54–58, 60, 61–62, 64–67; parent
organizations, 60

Manitoba Band Association, 26, 31, 59, 62, 63, 68n11
Manitoba Choral Association, 31
Manitoba Music Educators' Association, 31
McKellar, Donald, 94, 95
Memorial University of Newfoundland, 30, 33, 148–49, 157, 159–60, 202n1
Morton, Charlene, 11, 12–13, 15, 17n2
multiculturalism. *See under* Canada
Murray, Elizabeth, 7
Musical Futures, 139
music education: accessibility of and enrolment in, 7, 21, 23–27, 35, 126, 130, 157, 200; advocacy and support for, 11–12, 17n11, 28, 30–32, 36, 50, 51–52, 66, 97, 200; as aesthetic education, 9, 11, 12, 15, 52; band, viii, 22, 96–97, 106–14 (*see also* bands); Canadian content, 39–47 (*see also* John Adaskin Project); choral, 4, 89–91, 93–95, 138 (*see also* choral music); class and, 91, 93, 96, 97, 102, 109, 114, 129, 136, 143; community music in relation to, 2, 4, 9, 123, 125–26, 128, 129–30, 157, 158, 187–88, 199; creating a history of, 2–3, 5–6, 16; critical ethnography and, 193, 197–99; critical thinking and, 140, 144, 168–69, 170–78; curricula, 8, 11–12, 21–23, 34, 41–45, 61–62, 166, 172–78, 200 (*see also under names of individual provinces*); defining in Canada, 1–2, 186, 194, 197–201; as democratic, 7–9, 109, 143, 170; early history of, 1–2, 4, 7, 90–92; e-learning, 147, 149, 156–61, 182, 183–84; elementary, 4, 22, 24, 41–44, 46, 55–56, 93, 97, 188, 199 (*see also under names of individual provinces under* music programs); epistemology and, 193,

197–99; gender and, 102–3, 108, 109, 113–14; globalization and, 12, 155, 182–84, 186–91; identity and, 47, 55, 76–77, 82, 124, 126–28, 130, 141, 155, 159, 161, 188–89; influential figures, 5; instrumental, 22, 93, 94, 96, 131n3, 138, 139, 183 (*see also under names of individual provinces under* music programs); lifelong learning and, 49, 61, 108, 125–26, 128; multiculturalism and, 12, 46–47, 186–88; 156; orchestra, 93–94, 95, 188; philosophy, 15, 46, 61, 194–95; politics and, 7–13, 17n13, 17n14, 24, 27, 30, 54, 64, 109, 130, 141–43, 196, 199; popular music and, 34, 47, 98, 135–41, 143–45, 188, 202; related to general education, 13–15, 49–50, 96, 200; secondary, 10, 11, 22, 24, 35, 41–42, 54, 95, 97, 135, 136, 138, 141, 156, 182, 202n2 (*see also under names of individual provinces under* music programs); subjects integrated with, 23, 34, 51, 53–54, 57, 64, 188, 200, 202n2; teacher training and qualifications, 21, 23, 26–30, 35–36, 45–47, 54–56, 61–62, 64–65, 66–67, 93, 97, 99n1; 136–38, 140–43, 165–66, 169–78, 199; university, 29, 46, 55, 64, 102, 106–7, 125, 128, 136–38, 165, 169, 171–78
*Music Education in Canada: An Historical Account*, 1, 3–5, 15
Music Educators' Associations. *See names of individual Music Educators' Associations*

**N**
National Symposium on Arts Education, 10, 11
New Brunswick: development of music education, 4, 30, 92; Les Jeunes

Chanteurs d'Acadie, 33; music programs, 25, 26, 33, 106, 126; New Brunswick Youth Orchestra, 33; teacher training and qualifications, 30–31

Newfoundland and Labrador: accessibility to education, 147, 149; development of music education, 4, 148–49; e-learning (arts), 150–61, 191n1; e-learning (general), 147–49 (*see also* e-learning); history of distance education in, 148–49; music curriculum, 22, 24, 26, 148–51; music programs, 25, 33, 127, 149–53; teacher training and qualifications, 26, 30, 149, 153, 155–56, 159

Newfoundland and Labrador Special Interest Council, 31

Newfoundland Music Educators' Association, 10

Nova Scotia: development of music education, 4, 7, 92; music curriculum, 22, 34; music programs, 22, 34, 125, 128; teacher training and qualifications, 28, 31

Nova Scotia Music Educators Association, 31

Nunavut, 72, 77, 85n5; Arviat Imngitingit choir, 32, 73; curriculum, 76, 78, 85n3, 86n13; music programs, 131n2; resettlement and colonization of, 74–77, 79, 85n6; traditional knowledge and teaching, 71–72, 74, 77–82, 84–85n3, 197. *See also* Inuit

**O**

Ontario: development of music education, 4, 17n11, 24, 27; music curriculum, 22, 23, 41–42, 44; music programs, 24–25, 26, 40, 127, 128; teacher training and qualifications, 24, 27, 28, 29, 31

Ontario Music Educators' Association, 10, 31, 40–41

orchestra, 91, 93–94, 95, 102, 104, 105, 115n6, 126, 128, 188

**P**

Paynter, John, viii

Plato, vii, 194

popular music: attitudes toward, 94, 98, 135–38, 202; challenges of teaching, 140–44; as curriculum content, 34, 135, 137–41, 202, 143–44; informal learning practices and, 139–40; large ensemble music programs and, 138–39; popular vs. mass culture, 136; role in music education, 140, 144–45; teacher training and, 135–38, 140–43. *See also under* music education

Prince Edward Island: development of music education, 4; music curriculum, 22; music programs, 24, 34; teacher training and qualifications, 26, 30

*Published Choral Compositions by Ontario Composers*, 40

**Q**

Quebec: development of music education, 4, 6, 92; music programs, 27, 127; teacher training and qualifications, 27

**R**

reflective practice, 141, 165–67, 169–71, 175–78

Reimer, Bennett, 8–9, 15

**S**

St. Francis Xavier University, 28

Saskatchewan: development of music education, 4; music curriculum, 23; music programs, 131n1

Saskatchewan Music Educators' Association, 10
Saul, John Ralston, 7, 17n7
Sefton, Henry, 4
Self, George, viii
Socrates, vii, 194
South America, ix
standards movement, 57–58, 96–97, 189, 200
Staples, Rj, 5
steel pan ensembles, 139, 182
Stein, Janice Gross, 7
Stubley, Eleanor, 47

**T**
Tanglewood Symposium, 15, 135
teacher training and qualifications. *See also under* music education. *See also names of individual provinces and territories under* music programs
technology. *See* e-learning
tradition bearer, 71, 72, 79, 156, 157

**U**
UNESCO, 11
United States of America, viii, ix, 8, 10, 15, 17n13, 41, 94, 96, 124, 131n4, 135, 166; bands and, 101–10

University of Manitoba, 67n2
University of Prince Edward Island, 30
University of Saskatchewan, 131n2
University of Toronto, 41, 92; Canadian Music Research Centre and, 41
University of Victoria, 29, 202n1
University of Western Ontario, 36, 90

**V**
Virtual Teaching Centre, 148, 149, 157
Vogan, Nancy, 1–2, 3, 4–5, 6, 14, 15, 17n2, 17n11

**W**
Watt, Charles, 4
Woodford, Paul, 7–8, 9, 12–13, 15, 17n12, 17n13, 141–42

**Y**
Yukon Music Educators' Association, 32
Yukon Territory: music programs, 25, 27, 32; teacher training and qualifications, 26–27; Whitehorse All-City Senior Band, 32